CW00765923

IT'S TIME TO CHANGE
MUSICAL THEATRE HISTORY

CREATING BACK TO THE FUTURE THE MUSICAL

Written by

MICHAEL KLASTORIN

Foreword by **ROGER BART**
Introduction by **BOB GALE**
Afterword by **ROBERT ZEMECKIS**

ABRAMS, NEW YORK

OFFICIAL REHEARSAL AND PRODUCTION PHOTOGRAPHY
Sean Ebsworth Barnes

SPECIAL MANCHESTER PHOTOGRAPHY
Phil Tragen

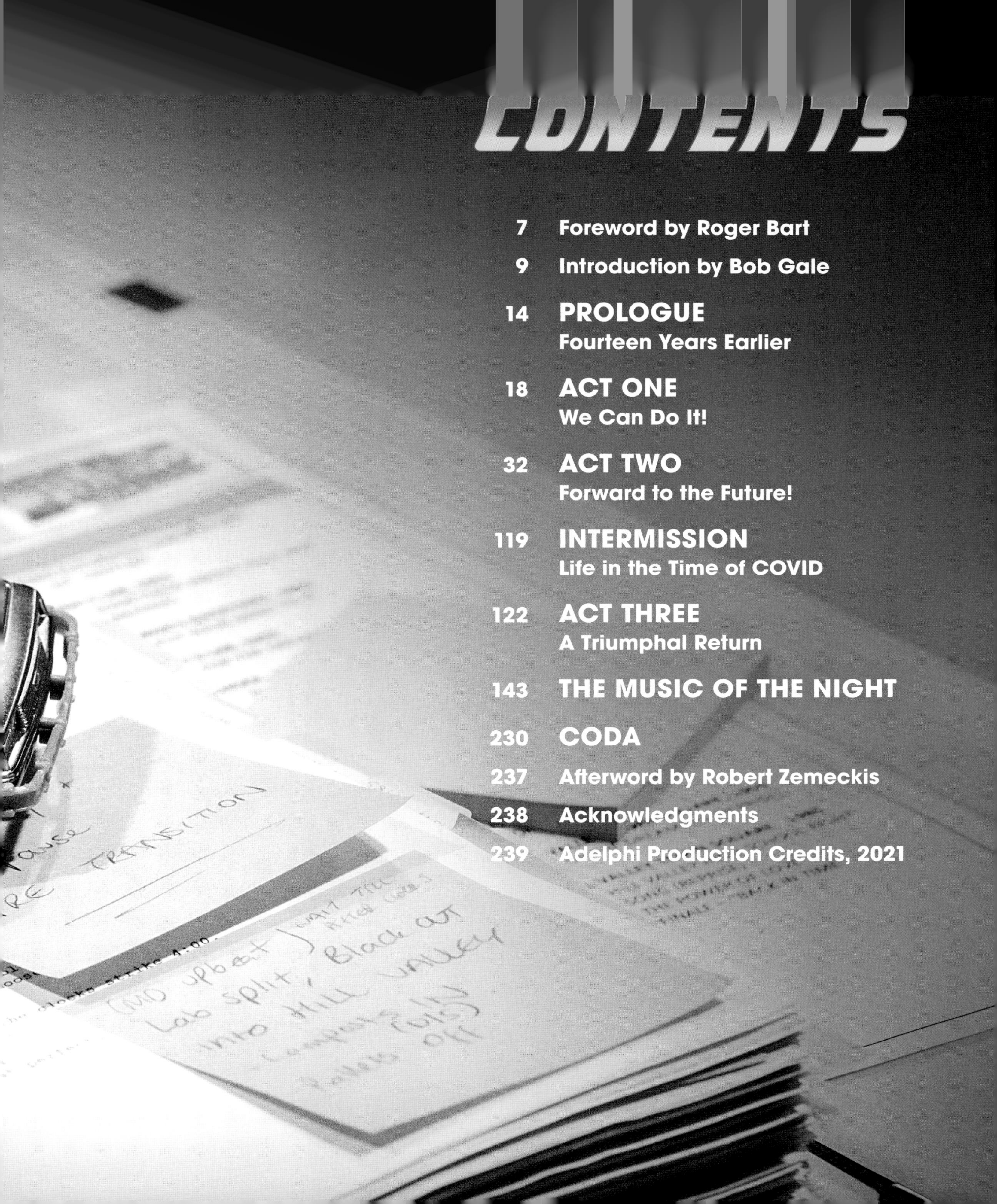

CONTENTS

7   **Foreword by Roger Bart**

9   **Introduction by Bob Gale**

14   **PROLOGUE**
Fourteen Years Earlier

18   **ACT ONE**
We Can Do It!

32   **ACT TWO**
Forward to the Future!

119   **INTERMISSION**
Life in the Time of COVID

122   **ACT THREE**
A Triumphal Return

143   **THE MUSIC OF THE NIGHT**

230   **CODA**

237   **Afterword by Robert Zemeckis**

238   **Acknowledgments**

239   **Adelphi Production Credits, 2021**

FOREWORD

by ROGER BART

GREAT SCO—

Nah, I'm not going to do that. It would be too easy, and probably the first words you'd be expecting to read from the man who has been fortunate enough to bring to the stage one of the most beloved characters in the history of motion pictures. But Doc Brown is far more than a famous catchphrase, and *Back to the Future The Musical* is far more than a bunch of actors trying to imitate the ones who did it in the movie and just regurgitating the same dialogue. Bob Gale and Robert Zemeckis and Alan Silvestri and Glen Ballard and John Rando, and everybody on that stage and backstage and in the wings, made sure of that.

That's not to say that when I got the call asking if I was interested in playing Doc Brown, I didn't jump up and yell out "Great Sco—" (no, sorry, still not going to go there), but I don't think I ever wanted to play a character so much in my entire career on the stage.

The Doc everyone knows from the films is a magical character, to be sure, and Christopher Lloyd has recounted on many occasions that fans have credited Doc Brown as the inspiration for them to embark on careers in the scientific world. For me, this is very much about making young people come to the theater and fall in love with science, be exposed to the limitlessness of a man's imagination and capability, as well as the unique relationship with a mentor and friend. Those things are what I wanted to reintroduce to young people. Not to mention an introduction to, and appreciation of, musical theater!

Back to the Future has been described, and rightfully so, as the perfect movie. This musical shares the pedigree, and the story that Gale and Zemeckis wrote so many years ago is being told in a way I think is ultimately successful in achieving what their goals were at the time. Not only didn't we get in the way of those goals, but in many ways we actually enhanced them. The added dimension of its being live theater takes it to a new and exciting level. The fact that we do this on a little stage at the end of a big box is extraordinary. The technology of this show is staggering, and what makes it even more remarkable is how John Rando was able to tie it all together so brilliantly. One of his greatest gifts is that he is unafraid of sentiment. There are elements of this show that are very moving, and there are directors who, when dealing with highly technical elements of a show, don't necessarily find the balance of the humanity. One of John's strengths was being able to have one foot firmly planted in an old-fashioned musical containing sentiment, emotion, and charm, with the other foot solidly in the technical part of the musical, which has some of the coolest stagecraft you've ever seen.

When I did my first interview for this book, Michael (the author) told me he hadn't been to see the show in Manchester before COVID forced its early closing, but he had

since seen it on a video stream and loved it. While I was gratified by his enthusiasm, I told him that a video can never capture the electricity inside the theater—actually feeling our voices, the music and the sound effects, the spectacle, and, most importantly, the heart. There is nothing like the combination of our spirits kicking around that space with the energy of the audience. And after being in the audience over the course of his many weeks with us, Michael wholeheartedly agreed.

I hope you'll enjoy this account of how it all came to happen, and that it will inspire you to experience *Back to the Future The Musical* in the way it was intended to be seen, live and in person.

If you're a fan of the movie, or even if you've never seen it, you're going to love the show. If you're a lover of musical theater, you're in for a magical time. Regardless, there are only two words to describe what you're in for . . .

Great Scott!

(Hey, I figured . . . what the hell?)

ABOVE The Marty to his Doc—with costar Olly Dobson.

ROGER BART
London
September 2022

INTRODUCTION

by BOB GALE

N EARLY MARCH 2019, AFTER A PERFORMANCE OF BACK TO THE FUTURE *The Musical* during our second week of previews in Manchester, a young man recognized me and approached. "Mr. Gale," he said, "I owe you an apology."

I'd never seen him before, so I had no idea what this was about. "You do?" I asked. "For what?"

"Well, I'm a huge fan of the movies. They were a really important part of my childhood. I still watch all three of them every year. And I always respected that you and Mr. Zemeckis swore never to make a part four, or a prequel, or a remake. So when you announced you were making a stage musical based on the first movie, I was horrified. I thought it was the stupidest idea I'd ever heard and a betrayal, and I was all over the internet trashing the whole idea of it. Honestly, I came here tonight to hate this show so I could really rip it apart on Facebook and Twitter and on every website where I could post. But I *loved* it. This show is *so* good, and it really is true to the movie, and I'm sorry I ever doubted you. So I promise you that I am going to go online and publicly eat my words and proudly say how wrong I was, and urge everyone to come see it."

I grinned, thanked him, and shook his hand.

It was a sentiment I would hear many more times, in Manchester and in London— and I still hear it. *I didn't think you could pull it off. The show exceeded my expectations.* Truth be told, the show exceeded *my* expectations too, as it all came together. And in this book, my friend Michael Klastorin documents the entire journey in a truly in-depth look at the creative process. It's a book that (I'm delighted to say) has also exceeded my expectations.

This book, of course, has an origin story too, and this is the only place I can tell it. It requires some background on the author. Michael Klastorin has had a long history with the franchise, first as a fan, then, starting in 1988, as our unit publicist on the sequels, then totally rewriting an eighty-page book about the trilogy in 1990, and then writing two scripts for the animated series that followed. In 2015, with the publication of his book *Back to the Future: The Ultimate Visual History* (which is the definitive book about the franchise), he claimed the title of "Official *BTTF* Historian." He has also been involved with numerous *BTTF* events through the years. Michael became a good friend over those decades, and loved the idea of a *BTTF* musical as soon as I mentioned it to him way back in 2010. That's why I invited him to our 2017 musical song showcase, the first time any members of the public got a taste of the musical (which you'll read about shortly). He was one of several members of our *BTTF* family on whom we could rely for honest, constructive feedback, which he provided.

In August 2019, I returned to California from our third London workshop, and Michael wanted an update. I told him how wonderful I thought the show was going to be, and he was especially thrilled because, with our thirty-fifth anniversary less than a year away, he had been asked to update his 2015 book with a new chapter covering everything that had happened since. And that would include major coverage of the musical, which would be opening in Manchester in early 2020, before the book would go to press. I was delighted, too—it would be great publicity for the show.

On my January 2020 return to London, I started telling our key people that Michael was going to update the book with a chapter about the show, and he'd love to interview them at some point down the road. Of course, they already owned the book, because it served as a valuable reference work, so they were more than happy to participate. And I started taking lots of photos, and enlisted Sandra Silvestri, Alan's wife, to do the same.

Those eight pages of that new chapter became the conceptual start of this book. Michael's interviews gave him far more material than could fit into those pages, and I knew there were many other stories to tell. With our successful opening in Manchester (despite our subsequent COVID shutdown), we knew "*the Future*" *would* have a future in London, and that, with extensive coverage of our West End production, the whole story, which goes back to 2005, could easily fill a book. Michael couldn't have agreed more and had approached me about doing just that. He found the publisher, and with their support, led by editor Eric Klopfer and with the support of everyone involved in the production, he has succeeded beyond our collective dreams.

I honestly think it's one of the most comprehensive chronicles of a musical ever written (and I've read quite a few). In addition to having access to early drafts of the book, early versions of the songs, photos, memos, notes, reports, concept drawings, and videos of the workshops, Michael traveled to London and was totally "boots on the ground." He attended rehearsals, previews, and our opening-night performance. He became part of our musical family. He went backstage, conducted even more interviews, took copious photos, and spent time with the technical people, the production team, and the musicians, as well as the cast. Michael is a perfectionist, so he was relentless in

How "The Future" Came to Be

In August 1980, while visiting his parents in St. Louis, Bob Gale accidentally found his father's high school yearbook. Paging through it, he was surprised to see that his serious-looking father-to-be had been class president. Bob immediately wondered if he would have been friends with this very straightlaced kid had they been classmates in 1940. Although he didn't have a time machine to find out, he had something better: his imagination.

CLASS OF JUNE, 1940

OFFICERS
MARK GALE - *President*

getting the information and images he needed, and it took him three trips to London to do it. But he had to get it right, not only for those who worked on the show, not only for those who have seen the show, but for those who are still awaiting their opportunity to see it. Is everything in here? Not quite. We asked him not to reveal certain secrets of our stagecraft. After all, the magic and romance of the theater must always be preserved. And good magicians never reveal their tricks!

As I said, this book has definitely exceeded my expectations. I hope it exceeds yours.

BOB GALE
Los Angeles, California
September 2022

ABOVE Bob Gale (center) with a "paradox," Christopher Lloyd (left) and Roger Bart (right).

PROLOGUE

FOURTEEN YEARS EARLIER

> ## "The idea of making a musical out of *Back to the Future* was beyond crazy. So naturally, I said, yes, I'm in!"
> ### —Alan Silvestri

Act One, Scene One

EXT. ST. JAMES THEATER NEW YORK - NIGHT
MID 2005

As native New Yorkers and tourists go about their business on West 44th Street, they pass the theater marquee and the smiling faces of Nathan Lane and Matthew Broderick in Mel Brooks's Broadway sensation, "The Producers." Now we hear wild applause coming from within the theater.

                                              CUT TO:

INT. THEATER

The audience is on its feet, cheering, as the curtain closes. Our focus is now drawn to a couple making their way from their orchestra seats to the aisle. LESLIE ZEMECKIS, award-winning writer, actress, and documentarian, and her husband, Oscar-winning writer/director ROBERT (BOB) ZEMECKIS, having just experienced an exultant evening of theater, smile broadly as they exit.

                    LESLIE (to Bob)
     You should make "Back to the Future" into a musical...

AND THE REST . . . IS "HISTORY"!

Decades later, Leslie remembers the evening, and her suggestion, quite well. "It wasn't like I thought of anything brilliant," she recalls. "To my mind, it was a no-brainer, and Bob was like, 'Hahaha. Yeah, sure.'" However, Bob Zemeckis did not summarily dismiss the idea. From 1990, ever since the words "The End" flashed on the screen, signifying the finale of both *Back to the Future Part III* and the film trilogy, Zemeckis and his cocreator, writer, and producer, Bob Gale, had been approached

with countless pitches of sequels, reboots, remakes, and 3D conversions, and myriad suggestions of how to prolong the series, but neither of them had any interest in doing so. But, as Zemeckis pondered Leslie's proposal, he found himself intrigued.

"*The Producers* started out as a movie, and then decades later became this triumphant Broadway show," offers Zemeckis, "and I think that's what Leslie was keying in on. What I certainly heard her say was 'If it's a musical, it doesn't have to be the movie.' That was a defining moment. It wasn't like we'd be remaking or continuing to make *Back to the Future* movies."

"It was certainly something that had never occurred to me," admits Bob Gale about Zemeckis sharing the idea with him. "I didn't hate it," he continues, "which is my usual reaction to other *BTTF* pitches, which were always obvious money grabs. But this was coming from someone (Leslie) who genuinely loved theatrical musicals. I hadn't seen *The Producers* onstage, but ultimately, the combination of seeing the movie version [released Christmas 2005] and my wife Tina's enthusiasm for the idea made me realize this was worth exploring." Motivating their decision was the unceasing popularity of the *Back to the Future* franchise, and the ever-growing fandom who showed no signs of losing interest in the adventures of Marty and Doc. "We knew people were hungry for more *Back to the Future*," says Gale of their initial thoughts. "We had made it clear that we weren't going to make any sequels or reboots, and this idea sounded like a way to create something interesting and hopefully entertaining, that would be *Back to the Future*, but it wouldn't affect the canon we had established. It was also important that the show be accessible and entertaining to people who had never seen the films." Most importantly, both men agreed that this show would have to live up to the stratospheric standards they insisted on for any project that carried the *Back to the Future* imprint. "If we weren't satisfied, we wouldn't move forward," clarifies Gale. "It was only worth doing if it was great!"

The New Fab Four

As far as the "Bobs" were concerned, there could be no *Back to the Future* musical without the involvement of Alan Silvestri, the Oscar-nominated, Emmy- and Grammy–winning composer who not only created the iconic scores for all three films in the *BTTF* trilogy, but had also composed the music for every film directed by Robert Zemeckis since their initial collaboration on *Romancing the Stone* in 1983. In addition, Zemeckis had another suggestion. For his 2004 fantasy-adventure *The Polar Express*, the director teamed Silvestri with multi-Grammy-winning songwriter and music producer Glen Ballard. Despite never having previously met, the two immediately clicked, and their fledgling partnership resulted in an Academy Award® nomination and a Grammy Award for their song "Believe," performed by Josh Groban. With that experience still fresh in Zemeckis's mind, he suggested the addition of Ballard to the team. "When he and Glen met," recalls

Silvestri, "Bob [Gale] immediately got it and said, 'Oh yeah. This man is one of us. He's a family member.'"

On February 5, 2007, the four men, with zero experience in musical theater, gathered in Zemeckis's office in Carpinteria, California, and decided to make a musical, taking their inspiration from the immortal words of Dr. Emmett L. Brown: "If you put your mind to it, you can accomplish anything."

At that very first meeting, the foursome agreed on a key tenet of the musical, recalls Bob Gale: "that we would not try to do this as a slavish adaptation of the movie."

As the creative juices flowed, no idea was discounted before its merits were weighed. Zemeckis had a thought for the Twin Pines Mall scene in which Doc explains the DeLorean time machine's workings to Marty: "The audience would see all kinds of goofy animation that was like the inside of Doc's brain, which was an example of how we could push the envelope," says the director. "We could go anywhere with this. It needs to be like the movie, but it's also a celebration of the film, and we wanted to do things never seen on a stage." Alan Silvestri proposed they take a cue from a then-current Broadway smash that had also originated on the silver screen. "At that time, *Wicked* had this amazing level of success, and it was a tremendous idea—connected to this archetype iconic story [*The Wizard of Oz*], and yet there was a point of view that was very unique. And with Bob and Bob, I have to say, from day one, they were always completely up for new ideas."

"For me," adds Glen Ballard, "the first thing was to take the Hippocratic Oath of 'First do no harm.' The idea was that we would be able to somehow capture the spirit of the movie but also expand and let the characters reveal themselves in a way that they couldn't do in the film. You kind of have to tiptoe into it, but then you have to be willing to just go for it."

Continues Silvestri, "After that first meeting, the mandate for both Glen and me was, 'OK, you guys go write some stuff.'"

And that's what they did.

TOP Bob Gale (left) and Robert Zemeckis on the set of the original *Back to the Future*.

MIDDLE (Left to right) Robert Zemeckis, Bob Gale, and composer Alan Silvestri at a 2019 rehearsal of the musical.

BOTTOM And Ballard makes four! Producer/songwriter Glen Ballard takes his place alongside Gale, Silvestri, and Zemeckis as part of the four original creative talents.

ACT ONE

WE CAN DO IT!

WHEN ROBERT ZEMECKIS BEGAN WORK ON *THE POLAR EXPRESS* IN 2004, it came as no surprise that Alan Silvestri would compose the score. Silvestri's agent suggested the project might further benefit by the addition of another of his clients: Glen Ballard. "The proposed collaboration," explains Silvestri, "was clearly built around the fact that I had achieved a certain level of success in the scoring world, and Glen had attained this amazing level of success as a songwriter and producer in the music industry."

Their initial session gave birth to a relationship that continues to deepen after nearly twenty years. "I had essentially never collaborated with anyone, and didn't know what to expect," admits the composer. "What I found was the most open, talented, brilliant artist whose literary sensibility was magnificent. On our first day together, I started off playing guitar, and Glen picked up a yellow legal pad. Half an hour later, Glen had the guitar, and I had the pad. Then we both had the legal pads, and finally, we both ended up with guitars in our laps. It's been like that ever since." "From the very start we have worked in a way that's totally synergistic," adds Ballard. "Ultimately, I can never keep up with him musically, and in this case, let's face it—Al is 'Mr. *Back to the Future*,' but I do offer him music that he occasionally embraces. And Alan is a remarkable lyricist. It's hard to say who wrote what, and we don't care." "We don't have 'words by one, music by the other.' That's not how we work," confirms Silvestri. "It's just us, and we've got a puzzle in front of us. How do we solve it?"

What Rhymes with "Flux Capacitor"?

When a songwriting team begins work on a show, they usually have the full book (script) of the production. Silvestri and Ballard chose not to wait before diving into the task.

Instead, they viewed the film a number of times, and then, along with Bob Gale, went through the script to determine what "roads" to pursue. "We went scene by scene to figure out the best places for songs and what they might be," says Gale.

"When you're going into a new iteration of *Back to the Future*, you first empty your pockets on the table and see what you've already got," explains Silvestri. "We have Doc and Marty, we have all our beloved characters. We have the DeLorean. What else do we have? All those resources are there to be revisited as appropriate."

One of the most valuable resources they had was Silvestri's majestic and instantly recognizable score.

Ballard knew that the opening song of the show should make use of Silvestri's iconic theme in a way no one had ever heard it before—with lyrics. Its immediate presence in the opening number would assure the fans that this was indeed *Back to the Future*. "It was a natural thing to explore," allows Silvestri, "so we went for it.'"

Aptly titled "A Matter of Time," the song introduces the town of Hill Valley, California, and its citizens circa 1985. As it had been depicted on-screen, the town is in decline, but the citizens cling to the belief that better times are ahead:

HILL VALLEY TOWN SQUARE, OCTOBER 1985

The set is dominated by the Hill Valley Clock Tower, atop a courthouse-like building which is the Hill Valley Department of Social Services. The clock is stuck at 10:04. Citizens of Hill Valley converge and fill the square, and our opening number begins: "A Matter of Time/I've Got No Future."

CITIZENS (singing)
'CAUSE IT'S ONLY A MATTER OF TIME
AND TODAY WILL BE LEFT FAR BEHIND
YOU CAN ONLY GO THROUGH IT
NEVER REDO IT
'CAUSE THAT'S ALL YOU GET FOR YOUR DIME.

IT'S ONLY A MATTER OF TIME
YOU CAN MAKE IT OR GET LEFT BEHIND
YOUR CHANCE TO BE GREAT
IS LOST IF YOU'RE LATE
IT'S ONLY A MATTER OF TIME.

DESTINY.
IS IT LUCK? IS IT FATE?
WHETHER EARLY OR LATE
YOU'LL CHANGE WHAT IT WILL BE.

HISTORY.
JUST A TIME AND A PLACE
IN THIS STRANGE HUMAN RACE
BUT THERE'S NO "MEANT TO BE."
'CAUSE IT'S ONLY A MATTER OF TIME
TICKING ON WITHOUT REASON OR RHYME.

IT'S A THING THAT WE MEASURE
A THING THAT WE TREASURE
A THING THAT WE NEVER CAN FIND.

IT'S ONLY A MATTER OF TIME.
SO RIDICULOUS AND SO SUBLIME
HOW THE FURTHER YOU'RE GOING
THE FASTER YOU'RE SLOWING
THE PHYSICS WOULD JUST BLOW YOUR MIND.

GOLDIE WILSON and his CAMPAIGN COMMITTEE quickly set up a lectern for the first part of his number. On it is a big picture of Goldie with "Goldie Wilson for Mayor."

GOLDIE WILSON (sings)
LOOK AT ME.
GUARANTEED IN ADVANCE
JUST GIVE ME THE CHANCE
I'LL SERVE YOU FAITHFULLY.

I BELIEVE
THAT THE FUTURE IS BRIGHT
AND NOT ONLY WHITE
YOU'LL SEE... JUST VOTE FOR ME.

'CAUSE IT'S ONLY A MATTER OF TIME
AS YOUR MAYOR I'LL STAMP OUT ALL CRIME
I'LL INSPECT IT, DETECT IT
THE CROOKS WON'T EXPECT IT
YOU'LL SLEEP KNOWING EVERYTHING'S FINE.

The lectern is collapsed and Goldie breaks into a dance.

IT'S ONLY A MATTER OF TIME.
WHEN YOU LOOK AT A STORY LIKE MINE
IT WAS TIME FOR A BLACK MAN
TO TAKE UP YOUR SLACK, MAN,
IT WAS ONLY A MATTER OF TIME.

Also in attendance is the Clock Tower Lady, flanked by two women carrying picket signs urging "Save the Clock Tower," who add their own informative lyrics regarding their agenda:

TIME STOOD STILL
WHEN THAT LIGHTNING BOLT STRUCK

```
AND THE CLOCK HANDS WERE STUCK
NO TICK TOCK ANYMORE

PLEASE HELP OUT
WE'RE PRESERVING THE TOWER
TO REMEMBER THAT HOUR
EXACTLY AT TEN-OH-FOUR.
```

Interspersed with these lyrics is the entrance of Marty McFly, taking center stage to sing "I've Got No Future." In this first original version of the song, Marty informs the audience about his current state of mind after a disaster of a band audition:

```
                    MARTY (sings)
I'M SICK OF THIS TOWN
EVERYTHING HERE IS SLOWING ME DOWN
SAME OLD STORY, NIGHT AND DAY
MAKES ME WANT TO SKATE AWAY.

WON'T MAKE IT, EVEN IF I TRY
JUST LIKE EVERY OTHER MCFLY
IT DOESN'T MATTER HOW I REACT
I'VE GOTTA FACE THE FACT...

I'VE GOT NO FUTURE
I'M NOT GETTING OUT OF HERE
DOESN'T MATTER WHAT THEY SAY
TODAY IS JUST LIKE YESTERDAY.

I'VE GOT NO FUTURE,
I'M JUST ANOTHER LOSER.
AND I'M GETTING NOWHERE FAST,
I BLINKED, THE FUTURE PASSED
AND WENT AWAY...

IT'S JUST ANOTHER BAD CALL
AND I'M STUCK BEHIND THE EIGHT BALL
OUTLOOK NOT SO GOOD.
YEAH...

I'VE GOT NO FUTURE,
IT'S SHOT AND THERE'S NO GETTIN' THERE.
STUCK IN 1985
SWEET SUBURBAN SHUCK AND JIVE

I'VE GOT NO FUTURE,
I'LL ALWAYS BE A LOSER,
```

```
DOESN'T MATTER ANYWAY
THE FUTURE MIGHT AS WELL BE YESTERDAY...
```

The first "No Future" piece would change in subsequent drafts and be reprised in a number of places to reflect the turn of events. After writing the first few songs, Silvestri and Ballard met with Zemeckis and Gale to give them a sample. "I'll never forget that meeting," says Silvestri with a smile, "because those guys laughed their way through the few songs we played for them. The good kind of laughs. They were like, 'This is going to work. We can do this.' That lit a tremendous fire. Of course, it was a slow-burning fire that went on for twelve years!"

History Is Gonna Change!

In 1985, after the explosive box-office success of *Back to the Future*, Universal Pictures wasted no time asking Zemeckis and Gale for a sequel. When they finally agreed, Zemeckis had already begun preproduction on *Who Framed Roger Rabbit?* and was unable to fully devote his attention to co-writing the next adventure of Marty and Doc.

So Zemeckis and Gale developed the story together, and Gale wrote the screenplay (which would eventually include *Back to the Future Part III*). Some twenty years later, Zemeckis's schedule had not eased up, so they again agreed that Gale would handle the writing. Says Zemeckis, "I have always had the utmost trust in Bob not only as a writer and my cocreator of the films, but as someone who has diligently served as the keeper of the flame and guardian of the franchise."

That didn't mean Zemeckis wouldn't be a major contributor to the project. "Every couple of months, Bob and Al and Glen and I would have these meetings where we would discuss everything that had been done so far and continue to discuss every aspect of the show—the story, the songs, what we thought the audience would want to see onstage, and what we couldn't have. We talked endlessly about the style and the scope, and how the show had to have spectacular stage illusions," he says, smiling. Meanwhile, Gale dove headfirst into his new endeavor. His extensive research included reading *The Secret Life of an American Musical: How Broadway Shows Are Built*, *Broadway Anecdotes*, and *Show and Tell: The New Book of Broadway Anecdotes*, among many others. On numerous trips to New York, he (on occasion accompanied by Zemeckis) immersed himself in the theater scene, where he was able to get firsthand experiences of

had set out to do. "We weren't trying to get everything figured out," explains Gale. "We saw it as a tool to get the right producer involved."

How Not to Succeed in Business...

While Silvestri and Ballard toiled away on the music, Gale and Zemeckis made sure they were legally able to proceed. "Theoretically, we could have done it without Universal," explains Gale. "The Writers Guild contract for an original screenplay gives the writer(s) what is called separated rights: complete control and ownership for subsequent versions of the project in certain other mediums, including theater. But having Universal involved always made sense from the beginning, because the ownership of some elements was in a gray area, and others, like the logo and music publishing, were theirs. Plus, they had a

the pitfalls, the possibilities, the perils, and the promise of what he had hoped to be his future.

The musical *Billy Elliot* left Gale feeling that, despite amazing performances, it was a too-literal retelling of the original film, something he and Zemeckis wanted to avoid. At the same time, Gale thought *Matilda* added elements that distracted from the core of the story. "*The Book of Mormon* was the best show of all the things that I saw," reflects Gale. "I had no expectations about it, so everything in it took me by surprise. It used a lot of elements of classic musicals, with an updated sensibility. It was clear that it was an approach that could work."

In 2006, Gale began the writing process with a rudimentary outline that was used for the initial discussions about the show with Zemeckis, Silvestri, and Ballard.

When he moved on to the first full draft of the book, he included sequences from the film that he knew would ultimately be either removed or revised as the show evolved. It was, essentially, *Back to the Future: The Kitchen Sink*.

Dated October 22, 2010, the draft included the first songs penned by Silvestri and Ballard and became the starting point from which Gale began the true transmogrification of the film's screenplay into the musical's book.

There would be dozens of rewrites to come, but with this first draft, Gale and Zemeckis accomplished what they

TOWN SQUARE 1985

Opening number: "(Good to be alive in) 1985." Cultural references.

Reagan is president, home computers are new, small camcorders are new.

Enter Marty (on a skateboard) to complain that "I got no Future."

His failed audition.

His family: dysfunctional. (Biff's song—"Anybody Home?")

(Lorraine's song: "Enchantment.")

THE MALL

"Connections." A look inside Doc's brain.

"Time Machine"—Doc Brown sings about his experiment and how the time machine works. He should, in answer to Marty's question about how did he build it, say "if you put your mind to it, you can accomplish anything."

Should Doc sing about "The Future"—envisioning 20 years ahead, the world of 2005 with lots of ridiculous predictions?

Perhaps Doc could Doc rattle off lyrics like Robert Preston in *The Music Man* ("Trouble in River City")?

Note: since we can't see the Time Displays, the DeLorean could have talking time circuits.

theatrical department, which we hoped would make a good ally and give us more credibility."

Indeed, two executives at the studio helped facilitate their plans. "We were all so green," admits Gale. "We wanted to find an experienced Broadway producer who believed in it and go from there." So the executives arranged a meeting between the *Back to the Future* team and a producer whose first musical production was a huge hit on Broadway. (SPOILER ALERT: It doesn't go well.)

"We waited three weeks for the meeting," Gale remembered. "The guy was late, rude, arrogant, and unprepared—he hadn't seen the movie since it came out. He told us he didn't think it could even be translated to the stage, and besides, 'You guys have no experience. What makes you think you could do it?' We couldn't get out of there fast enough."

In early 2010, among the myriad of introductions and meetings, two New York producers with an impressive Broadway track record actually understood the appeal of a *Back to the Future* musical and flew into Los Angeles for a dinner with the Bobs to discuss it. To further demonstrate their interest, they brought along the director of their current hit show. As they chatted, the director shared some of his vision, beginning with the thought of contemporizing it by starting the show in the year 2011 instead of 1985, as in the movie. "Bob and I gave each other a sideways glance," remembers Gale. "I asked, 'What happens in 2012 when the show is still playing? Does the opening of the show each night correspond with the actual date on which you'd be seeing the show?' He had no answer." Then, when the Tony-winning director wanted to include *Back to the Future Part II*'s iconic hoverboards in the mix, the conclusion was obvious. "He just didn't get it," says Gale.

Despite their disappointment with the director, the Bobs were still very open to partnering with the producers. "They said all the right things, and their courtship of us lasted several months," says Gale, "but they never responded to my drafts of the book." The reason soon became clear. On his and Zemeckis's next meeting in New York, they were surprised to find that the producers had invited another playwright and a composer,

both veterans of their previous musicals. "Their pitch was, 'Just give us the property, let us run with it and see what we come up with. It isn't going to cost you anything.'" Gale and Zemeckis responded by asking the producers to meet with Silvestri and Ballard before they would consider the proposal. To their amazement, the producers flatly denied the request, because neither the Academy Award–nominated composer nor the multi-Grammy-winning songwriter had any musical theater experience, and they would not work with these "untested guys."

That meeting was followed by a letter signed by Gale and Zemeckis informing the producers that "they were regrouping because the chemistry just wasn't right." States Gale, "It was a polite way of saying 'drop dead.' No one was going to bust up our team."

Glen Ballard Sees a *Ghost*...

Over the musical's development period, each member of the team would occasionally take a step back and tend to their "day job." Zemeckis would helm several films, and Silvestri would inevitably score them, along with other blockbuster movies, while Gale would keep occupied with additional *Back to the Future* ventures. In 2009, Ballard accepted an "outside" opportunity that would ultimately have a profound and beneficial effect on *Back to the Future The Musical*.

RIGHT Dave Stewart (left) invited Glen Ballard to team with him in the writing of the songs for the stage version of *Ghost: The Musical*.

Ballard was contacted by a longtime friend and colleague, the songwriter, producer, and performer (with the Eurythmics) Dave Stewart, with whom he had shared a studio for many years. Stewart had been engaged to write the songs for the upcoming musical adaptation of the Academy Award–winning box-office smash *Ghost* and wanted to partner with Ballard on the project. The book for *Ghost* would be written by the film's screenwriter, Bruce Joel Rubin. After a meeting with Stewart and Rubin, Ballard signed on and became the first of the *BTTF* core group to experience the musical process from the other side of the curtain.

"I got my theater education from a genius director named Matthew Warchus (*Groundhog Day*, *The Lord of the Rings*, *Matilda the Musical*)," he relates, "and he was willing to lay the whole thing out for us. There were definite parallels to *Back to the Future*, starting with the difficult task of adapting source material that's well known to the film audience."

Unbeknownst to his colleagues, Ballard actually did have some prior musical theater experience. "I directed my high school musical, *Once Upon a Mattress*," he confesses, "and that was it until *Ghost*. It was like reawakening a long, underused muscle. As an overview, it's basically a two-hour continuous live shot, and it's the hardest thing in the world. The music, the dance, the dialogue, the lighting cues, the choreography all have to be down to the millisecond. The most important concept Matthew taught us was that in a movie, you have thousands of images, literally thousands of ways to tell a story, while in theater, you're only going to have about ten or fifteen 'pictures' to look at right in front of your eyes and that's it. It's a matter of boiling everything down to its essential dramatic essence, and then using song to provide the insights into the characters and represent close-ups."

On working with screenwriter Rubin, Ballard says, "I was collaborating with somebody who had won an Academy Award for his writing, and we were on his sacred ground, but soon Bruce realized Dave and I were going to respect the essence of his work, so we earned his complete trust to do what we had to do to get it onstage. It's been like that with Bob Gale as well. In both cases, Dave and I with *Ghost*, and Alan and I on *Back to the Future*, started to create materials for characters before we really had the complete way to do it onstage. It was an act of faith. We didn't have the book, so it was trying to understand what you can leave out of a hit movie and still have it work onstage.

Ghost: The Musical had its first public preview on March 28, 2011, in Manchester, England, running through May 14. It moved to London's West End on June 24 of that year. As it continued its UK run, director Warchus brought another production of the show to Broadway, beginning previews on April 23, 2012, followed by engagements in dozens of countries around the world.

...And Scares Up a Producer!

While working on *Ghost*, Ballard maintained close contact with the *BTTF* group, and both he and Silvestri made time within their busy schedules to continue their musical efforts in Hill Valley. As he settled into the *Ghost* production, he found himself impressed by the show's producer, Colin Ingram, who had worked for Cameron Mackintosh and Disney Theatrical Productions before producing *Billy Elliot: The Musical*, Billy Joel's *Movin' Out*, and *Breakfast at Tiffany's*, among many others. "From the beginning, I closely observed how Colin went about producing the show," says Ballard. "British theater is just so robust, and the talent level in every department is astounding, and Colin is very fluent in every aspect of the British stage." Given that *Back to the Future* shared a great number of sensibilities with their adaptation of *Ghost*, Ballard made his thoughts about Ingram known to Silvestri in August 2010, who relayed the information in an email to Gale and Zemeckis:

> Hi Guys,
>
> Sam Schwartz [Glen and Al's manager] was in London a short while ago with Glen, while Glen and Dave Stuart were workshopping "Ghost." Sam mentioned (very discreetly I'm told) the fact that we were looking to take BTTF to Broadway. He said Colin's reaction was "exuberant" to say the least. Colin asked that we please keep him in mind as we move forward through the process. Glen has been working with him for over a year and has nothing but great things to say about him.
>
> Alan

Being that *Ghost* wouldn't make its debut for another year in the UK, to be followed by its transfer to Broadway, Ingram would not have been available to take on the job, not to mention that Zemeckis and Gale were still in ill-fated talks with the aforementioned Broadway producers.

Two years later, with *Ghost* in previews in New York, Ballard invited Bob and Tina Gale to a performance, where they were introduced to Colin. By that time, Ingram was looking for his next opportunity, and he had his sights firmly set on *Back to the Future*. While acknowledging how much he enjoyed working with Glen Ballard on *Ghost*, and wanting to continue their professional relationship, Ingram admits that his motivation dated back to his youth. "First and foremost, I loved the film. I was fifteen, and I remember I saw it on Christmas Eve when it first came out in the UK. A couple of months later, I went back to see it again with a friend. At that time, when you saw a film in the cinema, one didn't generally go back and see the same film again. It was one of the very few times I did that, and it's always been with me."

In addition to his love for the classic film, his experience on *Ghost* gave Ingram the confidence that he would be the perfect fit for the *Back to the Future* team. "There was a lot of technology in it," he explains of the paranormal thriller. "We had a lot of LED, video, and a lot of stagecraft and spectacle. I love the spectacle side, the big set pieces. I felt that *Back to the Future* would embrace all of those same elements. I knew who to hire, as well as how much preparation and development would need to be done. That's why I was confident I could do it."

In 2013, with a stellar recommendation from Ballard, Ingram was invited to the United States to meet with Zemeckis, Gale, Silvestri, and Ballard, where he proceeded to outline those very reasons as to why they should bring him aboard as a producer. "We liked him," says Gale of the group consensus. "We were impressed with his enthusiasm and his very positive attitude. 'We'll figure out how to do this. We have to put this onstage,' as opposed to the guys who said 'You'll never be able to do that. You'll have to think of something else.' Colin's enthusiasm was a direct result of his having seen the movie when he was a kid and loving it as a fan. I think a lot of the other producers that we met were, in hindsight, too old to do this." Adds

Zemeckis, "He was the one guy who made us feel like we were in good hands."

And then there were five . . .

Ingram wasted no time in getting down to work on the project, with one of his first acts being a change of locale. Based on his decades of experience in producing shows on both sides of the Atlantic, Ingram felt strongly that *Back to the Future* should follow the path he had taken with *Ghost*—previewing in Manchester and then moving to London's West End. Among his many reasons for the shift were the following:

1. Colin was based in the UK. The daily commute would have taken an enormous toll (and a costly one, as well).
2. The development costs of doing a show on Broadway are extraordinarily high.
3. The legal bill alone would have been a fortune: "Every little thing in the States has to go through lawyers, whereas in the UK, we have a more informal way of doing things."
4. More resources: "I believe we have better designers here, and the places that build the scenery and do the engineering and automation are better here. If we'd gone to a Vegas shop [for special effects work] I can't imagine how much it would cost."
5. The *Back to the Future* films had/have a huge fan base in the UK: "The film was so beloved here that it would get a really great welcome."
6. The UK was more of a safe space: "Opening on Broadway is a very public thing, and because of the cost, you have to hit the ground running. Because if you're not making a million dollars a week, which is a whole lot of money to make, you're gone. I think they understood my argument in terms of it being a safe place to create the show and put it on."

"Doing the show in the UK made complete sense given Glen's experience on *Ghost*," says Gale. "There was never any reluctance on our part. As Glen also pointed out, it gave us the opportunity to do two versions of the show [Manchester and London] before we would presumably go to Broadway. And what could be better than opening our show in the country that gave birth to William Shakespeare?"

With the new location established, Ingram started his search for the right director. At the same time, he knew one of the most crucial components he could contribute was "front money," funds that would cover the early development of the show, pay for the writers, director, legal

costs, casting, workshops, and travel expenses, in getting the show on its legs.

Ingram contacted a number of producer/investors with whom he had past relationships to gauge their interest in *Back to the Future The Musical*. In New York, Donovan Mannato, who had worked with Colin on both *Ghost* and *Breakfast at Tiffany's*, was the first to pledge his involvement, closely followed by other former partners of the producer, including South Korean media conglomerate CJ ENM (who also expressed interest in producing a South Korean version of the show), producer Ricardo Marques (who had produced the Brazilian stage adaptation of *Ghost*), merchandising company Araca (also involved with *Ghost*), as well as producer Hunter Arnold, along with other members of the Independent Producers Network (IPN) from the United States.

Ingram's first round of fundraising garnered more than $750,000. "They took a big leap of faith," marvels the producer. "They invested solely on the basis of the title, and the idea of *Back to the Future* becoming a musical, and the fact that original creators Zemeckis, Gale, and Silvestri were involved along with Glen Ballard. They knew that the film's songs ["Power of Love," "Johnny B. Goode," "Earth Angel," and "Back in Time"] would be in the show, but they committed without ever reading a script, no proposed cast, or hearing any of the original songs."

The future was certainly looking good.

No, No Relation to *That* Lloyd . . .

Shortly thereafter, Ingram brought to the attention of the "Core Four" someone he thought might be an interesting prospect to direct the show. "At the time, Jamie Lloyd was one of the up-and-coming directors, on the cutting edge of theater in London," says Ingram. In conversations with the director, Lloyd had expressed great enthusiasm about the film, and the idea of the musical. "I felt he would bring something different to the project," and so he brought Lloyd to the United States to meet with the group.

Having already faced a number of disappointments in trying to find a director, Gale recalls what led to the meeting with Jamie Lloyd. "We learned that getting an established director to sign on for a show is really difficult in theater. They all have their specialties. Some are great at drama, but they can't do a musical comedy or a musical of any sort. And they're in great demand because there are so many shows in development that want to have a director attached as it helps get financing. Glen had already

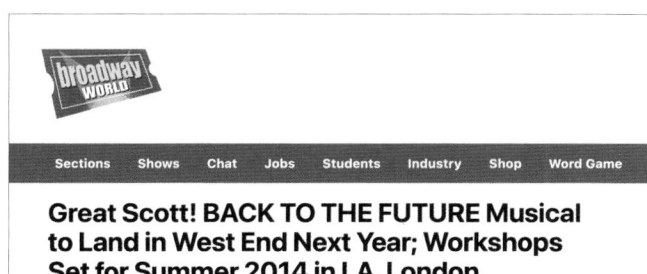

Great Scott! BACK TO THE FUTURE Musical to Land in West End Next Year; Workshops Set for Summer 2014 in LA, London

by Jessica Showers   Jan. 30, 2014

BACK TO THE FUTURE will be tuning its DeLorean time machine's "flux capacitor" to a different frequency when it travels to the West End in musical form next year.

According to the Daily Mail, BACK TO THE FUTURE will be adapted for the theatre just in time for the 30th anniversary of the film's release. **Bob Gale**, who penned the 1985 original, as well as its two sequels, is collaborating with the film's director **Robert Zemeckis**, theatre director **Jamie Lloyd** and producer **Colin Ingram** on the musical version.

"We met Brits, and we met Americans, but we decided on the Brits -- Jamie and Colin -- because they're seeing our material through slightly different cultural eyes," Gale told the Mail. Plus, BACK TO THE FUTURE is automatically suited to become a musical because, "you've got a main character who wants to be a rock musician," Gale added. "The script stands on its own. It's a different version of the same story."

experienced the benefit of collaboration with a capable director during his time on *Ghost*, and, coming from our movie backgrounds, we knew how much a good director brings to a movie. We also hoped we could premiere the show in 2015, in time for the thirtieth-anniversary celebrations of *Back to the Future*."

When Ingram approached them about Jamie Lloyd, they did some research about him and read reviews of his past directorial efforts. "He clearly was someone who was willing to take chances with established material, so we said, 'Why not?'"

In their meeting, Lloyd expressed the same enthusiasm he had displayed with Ingram. "He had read the last draft of the book," continues Gale, "and said, 'I think you guys are going in the wrong direction, and I see this in a completely different way.' He couldn't quite articulate it, but we were intrigued enough to say, 'Let's find out what he's got in mind. Maybe he's got something here that's going to make the show really wonderful.'"

As he assumed the helm of the production, Lloyd brought in several members of his creative team, and spent several weeks working on a rewrite of Bob Gale's book.

"He came to Los Angeles in August 2014 for some intensive sessions with Al and Glen, as well as further discussions with me about the book," said Gale. "I found myself questioning a lot of his choices, and he was unable to convince me that he was right. His sessions with Al and Glen did not go well either, and he wanted to bring in another songwriter. None of us liked the way this was going, and it was clear we had reached an impasse, so I called Colin and laid everything out. He was 100 percent supportive."

Creative Differences

English Noun

creative differences pl (*plural only*)

1. (euphemistic) Interpersonal disagreements within a collaborating group of musicians, authors, or other artists, especially as resulting in a collapse of the collaboration.

AUGUST 28, 2014

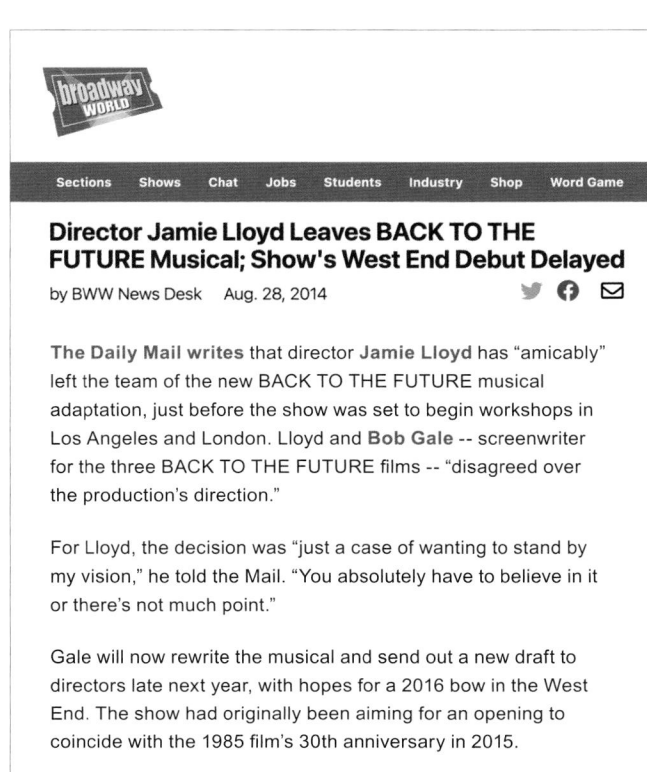

Director Jamie Lloyd Leaves BACK TO THE FUTURE Musical; Show's West End Debut Delayed

by BWW News Desk   Aug. 28, 2014

The Daily Mail writes that director **Jamie Lloyd** has "amicably" left the team of the new BACK TO THE FUTURE musical adaptation, just before the show was set to begin workshops in Los Angeles and London. Lloyd and **Bob Gale** -- screenwriter for the three BACK TO THE FUTURE films -- "disagreed over the production's direction."

For Lloyd, the decision was "just a case of wanting to stand by my vision," he told the Mail. "You absolutely have to believe in it or there's not much point."

Gale will now rewrite the musical and send out a new draft to directors late next year, with hopes for a 2016 bow in the West End. The show had originally been aiming for an opening to coincide with the 1985 film's 30th anniversary in 2015.

We've Got No Future...

With no director, the "future" of the musical suddenly didn't seem very bright. Having it ready to open in 2015 was no longer a possibility, and everyone was concerned that the project could be "erased from history." Contractually, without a showcase on the horizon, the rights to produce the show reverted back from Ingram to Zemeckis, Gale, and Universal. Colin decided to step back for a period, taking a job at New York's Madison Square Garden.

"We again wondered if the show would ever happen," reflects Gale. "But looking back, we realize it was an important learning experience. We had made a mistake in thinking we could rely on somebody from the outside to bring us the answer to what we needed on the project. Nobody knew *Back to the Future* better than the four of us, nor what the musical ought to be. We preferred there be no musical at all if we weren't totally excited about it." It was during this time that Robert Zemeckis considered the possibility of directing it himself.

Both Gale and Zemeckis had thoroughly enjoyed *The Book of Mormon*, co-directed by *South Park* co-creator Trey Parker, along with esteemed choreographer Casey Nicholaw. Prior to *Mormon*, Parker had no previous experience in theater, and Zemeckis thought that with an equally talented choreographer at his side, he too could add the title of stage director to his illustrious credits. Ultimately, it was a brief flirtation, due to his film commitments. The project then languished in limbo for almost two years until Glen Ballard called upon his *Ghost* musical experience with a suggestion . . .

Let's Put On a Show(case)!

In 2016, it occurred to Ballard and Steph Whittier, his partner in Ballard's Augury music-based production company, that hardly anyone had actually heard any of the songs that he and Silvestri had composed. "We knew the songs worked, so we thought, why not play them for other people," something that had been done on *Ghost* to great effect in attracting additional talent and financial backing. "We didn't have the libretto yet, but we had the movie, and we had ten or twelve songs we felt were entertaining in their own right." They took the idea to Bob Gale, who enthusiastically went to Universal with it, and the studio loved it to the tune of a promised $30,000 to produce the event.

Ballard and Whittier took immediate charge. "We found a venue in a large recording studio space in LA's San Fernando Valley," recalls Ballard. "We have connections with some of the great musicians in town and put together a band. Six of the best singers, who do all the commercials

```
        Wednesday, June 7, 2017 @ 7 p.m.

       The Woodshed Studios, North Hollywood.
    Located just off the 170 Freeway, south of Sherman Way
    and east of Laurel Canyon Blvd. Very limited parking
    in alley east of the venue; street parking available.
                  Enter thru the alley.

       Soft drinks, beer, and wine will be provided.

     This presentation is a work-in-progress and is NOT
   open to the public--it's for a very select group. Your
   name will be on a list; please do not bring additional
   guests unless they have been cleared. We ask that you
   not discuss this with anyone ahead of time, and there
   can be no recording of any type of the presentation.

    Note: This is a recording studio, not a performance
    venue. There is some seating, but many of you will be
        standing at tall bar-style cocktail tables.

   We anticipate the presentation will be under an hour.

            The Future is gonna be great!

                    The Songs:
      1. "Power of Love" Marty McFly and the Pinheads
      2. "Only a Matter of Time/I've Got No Future"
                 Marty and Ensemble
      3 "Wherever We're Going" Marty and Jennifer
         4. "Hello, Is Anybody Home?" McFly Family
         5. "It Works!" Doc Brown and chorus girls
             6. "It's What I Do" Biff Tannen
      7. "You Gotta Start Somewhere" Goldie Wilson
               8. "Future Boy" Marty and Doc
      9. "Something About That Boy" Lorraine and girls
         10. "Earth Angel/Johnny B. Goode" Ensemble
      11. "Power of Love/Only a Matter of Time" Ensemble
```

TOP A group of talented actors and singers perform a selection of songs from the musical for the first time to an invited group of friends, family, studio executives, and investors.

BOTTOM Back row (left to right) Fletcher Sheridan, Beverly Staunton, Sandie Hall, Rick Logan, Randy Crenshaw (crouching), Payson Lewis (crouching), Danny Wirick, Scott Heiner, Michael Blasky, Randy Kerber, Jonathan Sim. Front row (left to right): Monique Donnelly, Rodrigo Moreno, Malia Civetz, Steph Whittier, Bob Gale, Glen Ballard, Alan Silvestri.

in town, were hired to perform the numbers. We set up screens and projected select *Back to the Future* images from the film to lead into the songs. That was the whole approach. That was our 'musical.'"

"Every day of rehearsals made us increasingly optimistic," says Gale. "Our performers were top notch, and they really got into it, bringing their talent, their humor, and their personalities into the room. Glen brought in an experienced arranger, and in the end, it was the difference between a dirty, old black-and-white image versus full high-definition color."

"It's a fascinating process," says Zemeckis of the event. "You present the tone and feel of what you're doing with the music. And basically we're saying, 'This is a pitch for us to now develop the whole show.'"

Ballard, Silvestri, Gale, and Zemeckis invited a select group of producers, friends, studio executives, and assorted members of the *Back to the Future* community for the exclusive performance. Colin Ingram was also invited and happily made the trip from the UK to attend.

After the forty-minute presentation, the group got the concrete answers they were seeking. "I think you live or die at that moment," continues Zemeckis. "If it falls flat, then everyone goes 'well . . . I don't know . . . I don't know.' We were a resounding success! It just kicked us up to the next level."

"This was a true demonstration of the power of the live performance," adds Ballard. "You can evaluate something on a page. You can listen to a demo of a song. But being in the room is loud, it's vibrant, it's people singing their butts off. There had been just too much talking about everything—what we've done wrong, what we've done right. It was

time to just play some music. Once we did that showcase, everybody involved in it said, 'Oh, there's hope!'" Another true testament to the music performed at the showcase was that, with sporadic modifications, almost every song presented that night remains in the show.

"We put this material in front of an audience," says Silvestri, "an audience who had no idea what they were going to hear, and the reaction was everything we had hoped for. 'Keep going.' That was the message." The energy and positivity of the evening was not lost on the studio executives from Universal. "They loved it!" relates Bob Gale. "Chris Herzberger said that he'd been to a lot of these type of things, which were generally some performers in a room with somebody playing a piano, as opposed to

having a band, a semblance of costumes, and video screens to create the ambiance of a scene. He said he'd never seen any show at this stage that was as far along as we were." Their expressed admiration of the showcase emboldened Gale. "I asked them if they wanted to finance the whole thing. They said no," he says, laughing. "But that didn't faze us."

The energy they received from the song show-case pulled the foursome out of their creative malaise and made them even more determined to realize the show they had first conceived some ten years earlier. One of the first steps was to invite producer Colin Ingram back into the fold. He didn't have to be asked twice.

Meet John Rando…

Upon reclaiming the title of producer, Ingram dove back into the job with fervor. He received a flurry of calls from directors hoping to get a meeting to pitch themselves for the show. Most of them, recalls Ingram, were far too green for consideration. In January 2018, he returned to Los Angeles, where he, Bob Gale, and Glen Ballard supervised a table read of the book, accompanied by song, and put it on video. Along with an edited version of the song showcase from the previous summer, Ingram used both videos for meetings with potential directors.

Compiling a list of promising candidates, Ingram took a few meetings, but one name stood out. "I had decided the director for this show should be American, a little older, and with extensive experience in musical theater."

John Rando ticked off all three boxes, and a few more. The winner of a Tony Award for his 2002 production of *Urinetown*, Rando boasted directorial credits on a number of shows that were derived from films (or stage-to-film-and-back-to-stage revivals), such as *A Christmas Story*, *The Wedding Singer*, *A Thousand Clowns*, and *On the Town*, for which he was also nominated for a Tony. Their first meeting confirmed Ingram's instincts. "I was absolutely convinced that he would get along with the group. He was younger than them, but much closer in age. He was very unpretentious and accessible, and most of all, he really understands comedy. Of all the people I met with, he was the only one I put forward to the guys just on the strength of that first meeting."

In recalling that meeting, John Rando was equally impressed with Ingram. "We had never met before, but he knew my work, and he asked if this was something that might interest me. At the time, I was given the first draft of the book, and the video from that garage reading they did with the music [the song showcase]. As a director of musical theater, I'm always curious how things are going to get produced—how well they *can* be produced, especially such an enormous title as *Back to the Future*." As he had originally done with Zemeckis and company, Colin explained his intention of putting the show onstage first in Manchester and then moving it to London. "When I heard that, I was in," recalls John. "You want to protect this property as best you can, so I knew we could develop production there, without the glare, and there wouldn't be a million eyes on it right away. Having known the movie since it had come out, I knew it was a very good story to tell and could be told through music, as music is intrinsically interwoven through the story . . . The 1950s are a very good time in which to base a musical," he explains. "I knew that I could bring my Broadway know-how to create a musical that reflected the period."

Not long after their first meeting, in February 2018, Colin flew from London, and John from New York, to meet with Bob Gale and Glen Ballard (Zemeckis and Silvestri were unable to attend). "I went into the meeting with real, concrete notes about how to develop what was already there into a musical," says Rando. "I think he spoke pretty much uninterrupted for half an hour," recalls Ingram. "He was very passionate and animated."

"At the very end of the first meeting," relates Rando, "I grabbed Bob by the shoulders and said, 'I love these people.' It's not whether you love the movie or not. It's truly whether you love the people. The McFly family, and Doc and Biff, are those people. And I told him I would take very good care of his family, because that's truly what I believe writers need to get from a director."

Gale and Ballard were more than impressed with Rando's thoughts about the show, and the passion he displayed for it, and Gale made it clear in an email to the director soon after that meeting:

From: Bob Gale

Date: Tue, Feb 13, 2018 at 7:56 PM

Subject: It was an absolute pleasure, John!

John, THANK YOU for coming out to see us—that speaks volumes about your enthusiasm—made all the more impressive by hearing your thoughts, ideas, and observations, which have certainly gotten my creative juices flowing. (Believe me, I've met too many folks that only got my bile flowing—I suspect you have, too.) So I'm excited and optimistic, and I have the gut-level sense that we'll all work well together. I just want to do a little homework on you. The BTTF property and characters are like my children, and like any responsible parent, I want to be fully comfortable they'll be in good hands. And if there's anything you've done that you'd like to share with me, I'd love to get more educated.

Thanks for your patience in this part of the process.

On to the future!

Best,
Bob

Rando wasted precious little time in responding, sending a list of his former productions, including links to videos of some. "He obviously came prepared, and he said all the right things," recalls Gale of that meeting. "In addition to discussing story and approach, he gave very clear, concise, and intelligent answers to a few questions I had about what might or might not work onstage. What was equally important was that *Back to the Future* was conceived to be a big crowd-pleasing musical. And Rando had done them, knew how to do them, and he had such knowledge and respect for the 'Golden Age' of musical theater. His very strong assurance to me at the end of the meeting about wanting to honor the show and the characters had been truly heartfelt.

"I did want to see a sample of John's work if I could. In the film world, it's pretty easy. If you want to check out the work of a director, a cinematographer, or others, you just watch their films. It's not that simple with theater. Even if there is a recording of a live show, it can't give you the full scope of the creative talent behind it. Even so, I got a great feeling from what I did see." The references given to him by Rando, to a person, were all totally effusive about his talents, and Universal also gave Rando an enthusiastic thumbs-up.

Glen Ballard was equally excited about the prospect of working with Rando:

Tue, Feb 20, 2018 at 10:37 PM, Glen Ballard wrote:

Bob

I think John is very strong. He seems very collaborative, and his skill set is complete, and he has a sense of humor!

He's hungry but not starving—perfect motivation . . .

I'm happy that many of our songs have a place in the show—now he can apply some active dramaturgy to get us stage-ready.

A workshop in August is doable for me, but let's see what evolves.

I'm very excited!

Best,
Glen

Although neither Zemeckis nor Silvestri had been able to attend the meeting, both men were completely comfortable with Gale and Ballard making the final decision.

As Doc Brown might have said upon entering the time coordinates in the DeLorean, "Here's a red-letter day in the history of *Back to the Future*: February 20, 2018. The day that John Rando became the director of the musical!"

ACT TWO

FORWARD TO THE FUTURE!

> ## "Who hasn't wondered about what their parents were like as teenagers? It's a universal theme that appeals to all generations and cultures."
> ### —Bob Gale, explaining the enduring popularity of the story

WITH JOHN RANDO OFFICIALLY IN THE DRIVER'S SEAT, THE *BACK TO the Future* musical would finally begin its proper journey to the stage, albeit with a slight delay. An experienced director is greatly sought after and, as a result, is simultaneously juggling multiple projects. Rando had three such obligations to fulfill before he could give his complete focus to the show. "I made it clear to Colin that I couldn't really, really start until I got through the next couple of months. I couldn't even begin to think about it because I was so busy," Rando explained. "That said, I was eager to get started."

Prior to Rando's engagement, Bob Gale had already removed elements of the original film for the sake of streamlining the story and replaced them with inventive twists that would play better onstage.

"Brittle Me This!"

From Gale's 2011 notes: "Cut exterior of Marty's house, and the wrecked car bit. Replaced with new version of the peanut brittle gag that was cut from the film with Biff's nephew Billy.

"Reason: The subplot of Marty needing a car and getting the truck worked great in the movie, but the truck payoff can't be effectively done onstage. Cutting the car bit saves a set. Doing the peanut brittle gag gives us something new, which also ties into the movie in a way that fans will appreciate."

The "peanut brittle" gag referred to a deleted scene in the film in which George was bullied into buying cases of candy from a coworker's son. It appears in numerous home video releases of the movie. The revised scene would introduce Biff extorting the money from George on behalf of the child and taking a generous "commission" for the sale.

RIGHT Biff Tannen (Aidan Cutler, right) delivers some overpriced peanut brittle to George (Hugh Coles).

"Dog Gone!"

It's long been acknowledged that working with children or animals can be problematic, to which Colin Ingram can attest, having featured a cat in his theatrical production of *Breakfast at Tiffany's*. For his 2016 version of the book, Gale saw the wisdom in that trope, with a dividend: Dropping Doc's furry pal, Einstein, led to a new, crowd-pleasing entrance for the scientist.

"Bob [Zemeckis] and I are both big aficionados of magic," says the writer. "I knew you could make a car appear or disappear—Lance Burton was doing that every night in Vegas, and I knew how the effect could be done. So the spectacle of Marty on a basically bare stage, greeted by three sonic booms, and the appearance of the DeLorean from out of nowhere, was a perfect entrance for Doc, who announces he has just become the world's first time-traveler. We were essentially shortcutting the scene in the movie but doing all the great stuff theater allows you to do. A spectacular magic trick, a fabulous entrance for an actor, and a wonderful lead-in for a song."

"Diplomatic Impunity"

When Colin Ingram came on board in 2013, he and Gale had a discussion about the infamous Libyan terrorists who shoot Doc in the feature film. "Colin said he didn't want any gunfire in the show. He was adamant about it, and it was totally understandable. He (and we) always considered it would be a family show, with very little violence, and I made sure there would be no stronger language than 'hell' or 'damn.' But it wasn't simply an issue of violence. Dramatically, if we had included the Libyans, the big issue was how to tie up that thread at the end. We didn't want the audience to think they were still a threat, but we didn't want to go back to the mall. Most of all, I felt that any stage version of a violent confrontation or chase would have been a mediocre version of what we did in the movie." But what to do? In 2017, Gale had an epiphany.

"I asked myself, what's the drama?" explains Gale. "Doc is dying. That's what's important. That's why Marty needs to speed off in the DeLorean. That begs the question, instead of being shot, with all the elements we already have, *how* can he be dying?" The answer came to the writer like a bolt

---

TWIN PINES MALL
F 19 AM

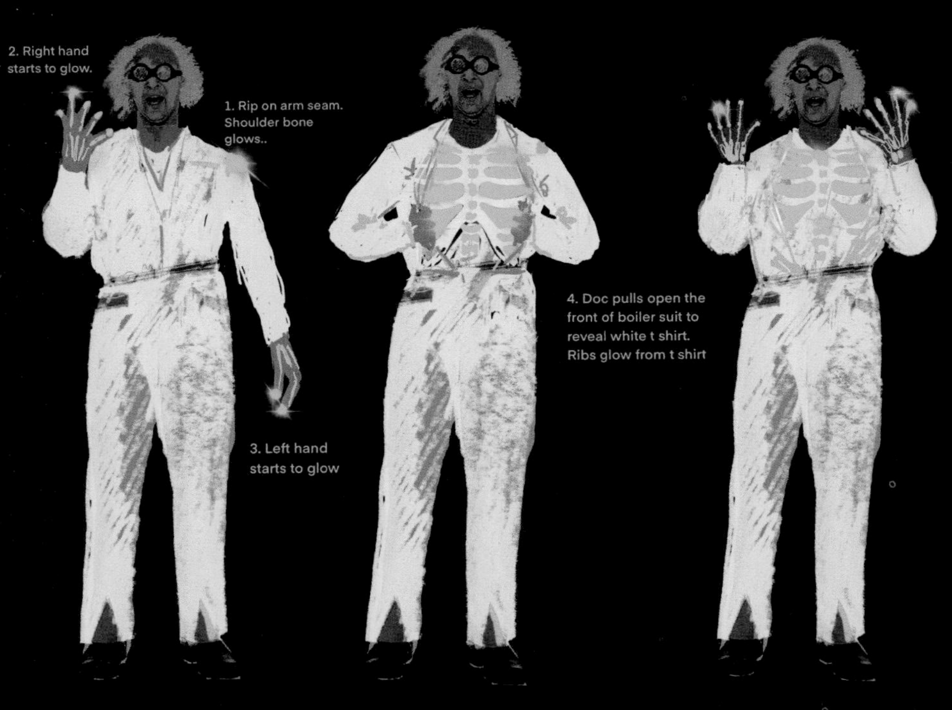

2. Right hand starts to glow

1. Rip on arm seam. Shoulder bone glows..

3. Left hand starts to glow

4. Doc pulls open the front of boiler suit to reveal white t shirt. Ribs glow from t shirt

of lightning. "Radiation poisoning. Doc is careless because he's excited about this monumental break-through, and he used a ratty old radiation suit he had from his Manhattan Project days, which gives us a little backstory on Doc as well. Everybody thought that was a great idea."

The writer thought out every aspect of the questions that could arise from this new scenario. Why wouldn't Marty just put Doc in the DeLorean and drive him to the hospital? "If Doc has radiation poisoning," he reasoned, "he can't be in close proximity to Marty and risk his friend getting exposed. Doc was in no condition to drive himself, so it was up to Marty to speed off in the car to seek help from the nearest hospital."

His thought process on whether the audience would accept this radical change hearkened back to the time he and Zemeckis met with the top executive of Columbia Pictures while in development on the original script. "Bob Z. asked [studio head] Frank Price whether the audience would believe that Marty travels through time. Frank's answer was one I've always remembered. He said, 'Yes, because they *want* to believe it. That's why they bought the ticket.' Will the audience believe Doc is dying from radiation poisoning? Yes, because they want to, and we're giving them clear reasoning for it."

In mid-2018, when his schedule finally cleared, Rando immediately settled into Hill Valley and got to work. As he had already stressed to Ingram, Gale, Ballard, and Silvestri, his first priority was to make sure the story and the music "worked." "I didn't care about the design," states Rando. "I didn't care about the technical aspects. I just wanted to make a really good musical. We could get into everything else after that. We set up a very good schedule, targeting August for our first major road marker: a reading, also known as a workshop, in London." Rando divided his time between collaborating with Glen Ballard and Alan Silvestri on the songs and score, and with Bob Gale on the book.

Rando had already expressed his admiration for Bob Gale's dedication to learning all he could about musical theater and his attempts to adhere to some of the tenets that separated writing for the screen from adapting to the stage. A major change that Gale devised before Rando came aboard was one that particularly delighted the director. He gave voice to the DeLorean. Literally. "In the very first versions of the book, I wrote, 'You see the time displays on video screens,'" says Gale. "At a certain point, I decided we shouldn't depend so much on video technology. I was

```
In the Mall parking lot, Doc explains how the time
machine works.

                    DOC
    The time vehicle is completely voice activated,
     and responds to my voice, and my voice only.
     (pulls a wired microphone from the car)
                "Start the car."

                 DELOREAN
            "Now starting the car."
The car starts and revs up.

                    DOC
              Time circuits on.

                 DELOREAN
            "Time circuits on."

                    DOC
          Now I use my voice to state
         the destination time and date.
       Say we want to see the signing of the
     Declaration of Independence. "July 4, 1776."

                 DELOREAN
              "July 4, 1776."
```

always thinking, what will people in the back of the theater actually be able to see? Having the DeLorean talk was a good way to solve that problem, and get exposition across at the same time.

"When I read that for the first time," adds Rando, "it really excited me and made me think, 'This is theatrical! This will be fun.' He knew that you couldn't see the dashboard and read the dates, and all that. We needed for it to talk, so if you didn't know the movie at all, you would love our musical nonetheless."

"Rhyme or Reason?"

While doing a revision on the musical's book,
A novel approach writer Bob Gale, he took.

When Doc would explain about traveling through time,
Gale decided the Doc would do it through rhyme.

He worked very hard, and it took quite a while,
But he thought, *It's a musical, do it with style.*

John Rando told Gale the rhymes didn't belong,
He said, "Save all the rhyming for Al and Glen's songs."

Gale used this format for both Marty's and Doc's dialogue, starting with Doc's unveiling of the time machine at the Twin Pines Mall in 1985, and then again when Marty finds the 1955 version of the scientist. Rando assured the author that so much of the classic dialogue that he and Zemeckis had created in the eighties should remain intact and that the audience would want to hear it.

But there was one couplet that Rando insisted remain, as Gale had slightly tinkered with a classic piece of dialogue from the film.

```
                    DOC
Once I've set the time and date,
I make the car go 88.


And when that magic number's hit,
You're gonna see some serious...
Shift in scientific thought!
```

Cast Away!

With work on the songs and book progressing to everyone's satisfaction, Rando needed to find the performers who would bring the characters to life. In 2014, the production had engaged David Grindrod, one of the UK's most prodigious casting directors, to begin the process for the previous director. Grindrod had worked with Colin Ingram many times over the years, most recently on *Ghost*.

The first step was the casting breakdown. Explains Grindrod, "It is a document which is the culmination of thoughts about each character from the producers, the director, the musical supervisor, and what is required movement-wise." That document was circulated to hundreds of agents and managers throughout the UK.

Although not specified in the written breakdown, the casting director notes that there was one important quality every cast member had to possess before they could even be considered: stamina!

"While there might be any number of recognizable faces from film or television that would seem to be a proper fit for a role, one has to bear in mind that, unlike in filmed entertainment, there is no starting and stopping, retakes, or long—if any—breaks in the course of a stage show. The stars of that show face the enormous prospect and responsibility of being onstage in front of an audience for a couple of hours at a time, for eight performances each week."

DOC BROWN (Male)

- Doctor Emmett Lathrop "Doc" Brown is the inventor of the DeLorean time machine. At various points in time, Doc helps Marty restore the space-time continuum and reverse the changes that were caused by time travel. Eccentric and characterful. Needs strong COMEDY. Strong character voice who is well versed in singing pop stylistically, as well as musical theater. [TENOR or HIGH BARITONE Belt A]
- Playing age 35–50
- Height: approximately 6'
- Appearance: Any

Grindrod began his quest for talent in the United Kingdom, beginning with the iconic role of Doctor Emmett L. Brown. After an initial search of local talent failed to unearth any viable contenders, the producers made a decision to extend their search "across the pond" with the help of esteemed New York casting director Jim Carnahan. "When it came to Doc Brown," says Colin Ingram, "we weren't sure if we wanted a comedic actor who could sing, or a strong singer who could act." Carnahan was able to provide a combination of the two when he solicited an audition tape from Tony Award–winning actor Roger Bart (*You're a Good Man, Charlie Brown*). Ironically, Bart had already been seen by *Back to the Future*'s director and cocreator Robert Zemeckis when he and wife Leslie had attended a performance of *The Producers* on Broadway in 2005. Bart had originated the stage role of Carmen Ghia, the very personal assistant to director Roger De Bris in the original production, and later took over the costarring role of Leo Bloom from Matthew Broderick.

"I was asked to put myself on tape," recalls the actor, "and to prepare three big, long scenes. It was a lot of material, but I memorized it, and threw on a bathrobe, and used a lampshade for the mind reading helmet. I had the lines written all over pieces of paper on top of the ladder that was holding the camera and created a fairly insane tape."

Roger Bart

In addition, Bart was asked to record a song. "I found a karaoke version of Talking Heads' 'Once in a Lifetime,' and I thought that would be an excellent number because it was talk-singing in a way:

"And you may ask yourself, 'How do I work this?'

"And you may ask yourself, 'Where is that large automobile?'

"And you may ask yourself, 'How do I work this?'"

"I realized this song was the perfect example of how Doc might explain time travel. The whole tape was very goofy and fun."

"He just nailed it," remembers Colin Ingram. "He was charming and funny and warm—everything you wanted in a performer." A week after sending off his audition tape, the actor received a call from the producer offering him the part. Unfortunately, disturbances in the space-time continuum resulted in the planned production being "erased from existence." "It disappeared," says the actor, "and I was disappointed."

Some four years later, when John Rando restored the timeline, Ingram asked the director if he'd be interested in seeing Bart's audition tape. There was no need. Rando had worked with Bart years earlier on a workshop for a musical. While that show didn't come to fruition, Rando and Bart had formed a strong mutual appreciation. "When Colin told me Roger was interested, and that Bob and Glen liked him, I said, 'We have to hire him!' I knew having Roger would be an enormous help in the construction of the show. His experience and talent would allow us to test songs to see how they might or might not fit into the show or what might make them better from the actor's point of view."

Bart was equally excited. "I was thrilled! We had always wanted to work together, so I said yes immediately and got on a plane."

MARTY McFLY (Male)

- Marty McFly is the son of George McFly and Lorraine Baines-McFly. Marty travels to the past, encountering his ancestors. Late teens to mid-20s. Geeky but charismatic and attractive. Must have a killer voice for this challenging vocal.
- [ROCK TENOR Belt C]
- Skateboarding and guitar skills helpful.
- Playing age 20–25
- Height 5'4"–5'9"
- Appearance: Any

Olly Dobson

In the first round of the 2014 audition process, it would take a great deal of time and effort to find an actor to occupy the iconic role of Marty McFly. "I think we saw hundreds of actors for Marty," recalls Grindrod. The process was an extremely thorough one, which was based on not only the actors' innate talents, but their learned skills as well. "It was not only the acting," says Grindrod. "Since it's a musical, the dancing and singing were part of it, and, originally, there was also talk of Marty having to do skateboard tricks, so that was another acquired talent which was taken into consideration."

It was also important for "Marty" to have a certain look and demeanor. "Sometimes it's about getting somebody who projects an aura of freshness, balanced with the talent and experience that can cope with the pressure of being a leading man and the enormity of eight performances a week. So we looked at people fresh from college."

One such candidate, who had just graduated from London's Arts Educational Schools (where Grindrod, as one of the facilities' vice presidents, had first encountered the student), was Olly Dobson. "When I first heard about the job, it was 2014, when I was still in college," says Dobson. "This was my very first audition since I had graduated, and I thought, I don't care what happens with this. *And then things got real*." The young actor showed so much promise in his first audition that he was asked back an additional six times for further readings. "They have to see that you can riff with the other actors, as well as handle a pressurized environment. At that time, I didn't have the guitar skills I do now, so that might have been a factor. Who knows?" Ultimately, despite his obvious talents, the role was offered to an actor from New York. Subsequently, however, Grindrod would use Dobson in productions of *Bat Out of Hell* and *Matilda*.

In 2018, when casting began again, Dobson was determined to portray Marty McFly. When his agent informed him that he had been asked to meet with production to be considered for the role of Marty's "cover" (also known as understudy), the actor refused. "I told him I cannot be the understudy." If he was to go back to audition, it had to be for the starring role and nothing else. "I wanted it soooo bad," he says, smiling. "I felt like I had had my preliminary round a couple of years before, so I wasn't nervous. And it paid off."

Grindrod put the auditions on tape and sent the three strongest candidates to Rando, Gale, and Ballard for their scrutiny. Along with Colin Ingram, the group unanimously agreed on Dobson. "I don't remember the other two guys. It was Olly," states Gale. "There were no ifs, ands, or buts about it." "Olly had a lot of things going for him," adds Rando. "First off, the guy could sing. Glen Ballard writes songs for some really big superstars, so you've got to sing them damned good if you're going to be in the show. Number two was his look. He had the right body type, the right style, and he had this great thing going on, which was that he respected Michael J. Fox and at the same time was showing that he could own the role."

Even though Dobson joined the company, he didn't consider himself cast in the role. In the world of the UK theater, the development of a production goes through many stages, known as laboratories and workshops. Over the course of a two-to-three-week period, the actors work with the director to develop their characters and then perform a very bare-bones presentation of the book. If all goes well, they are offered an extension that will take them to the end of the next presentation, until they reach a point when they are formally offered the role. "I managed to bag the job for the workshop for two weeks," says Dobson, "and every single time, they asked me to come back. It was a couple of months of giving them your attitude, giving them a sense of who you are as a person, and as an actor. But I was always aware that they might recast the role at any point. In the end, they chose me. When I got that call, I was over the moon!"

LORRAINE BAINES-McFLY (Female)

- Lorraine Baines-McFly is the wife of George McFly and the mother of Marty. Lorraine is portrayed in 1985 as middle-aged and unhappy. In 1955, Marty inadvertently alters history when Lorraine becomes infatuated with him instead of George. Much to Marty's surprise, in 1955, Lorraine repeatedly engages in behavior she later classifies as "looking for trouble" in 1985, such as parking in cars with boys, drinking liquor, and smoking. Mid-20s to play older (47) and younger (17). MUST have strong comedy bones. Must have a strong musical theater belt with flexibility across the range. [SOPRANO Belt Eb]
- Height: Any (but not taller than Marty McFly)
- Appearance: Any

Rosanna Hyland had been offered the role of Lorraine Baines McFly in 2014 immediately after her turn in the UK production of *Urinetown*. "I actually tried to back out of the audition," she recalls, "because I had a terrible chest infection and had no voice left—no steam in the tank. They told me that all I had to do was come down and read. I went and booked it. With one audition, it just kind of fell into my lap. Then the project got back-burnered. I thought, if and when it comes back with another director, either I'll have aged out of it, or they'll just want new blood. I wrote it off."

David Grindrod knew better. He had met the actress years earlier in Singapore, where she had trained at the LASALLE College of the Arts. After graduation, she moved to London, where Grindrod cast her in *School of Rock*, *Shrek*, *Carousel*, and *Sister Act*. "She's got a quirky sense of humor, and you either get it or you don't. She makes me laugh, and I think she's got a unique inner quality that shines through. Once you get to know Rosie, it's very difficult to find anybody else. You know that she is the one." Ingram agreed. He had seen and loved the actress in *Urinetown*. "She looked so much like Lea Thompson, and was so good in the show, we decided to put her in the workshop prior to Jamie's departure," relates the producer. "I remember very clearly telling John [Rando] we had found a great Lorraine and making sure that David put her in the mix for the audition."

"A few years later, I heard that *Back to the Future* was auditioning again," continues the actress. "It didn't even enter my mind to ask my agent to put me forward for it." He didn't have to, and Rosie was pleasantly surprised when

Rosanna Hyland

she was asked for a self-tape (much like Roger Bart had made). She was even more surprised at the outcome. Rando, Gale, and Ballard were in total agreement that they had their Lorraine. "I booked it again!" she says, laughing. "It's a role that seems to have wanted to happen for me." Adds Gale, "Like it was . . . meant to be."

GEORGE McFLY (Male)

- George is portrayed as weak and the main target of Biff Tannen's bullying; he is unable to stand up for himself. In 1955, George did not have any friends for support and was targeted not only by Biff and his gang, but also by other kids in school. A real nerd as a teenager, he has a penchant for science fiction and writes some of his own but never allows himself to share his stories to anyone due to his fear of rejection. As a middle-aged man, he is of low social status and will stay that way. Mid-20s to play older (47) and to play younger (17). Should be a strong character singer. Needs strong COMEDY [BARITONE]
- Playing age 20–30
- Height: Any
- Appearance: Any

It was at an audition session for a musical comedy stage adaptation of one of the UK's most beloved comedy series, *Only Fools and Horses*, where Grindrod found his George McFly. "Hugh Coles made us laugh a lot during that audition," says the casting director, "and he'd done quite a bit of television. While he wasn't the right fit for *Fools and Horses*, I thought he could be right for *Back to the Future*, even though he had never done a musical before; nor had he ever appeared in the West End."

"On the day I was turned down for the West End musical, my agent called me and said, 'I've got another audition for you.' I thought, great, fantastic! Maybe it's for television or a commercial, and he says, 'It's *Back to the Future The Musical!*'"

Hugh Coles

There was one other notable "first" that had to be addressed in order for the actor to properly prepare for the audition: Coles had never seen any of the *Back to the Future* films! "I knew they wanted to see me for George McFly, but I'd never actually seen the film! I knew of it because it's a cultural artifact of our civilization now, so I was aware of it, and knew roughly what it was about."

What he couldn't appreciate until viewing the film for the first time was the enormity of the role, the overall impact of the character in terms of the story, and the performance of the actor who created it. "I was honestly cowed a bit by Crispin Glover's performance," he admits. "I thought, they want me to follow *that*?" Undaunted by the task, Coles took his character's own advice and "put his mind to it."

"I thought, OK, I'll go in and I'll take the material I'm supposed to be doing, and I did it in my own way. I knew I wasn't a singer or a dancer, so what I ended up doing was taking the song they had given me ("My Myopia"), and I cut the words out and put it into a comic book and made this whole scene out of it. I had heard the guys before me [in the auditions] singing these amazing notes, and Nick Finlow [the show's music supervisor] would ask them, 'Can you sing one note higher than that? Just one higher,' and I was hearing these incredible notes coming out of them. I thought, *Oh my God, this had better work.* I went in and did this sketch comedy scene with the song." SPOILER ALERT: It worked. Hugh Coles was cast as George McFly!

BIFF (Male)

- Biff Tannen is a local bully who harassed George. He comes from a long line of bullies in Hill Valley, most of whom harassed members of the McFly family. MUST have a jock physicality—tall, beefy, imposing. Late teens/early 20s. Strong voice required.
- [TENOR/HIGH BARITONE Belt A]
- Playing age 20–30
- Height: 6'2" or taller
- Appearance: Any

It seemed like history was repeating itself in the search for überbully Biff Tannen. In 1985, hundreds of actors were seen for the part, but none was deemed a perfect fit until a casting director found Tom Wilson at another audition. He was the final piece of casting before the cameras rolled.

More than three decades later, Grindrod found himself in the very same position. "Biffs went on forever," he

recounts. The internet call reached out to more than the "usual suspects" and resulted in hundreds of submissions and subsequent readings. As he had done with the other roles, Grindrod sent a select number of the video auditions to Rando, Gale, and Ballard. "Everybody picked a different one," he says of the effort, "and we were going right down to the line"—the "line" being the first official workshop of the production. "It was difficult to find a guy who was physically imposing and had comedy chops," affirms Bob Gale. "Matt Corner, whom we hired, was a very good actor, and he was very funny, but he was actually a couple of inches shorter than George [Hugh Coles]. He had the attitude, and we used his goons to give him more presence. We brought him back for the second workshop as well, but Bob Zemeckis led the charge in urging us to get a bigger guy for Biff."

When the next full cast reading of the show took place, there was a new, more physically imposing actor to take the role, and the result was immediately evident to all. Continues Gale, "John Rando said, 'Oh my God, the difference is unbelievable. The physical presence makes such a huge difference.' Unfortunately, the actor was good, but he wasn't great." As the workshops and labs progressed, so did Grindrod's search for a new, improved Biff Tannen.

An actor just a few months out of school who had caught Grindrod's attention was Aidan Cutler. One of the last shows he had appeared in while in school saw him in the title role in the musical version of *Shrek*, which Grindrod had cast for the West End. "That production," notes Grindrod, "was one of the first school productions ever done of the show." Cutler's performance also attracted a representative with one of London's top agencies, who immediately signed him, and began sending him out on auditions. In August 2019, one of his first professional jobs out of school was in a musical revue celebrating the work of legendary composer and lyricist Jerry Herman. Aidan was singled out in reviews for his performance and vocal abilities. After the

show's limited engagement, the actor experienced what he remembers as "a bit of a dry spell." In November, the clouds opened up full force! His agent called, informing him that he had been invited to read for Biff. "I went straight in, sang one of the songs from the show, read two scenes with Olly Dobson, and that was it." "When we saw Aidan, we were blown away," says Gale. "He had it all. The physical presence, agility, and a tremendous singing voice." Continues Aidan, "A week later, I had the job, and two weeks after that, I was in fight workshops for the sequence at the end of Act One. This was all just before Christmas, and in January, we started rehearsals for the show in Manchester!"

GOLDIE WILSON/MARVIN BERRY (Male)

- Male actor with an incredible gospel voice. Will need to be skilled in vocal improvisation.
- [GOSPEL TENOR Belt C]
- Playing age 30–50
- Height: Any
- Appearance: Black—Other Areas, Black-Caribbean, Black-African, Mixed Race, African-American

When he moved to the UK from his native United States, Cedric Neal had already established himself on television in the TV series *Friday Night Lights*, and in dozens of shows across the country, as well as turns on Broadway in the Tony-nominated productions of *After Midnight* and *Porgy and Bess*. In his London stage debut, he took the West End by storm with his portrayal of Berry Gordy in *Motown: The Musical*. David Grindrod was among the many thousands of theatergoers to experience Neal's electrifying performance. He would go on to cast the actor in the first West End production of the watershed musical *Chess* in more than thirty years. There was never a doubt in Grindrod's mind that Neal would be the perfect choice for Goldie Wilson. In the original film, it was not one of the larger roles, but it proved to be a popular one that resonated with movie audiences around the world, as realized by actor Don Fullilove. When Gale started writing the book, it was a foregone conclusion that Goldie's role would be expanded, including a show-stopping number written by Ballard and Silvestri.

"I couldn't have been more excited, proud, happy, and humbled to have been welcomed into this family, and to be a part of the *Back to the Future* legacy," states Neal. "I'm a part of that, and it blows my mind."

He would have an even bigger part of that legacy when Rando, Gale, Ingram, and Ballard approached him

with a proposition. "They pulled me to the side and basically said, 'We know this role [Goldie] is really small for a performer of your stature. How would you feel about doubling as Marvin Berry?'" Explains Ingram, "I was convinced that he wouldn't play such a small role. He was a principal player who had just appeared as the Arbiter in *Chess*, and even if he did the first workshop [as Goldie], there was no way he was coming back. I always worry about that because investors and theater owners latch on to people in the workshop and can't imagine it done differently."

In taking on the additional role as Berry, Cedric would also appear in the momentous Enchantment Under the Sea dance extravaganza and croon "Earth Angel" when Lorraine and George would share their space-time continuum–altering first kiss. A further enticement would be getting to perform yet another original Ballard/Silvestri composition to open the dance. He didn't need any time to mull it over. "Let's do it!"

The Perfect Ensemble for Both Afternoon and Evening...

In a theatrical musical, it is a given for there to be a number of skilled singers and dancers as part of the company. In addition, some of the members of this "ensemble" would be cast in roles important to the story, but not large enough to have the performer be dedicated to that role and that role only. In the *Back to the Future* cinematic world, Marc McClure, Wendie Jo Sperber, James Tolkan, and Claudia Wells portrayed the McFly siblings Dave and Linda; Hill Valley High's disciplinarian, Mr. Strickland; and Marty's girlfriend, Jennifer, and each of these actors worked a limited number of days filming their parts in the movie. Their musical counterparts, however, would need to be present and onstage for every performance. Having them sit idle for the majority of the show would be not only a waste of their full talents but be a greater expense to the budget of the production.

To that end, some members of the ensemble would portray the supporting characters, and also serve as the all-important "covers," or understudies, for the main roles (Marty, Doc, Lorraine, George, Biff, Goldie, etc.). If one was needed to take over the role of a leading character, the covers themselves would then be covered in their ensemble roles by another group of performers, known in the theater world as "swings." In all cases, the characters would have yet a second cover, in the event their main primary understudy was unavailable as well.

"It's quite a jigsaw puzzle," observes Grindrod of the process. "To get the principals is absolutely fantastic, but it's those people below, and how they fit into the show, that's really intriguing." In addition to learning all of their musical numbers and their speaking roles, the understudies immediately go into separate rehearsals as the characters they might have to replace at a moment's notice. Each would also be fitted for costumes of that character, as well as wigs and other accoutrements. "It's a major expense," admits Grindrod, "but, of course, it's insurance." Hundreds of applicants were broken down into groups of forty and personally put through their paces by choreographer Chris Bailey, who whittled down the candidates to eighteen (not including the four who would appear in featured roles).

JENNIFER/ENSEMBLE (Female)

- Jennifer Jane Parker is the girlfriend of Marty McFly. Pretty all-American girl. Ethnically diverse teenager. Has a heart of gold and is smart, too. The character is 17 years old; the actress can be in her late teens or early 20s.
- NEEDS A BRILLIANT **POP** SINGER. Must have a pop voice with belt, warm in the lower register and able to sing straight tone. [MEZZO Belt D] Looking for a range of dance styles from contemporary musical theater as well as varying '80s genre and '50s rock and roll. Partnering skills also will be explored. Break-dancing skills are a bonus.
- Playing age 20–25
- Height: not taller than Marty McFly
- Appearance: African-American, Black—Other Areas, Black-Caribbean, Black-African, East Asian, Pakistani, Asian, Indian, Filipino/Malay/Thai, Chinese, Japanese, Korean

As Olly Dobson had noted of his own experience, each member of the cast or ensemble would be hired for a two- to three-week rehearsal period, culminating in a rudimentary showcase, and then hopefully be invited back/hired

for the succeeding one. The rehearsals allowed Rando and the production team to gauge the actors' affinities for their characters and their chemistry, to test out new material from Gale, Silvestri, and Ballard, and to make sure that each voice in the chorus and footstep of a dancer would complement the others onstage. For any number of reasons, at times, one or more of those "jigsaw pieces" needed to be replaced with a better-fitting one.

After the first showcase, actress Courtney-Mae Briggs was invited to audition for the next one, an invitation she was happy to accept. She worked with the company for several days, but unfortunately, a prior commitment to the London production of *Hamilton* forced her to miss the final days, including the actual performance. Although another actress would play the part in the showcase, Grindrod knew that Briggs's talents made her a top contender for the role. "The part of Jennifer is relatively small, but a key role nonetheless," he explains. "It was a matter of finding someone who could play the role, then appear in all the numbers as part of the ensemble, go back to Jennifer, and back into the ensemble again." For Courtney-Mae, the prospect of going back and forth from Jennifer to the ensemble was a bonus. "I love being in the ensemble," she states. "I love to dance, and what I find when you're playing a leading role, you're not as involved with everyone onstage. Those kinds of shenanigans are a big part of being involved in the company." As Jennifer, her chemistry with Olly Dobson came naturally. "Olly and I trained together at Arts Educational Schools, London, in Chiswick, where we both got a BA honors degree in musical theater. We were in the same year, were close mates, and graduated together in 2014."

She never appeared in another workshop, but when it came time for the company to decide upon their Jennifer Parker, they went directly back to Courtney-Mae and formally offered her the role. "It was the balance of what she could do in the ensemble, as well as what she could do as a principal," affirms Grindrod of the decision.

COVER DOC (Male)

- This is a brilliant multifeatured character track with an awesome first cover to the lead role of DOC BROWN!

MR. STRICKLAND/LOU, DINER OWNER

- Versatile character actor with good vocal chops needed to play multiple features. Mainly MR. STRICKLAND, the uptight authoritarian headmaster at Marty's high school. As well as scene features of Town Square Bum, 1955 Mayor Red Thomas, and Diner Owner Lou.
- Needs good comedy chops and a good voice. [TENOR or HIGH BARITONE Belt A]
- Playing age 35–50
- Height: approximately 6'
- Appearance: Any

Although the majority of the casting leaned toward younger performers, a number of supporting characters required a gentleman with slightly more life (and theatrical) experience. Grindrod found all those characters in the singular person of Mark Oxtoby. "I've known Mark for quite a while. We did *Joseph and the Amazing Technicolor Dreamcoat* over twenty years ago, and a production of *Phantom of the Opera* as well. What I love about Mark is that he's a gentleman of a certain age. I know he can sing and dance, and he's just got funny bones."

After getting the call from his agent, the actor happily went off to meet with Rando and Ingram, ostensibly for the role of Mr. Strickland. He soon discovered the production team had much more in store for him. "I remember there was lots of music that was sent to me, as well as a lot of script to learn. It became apparent that this audition was also as the cover for Doc Brown. It was one very long day where I read the script, sang some of the songs, and did some work with John Rando. I had to go back the next day to meet with

Nick Finlow, the musical supervisor, which is a funny point in the auditioning process, because you never know whether you're singing yourself into a job or out of it!" Not only did the actor sing himself into the roles of Strickland and understudy for Doc, he would also take on the additional roles of diner owner Lou Carruthers, and 1955 Hill Valley mayor Red Thomas.

DAVE/ENSEMBLE/COVER MARTY (Male)

- Marty McFly's older brother.
- Male actor with a very strong high tenor. Equally comfortable singing in both musical theater and pop styles. [ROCK/MT TENOR Belt C] MUST be excellent, versatile singers capable of singing in both musical theater and pop styles. Solid experience of harmony work needed.
- Looking for a range of dance styles from contemporary musical theater as well as varying '80s genre and '50s rock-and-roll. Partnering skills also will be explored. Break-dancing skills are a bonus.
- Playing age 20–25
- Height: Under 6'
- Appearance: Any

As had happened with finding Hugh Coles at an audition for another show, at the same set of auditions David Grindrod spotted another potential member of the McFly family.

"I was auditioning at the time for *Only Fools and Horses*," recalls Will Haswell, "and at the beginning of the process, my agent mentioned that *Back to the Future* was coming around. They had gotten me an audition, and did I want to go? I went but didn't hear anything. On the day of my final audition for *Fools*, my agent called and told me I had

been offered the first two-week workshop for *Back to the Future*." Haswell never made it back to the other audition, immediately opting for the chance to not only play Marty's brother Dave, but to also serve as the understudy to Olly Dobson's Marty McFly. He would also be cast as "Slick," one of Biff's two (marked down from three) goons, along with ensemble song and dance duties in every major musical number in the show. "As actors," Haswell reflects, "we all have different checklists of things we would like to accomplish. When I left college in 2012, I knew I always wanted to be part of an original show, to be able to build something from the ground up. To have the chance to do it with this show was such an amazing and rewarding experience. It's a privilege to be even a small part of the *Back to the Future* family."

LINDA/ENSEMBLE (Female)

- LINDA is Marty's older sister. MUST have a very strong belt. [SOPRANO Belt E with strong mix in the upper register] Needs good comedy. MUST be excellent, versatile singer capable of singing in both musical theater and pop styles. Solid experience of harmony work needed.
- Looking for a range of dance styles from contemporary musical theater as well as varying '80s genre and '50s rock and roll. Partnering skills also will be explored. Break-dancing skills are a bonus.
- Playing age 20–25

In March 2020, after three workshops had already been completed, Emma Lloyd was brought in to audition for the final workshop, which would lead to the Manchester stage. Already acknowledged as an accomplished singer and dancer for the ensemble, the actress had been asked to audition as the primary understudy to Rosie Hyland for the character of Lorraine. At one point in the reading, the actress was stopped. "They said, 'Do you mind if we give you this script, you go out and take a few minutes to read through it, and come back?'" The pages handed to the actress were for the role of Linda McFly, Marty's older sister. "I went out and came back again and

FAR LEFT Will Haswell

LEFT Emma Lloyd

Rhianne Alleyne
Ensemble

Amy Barker
Swing

Owen Chaponda
Swing

Jamal Crowford
Ensemble

Nathaniel Landskroner
Swing

Bethany Rose Lythgoe
Swing

Cameron McAllister
Ensemble

Alessia McDermott
Ensemble

Laura Mullowney
Ensemble

Oliver Ormson
Ensemble

Katharine Pearson
Ensemble

Jemma Revell
Ensemble

Jake Small
Ensemble

Justin Thomas
Ensemble

Mitchell Zhangazha
Ensemble

actually read with Olly Dobson, who was playing all the other characters in that particular session. It was strange with him being Lorraine as I was being Linda." She laughs. "But at the end of it, I was offered the last workshop!" Adds Bob Gale, "As a bonus, it seemed appropriate for *BTTF* to have a performer named Lloyd!"

When the initial round of casting was done, the *Back to the Future* team had accomplished a feat relatively rare in theater. Five main cast members (Roger Bart, Olly Dobson, Hugh Coles, Rosanna Hyland, and Cedric Neal) and

one cast/ensemble member (Will Haswell) went from the very first showcase in 2018 through the entire process, to taking the stage in Manchester and beyond. "I have never done a show where we had most of the principals cast by the first workshop," states producer Ingram. "We got incredibly lucky!"

During the casting of the ensemble, and just prior to the first workshop, John Rando had an idea and took it to Bob Gale for his thoughts. Recounts Gale, "John proposed having the actors playing Dave and Linda McFly also play

Lorraine's parents, Sam and Stella Baines, in 1955. He thought it was a perfect way to depict 'family resemblance' through the generations. I thought it was a brilliant idea and endorsed it immediately!"

Let's Workshop It!

With the cast set, Rando worked at a blistering pace toward the first crucial hurdle in the race to the stage: the initial reading/workshop of the entire show—book and songs. This presentation would be bare-bones in a rehearsal studio of London's classic art deco Dominion Theatre. Along with the key cast members, the director had an ensemble of eight performers to "flesh it out" and a few musicians to provide accompaniment. "This is kind of like a little concert version of the show," states Rando. "You usually have about twelve days of rehearsal to get there. I had eleven.

"The audience sits on chairs about seven feet away from the cast," details Rando of the procedure. "There are eight music stands spread out about three feet apart. The actors are seated, scripts in hand. They go up to the music stands, play out the scene, and then sit back down." Because the event came

so closely on the heels of most of them being cast, and because the book and songs were changing almost every day, the actors weren't required to memorize their dialogue for the reading. "They know a bit of their lines, they know a little bit of the music, but they also have to read and sing a lot, so that's how it works." Choreographer Chris Bailey had not yet begun his work on the musical, so the director improvised some basic staging, or what he referred to as "silly dances" for the cast and ensemble to play with for the audience.

Glen Ballard had been through this process on *Ghost* and had a fundamental idea of the way everything worked over the course of those first ten days leading up to the performance. "We run through all the material," he explains, "and we figure out what we need to work on. Sometimes I'm sitting at a keyboard changing stuff, sometimes Bob is at his computer doing the same for the book. The actors have to learn it, we have to teach them the new parts musically, and it's this serious round-robin kind of thing.

"We were able to put new lines in front of the actors within thirty minutes. It's really a fantastic process, but it's completely mentally taxing. I don't think there's anything harder than that part of it. It's where the rubber meets the road. It's also a wonderful thing when something solidifies and it feels right; you see it take shape right in front of you."

It Didn't Work (at First)…

One of Ballard's assignments was to rework Doc's celebratory song, "It Works!" "Roger [Bart] had expressed some reservations about the number in its first iteration," recalls Bob Gale. "This was a prime example that demonstrated the importance, the effectiveness, and immediacy of this workshop process. Roger and John had a meeting with Glen, who stayed up all night and wrote a new version."

When he and Silvestri originally wrote the song, "it had more of a fifties 'Rockettes' high-kicking style to it. I agreed it needed to be revised," says Ballard. "The workshop was key in helping to visualize what was going to actually be happening at the point the song would be featured." "When Glen walked in with 'It Works' on the second day of rehearsals at the Dominion," says Rando, "it was so clear that Glen had Roger's sound in his head already and was writing specifically for Roger!" "We made it a little funkier, gave it more of an eighties feel, because it *was* taking place in the eighties, and once we did, it started to click," states Ballard. "We added the dancers about half an hour

CLOCKWISE FROM TOP LEFT Finlow rehearses the ensemble; Bart and Dobson prepare for their workshop performance as Doc and Marty; Roger Bart makes his very first public appearance as Doc Brown at the Dominion Theatre; the Dominion.

before we did it!" adds Roger Bart. Further development and changes to the number would occur down the line, but for the purpose of the workshop, the song was already remarkably close to the polished version that Bart would deliver on the Manchester and later the London stage.

Since the very first workshop, Roger Bart proved himself to be an important collaborator, generous with his musical experience, of which John Rando couldn't have been more appreciative. "We tested several songs through Roger," notes

Rando, "and it became a great partnership. We were able to recognize when we had struck gold and when we had missed the gate entirely on various songs that we tried to do for Doc. We would have really hard discussions about whether a song was in fact doing what it was meant to do. Roger was really key in terms of that."

"I do bring a lot of ideas to the table," admits Bart. "My skill set is that I like to live both in the character and in the putting together of the show. I care about the show, because hopefully I'm going to be doing it a long time." The actor makes it clear that his thoughts and ideas about the development of the show are not only those that affect him in particular. "What we're going to serve up is quality for everybody and every character. If anything, I'll remove myself if I think I'm stinking up the joint!" he says, laughing.

Something About That Back in Time

When Bob Gale was writing his first drafts of the book, he chose to drop the film's skateboard chase. "The practicality and potential for injury to the cast dictated that we *not* do it." In its place, Gale proposed a sequence in the school lunchroom where Biff and his goons would chase Marty, who would elude them in stylish moves that would frustrate the bullies, leave Biff humiliated, and further enthrall Lorraine. It would end Act One.

The song that accompanied the chase, "Something About That Boy," was one that caught Rando's fancy. "It was a really good musical hook," muses the director. "It was fresh and lively. At the time, it was just Lorraine singing. But it felt after we had sung the first chorus, and then repeated with another version of the chorus, it was sort of over. It wasn't doing enough, and I was concerned there wasn't enough story embedded in it. For the staging, we did a quick little chase around the rehearsal hall that was very silly."

Rando saw the potential for the song to be a rousing closer for the act, but he knew there was not enough time to get it into shape for the rapidly approaching reading. "In that room, there would be about sixty very discerning people who were essentially going to tell us what our future was. Either you're going to move forward, or you're not going to

TOP Bob Gale (center) observes as Glen Ballard (left) goes through a musical arrangement with Roger Bart.

BOTTOM (Left to right) John Rando, Glen Ballard, and Bob Gale.

get any money and you're going to fall on your face." The audience for that performance was comprised of potential investors, executives for theater owners, and creative talents that Rando invited in the hopes they would want to lend their award-winning expertise to the production. "From my own experience, I knew how hard it was to convince them we had the right show. Essentially, we were auditioning directly for them." His experience also told him exactly what he needed to win over his demanding audience. "I knew that if at intermission there isn't a buzz, it doesn't matter whether Act Two is the best thing you've ever seen. At intermission, you can get the money you need in order to fund your show if Act One goes out on a high." Rando realized he did not have that guarantee of a unanimous audience high with "Something About That Boy," and that he had no time. Until it dawned upon him that in fact, he did have time.

"Back in Time."

Huey Lewis's 1985 single was written expressly for the film and was featured over the closing credits. The feel-good hit also became the singer's official encore number for his live concert appearances, and it had been slated as the closing number for the musical. For this occasion, Rando decided to "borrow" the tune and move it to a place where he felt it would have a positive effect on the spectators. "We had established in 'Something About That Boy' that Marty had 'poked the bear.' Biff was angry and out for revenge. I quickly created a scene where Marty runs back to Doc's lab and says, 'Doc, you've got to get me the hell out of here,' and then sings 'Back in Time.'" Bob Gale wrote the revised lyrics, which were approved by Rando and Huey Lewis.

MARTY runs out of the school and begins a
cosmic duet, accompanied by an infinite number
of Martys and Docs.

                    MARTY
    HELP ME, DOCTOR,
    AND GET ME OUTTA THIS TIME
    OUT OF THE FIFTIES
    AND BACK TO 1985.
    ALL I WANTED TO DO
    WAS PLAY MY GUITAR AND SING

    SO TAKE ME AWAY,
    USE YOUR MIND
    BUT YOU GOTTA JUST PROMISE ME
    I'LL BE BACK IN TIME
    GOTTA GET BACK IN TIME...

                    DOC
    DON'T BET YOUR FUTURE
    ON ONE ROLL OF THE DICE

                 DOC & MARTY
    BETTER REMEMBER
    LIGHTNING NEVER STRIKES TWICE

                    DOC
    WHEN YOU DRIVE 88

                   MARTY
    DON'T WANNA BE LATE AGAIN

                 DOC & MARTY
    WE KNOW THERE'S A WAY

                   MARTY
    USE YOUR MIND
    BUT YOU GOTTA JUST PROMISE ME
    I'LL BE BACK IN TIME

             DOC, MARTY & ENSEMBLE
    GOTTA GET BACK IN TIME
    GOTTA GET BACK IN TIME

                        CURTAIN--END ACT ONE

Thus, on September 7, 2018, before sixty invited guests at the premiere workshop of the musical, "that's how we ended the first act," says Rando. "Every member of the cast and ensemble got up and danced and sang along to end Act One. And that made the room buzz like crazy. Everybody was happy. Everybody was joyful. We won them."

"Dominion was the most nerve-racking thing, and also the biggest jump in the whole process," reflects Ingram. "We actually had someone offer us a theater immediately after that, but it wasn't a good fit."

The success of the Dominion reading also did what Rando had hoped, by attracting some behind-the-scenes creative talent to commit to joining the production. "[Production designer] Tim Hatley came up to me and said, 'How dare you do that song ["Back in Time"] in the first act? The whole thing is so good. I'm in,'" says the director with a laugh. "[Co-lighting designer] Hugh Vanstone essentially said the same thing. They were upset because they really didn't want to like it or get involved in the show. That began an amazing collection of artists, because once Tim and

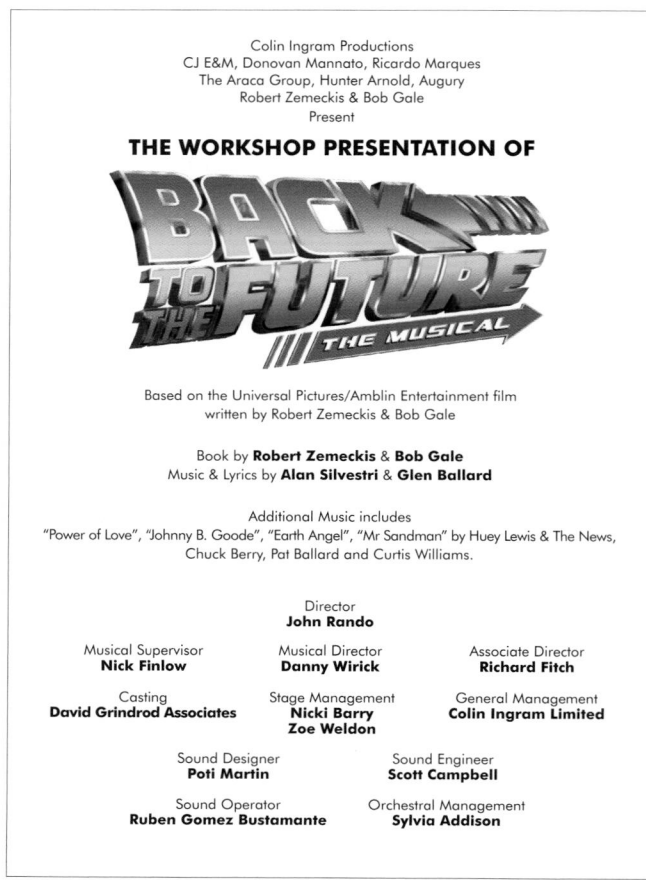

Colin Ingram Productions
CJ E&M, Donovan Mannato, Ricardo Marques
The Araca Group, Hunter Arnold, Augury
Robert Zemeckis & Bob Gale
Present

THE WORKSHOP PRESENTATION OF

BACK TO THE FUTURE
THE MUSICAL

Based on the Universal Pictures/Amblin Entertainment film
written by Robert Zemeckis & Bob Gale

Book by **Robert Zemeckis** & **Bob Gale**
Music & Lyrics by **Alan Silvestri** & **Glen Ballard**

Additional Music includes
"Power of Love", "Johnny B. Goode", "Earth Angel", "Mr Sandman" by Huey Lewis & The News,
Chuck Berry, Pat Ballard and Curtis Williams.

Director
John Rando

Musical Supervisor | Musical Director | Associate Director
Nick Finlow | **Danny Wirick** | **Richard Fitch**

Casting | Stage Management | General Management
David Grindrod Associates | **Nicki Barry** | **Colin Ingram Limited**
| **Zoe Weldon** |

Sound Designer | Sound Engineer
Poti Martin | **Scott Campbell**

Sound Operator | Orchestral Management
Ruben Gomez Bustamante | **Sylvia Addison**

Hugh were on board, we were able to collect the best from every department!"

The entire experience had been a profound one for the director, especially in the beginning stages of getting to know and get comfortable with his cast and hearing them sing in character for the first time. "I was deeply excited," he recalls. "With each passing hour of rehearsal, I felt over and over again that we had something special. I knew we had work to do, but at the time, Dominion was truly inspiring to everyone involved."

Bob Gale couldn't have been more excited about the performance. "I had heard some of the songs done quite well at our 2017 showcase in Van Nuys, a step beyond Glen's demo versions. What really blew me away at the Dominion workshop was the brilliance of Nick Finlow: how he arranged the vocals and got so much out of the performers. The material was performed as 'songs' at the showcase, but they became 'numbers' at the Dominion, and after a few rehearsals, they sounded and felt like a real musical. Nick was incredibly patient with the cast. He quickly picked up on what everyone could do and got them to use their talents and abilities in the best possible

way. It was like going from two dimensions in Van Nuys to immersive 3D at the Dominion."

Gale was further gratified by an exchange with Rando immediately after the event. "John and I were walking back to our hotel, and he said, 'You know, this isn't finished.' I replied, 'As Bob Zemeckis always says, the movie is not finished until it plays on cable TV. This won't be finished until opening night.' And John smiled broadly, knowing that I really got it. It was a memorable moment, because I'm sure he's worked with writers who don't want to change anything." "*I loved that walk home!*" agrees Rando. "It was a wonderful night, and the real start of something special between Bob and me."

No "Time" to Lose!

With the rousing success of the Dominion workshop, everyone had been energized by the audience reaction to the first public presentation of the material. But as Rando had remarked to Gale, there remained much work ahead of them until the director was confident he had the book and the score up to his critical and demanding satisfaction. "John had already done an enormous amount of work on the show in the eleven days leading up to the Dominion workshop," observes Ingram. "The beginning of September 2018 until the second workshop at the end of January 2019 was the most intense and productive period of time of the entire show."

"We knew we needed a bigger workshop/lab than we had just completed, and we ultimately agreed on the end of January 2019 as the target date for that presentation," recalls the director. "We would work exclusively on further developing the songs and the book, as well as creating new songs to replace those we felt fell a little short at Dominion," he explains. Rando also negotiated with Ingram for an additional one-week period in November 2018 for what he referred to as a laboratory in which he would do a closed reading consisting solely of those new materials. Rando and the producers had determined which of the cast members would return, and the roles in which they wanted to see new candidates. Roger Bart, Hugh Coles, and Cedric Neal all had scheduling conflicts during that time, and their roles would be read/sang by temporary replacements.

As Gale and Ballard had returned to Los Angeles immediately after the showcase, New Yorker Rando asked Colin Ingram for a further courtesy in allowing him to fly to the West Coast and spend a few days working closely with Bob and Glen. Ingram graciously consented.

Ch-Ch-Ch-Ch-Changes!

For the Dominion reading, Act Two had opened with a song by Doc and the ensemble entitled "Time Travel Is a Dangerous Thing," in which Doc sang of the perils and pitfalls of traversing the space-time continuum. He was aided in his lyrical discourse by the ensemble, assuming the identities of a plethora of historical figures, including Benjamin Franklin, William Shakespeare, Galileo, Henry Ford, Charles Lindbergh, and Frank Sinatra. It was determined that the song's title, and Doc's musical explanation, was knowledge of which every savvy time-travel fan was already aware and didn't add anything new or informative to the show.

DOC

TIME TRAVEL IS A DANGEROUS THING
'CAUSE ONCE YOU GET THERE
YOU MAY NEVER GET BACK AGAIN
WHATEVER YOUR TOMORROW MAY BRING
TIME TRAVEL
CAN UNRAVEL
TIME TRAVEL IS A DANGEROUS THING
BACK IN YESTERDAY
ANYTHING YOU REARRANGE
WILL GUARANTEE TOMORROW WILL CHANGE
BE CAREFUL OF
TIME TRAVEL
...
FRANKLIN MAY NOT FLY HIS KITE
SHAKESPEARE MIGHT NOT LEARN TO WRITE
HITLER MIGHT WIN WORLD WAR TWO
AND SLAVERY MIGHT STILL BE HERE TOO

"It was witty, and I liked it," says Roger Bart, "but I think the song didn't completely work. In the context of the show, I spend a lot of time warning Marty that if he changes anything in the past, the future is going to be different. So I didn't think we needed an entire song about that same concept. I know we probably saved ourselves a lot of money on costumes by cutting those characters."

The actor's instincts matched those of his director and producers. "Glen wrote this other song to put in that spot, called 'Connections,'" remembers Gale, "and it was Doc singing about how all different things in science are connected to one another, and how the space-time continuum is connected to everything."

DOC

YOU'VE GOT TO MAKE THE RIGHT CONNECTIONS
BECAUSE INFORMATION GETS CONVEYED
FROM ANCIENT TIMES, FAR AWAY
AND SOMEHOW ENDS UP HERE TODAY
...
SOME REVELATIONS STAGGER US
THE MATH OF GREAT PYTHAGORAS
WAS LEFT FOR PLATO TO DISPENSE
THEN EUCLID ADDED HIS TWO CENTS

After watching a video of the Dominion presentation, Robert Zemeckis suggested to Rando that when Marty arrives in Hill Valley in 1955, instead of using the song "Mr. Sandman," as in the film, there was an opportunity to do an original number that would communicate in song the visuals that had been utilized in the movie. Rando immediately embraced the idea and also requested that Ballard and Silvestri pen an original composition to replace the instrumental "Night Train." Those replacements came in the form of "Cake" for "Mr. Sandman," and Cedric Neal as Marvin Berry would now croon the number "Deep Diving" to open the Enchantment Under the Sea dance.

One new song came as a complete surprise to Rando and Gale when they arrived for a meeting at Ballard's Hollywood studio. The multi–Grammy winner handed them a sheet of paper with the lyrics for a new, totally unsolicited song for Doc Brown called "For the Dreamers." "I asked for a lot of different things," says Rando, smiling, "but I didn't ask for a solo song for Doc in Act Two, nor had I said it was something we needed. Glen took us over to the piano, sang it for us, and Bob and I were completely floored. It's just so beautiful, so moving, rich, complex, with dense lyrics, and I can't believe this is going to be in our musical." "It felt to me," says the songwriter, "that in the second act, Doc had this burden on him of being told that he created this incredible invention that worked so beautifully but that he may not be able to return Marty back to 1985. It was a way to express the tension he's feeling. There are pictures of Doc's scientific muses in the lab. While they're Doc's heroes and serve as an inspiration, my feeling is he doesn't necessarily number himself among them yet. The whole idea of the song was like, 'I'm probably a dreamer, and maybe I'm not going to be the one that gets remembered.'"

The only problem was, where to put it in the show? Gale would try it in various places in the second act, at one point using it as the curtain raiser. It didn't stay there long. At the one-week laboratory at the American Church in London in November 2018, Rando tried connecting it to Doc watching the prelude to his death on video. But that wasn't quite right either. Ultimately, Gale realized it should be married to the model scene, which could be separated from Lorraine's visit to the lab. "The song was so good that it was worth restructuring Act Two to give it its due and make it the star of its own scene," said Gale.

Something (Else) About That Boy!

Having previously noted the potential for "Something About That Boy" to be a crowd-pleasing closer for the first act, Rando began to consider ways to improve and enlarge an already infectious song. The first thought that came to mind was *WWBD?*

What Would Biff Do?

"I knew I needed a bigger production number, especially if I was going to do a chase," explains the director. "So we needed to further develop the confrontation. I asked Glen to think about the song from Biff's point of view."

Ballard understood the concept immediately. "Lorraine is singing 'There's something about that boy' through

lovestruck eyes. Obviously, Biff wants to know who the hell is this stranger that stood up to him and cold-cocked him in front of everyone. So each character has their own musical iteration of 'Something About That Boy.'"

The trope of two characters (or groups) singing the same song from opposing viewpoints had precedents in a number of classic musicals, including *West Side Story*, *Bye Bye Birdie*, *How to Succeed in Business Without Really Trying*, and *Grease*. Ballard expediently knocked out Biff's lyrics of the song, which included some participation from his goons, and sent them off to musical arranger Nick Finlow.

Like his director, Nick had always believed "Something About That Boy" could be worthy of dropping the curtain to end the first act. He eagerly went to work to add Biff to the existing arrangement. "I had a very happy accident with this song," he admits. "Glen had written a verse for Biff and his goons, which I dutifully arranged, gave the goons some answering phrases and a bit of fun to do vocally with Biff. I realized that once Biff had finished, Lorraine came back in with her entourage of girlfriends, and then the song needed to start building to the end. We needed Biff to be there at the end, too, to sing something. I was playing around at the piano and suddenly realized that Biff's melody for the verse fit in with a few really choice harmonic changes. His melody fit perfectly with Lorraine's melody for her chorus. Suddenly I had a built-in duet. I didn't have to write almost anything."

BELOW Biff and his goons provide a counterpoint to Lorraine and her girlfriends in the number "Something About That Boy."

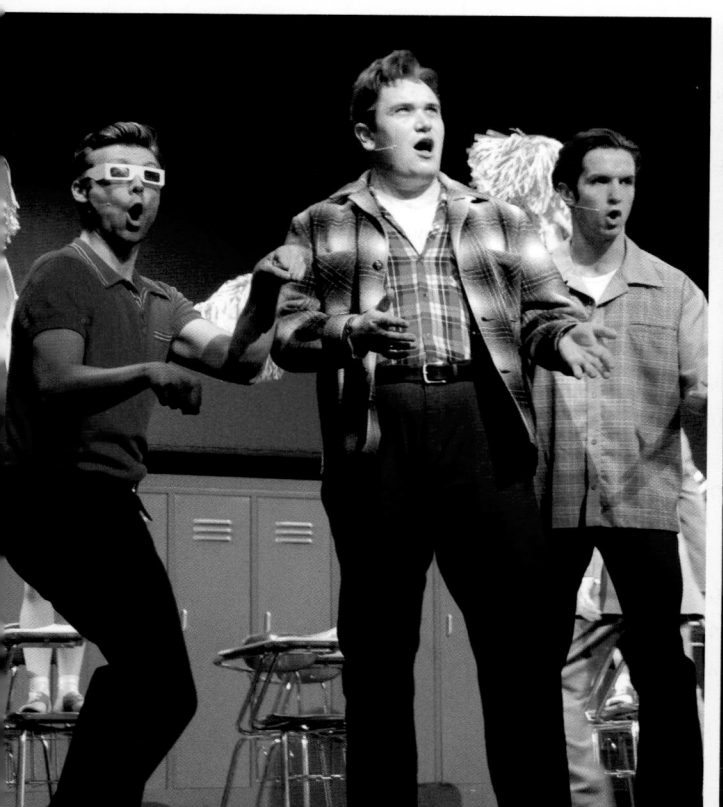

"As it builds," continues Finlow, "there's a key change in the song that lifts you into that duet, and you hear the two melodies. In the staging of the song, they're singing their own melodies at each other, and yet make this glorious noise which I thought was a happy accident. I sat at the piano and thought, *These work together*. I knew we had the end of the act when I arranged that."

While Ballard and Silvestri toiled away on the music, Bob Gale was making changes large and small in the book, in constant communication with Rando. From his notes at the time:

ACT ONE

New opening scene, as discussed, in Doc's lab Sets up lab, sets up Twin Pines Mall exposition, radio broadcast sets up stolen plutonium, we hear Doc stating his advice. Speaker gag gives us some spectacle to start. Marty skateboards down center aisle of theater.

Town square Goldie says "Third time's the charm," indicating he has run for mayor twice before but never won, thus setting up the surprise that he will be mayor at the end.

Revised Jennifer Marty scene. [They sing "Only a Matter of Time."] *At the urging of Colin Ingram, it is determined there will be a duet between Marty and Jennifer through time in the second act. Marty will be singing in Lou's Café, but in 1985, no such business exists in Hill Valley. Gale sets this introductory scene in a 1985 7-Eleven, and it will return in the second act from where Jennifer will sing to Marty.*

New element: Jennifer says her uncle Huey, with record company connections, is in town, and she has arranged an audition for Marty tomorrow. This raises the stakes for Marty to want to get back and will pay off nicely at the very end.

1955 café Marty says Goldie is going to run for mayor (as opposed to being mayor).

Lunchroom scene Marty asks George if he's ever considered writing about time travel. Lorraine vows to find out all about Calvin Klein.

ACT TWO

Doc's laboratory New logistics for the plan, replacing the turntable gag. Doc demonstrates this as a large-scale model, like in the movie, with fire gag.

Doc's plan to send Marty home returns in a form similar to the movie, with a model for which Doc apologizes, and a toy car that bursts into flame. At this point in time, no work has begun on the construction of the sets, so the description of Doc's plan, and how the audience sees it, is written in a looser form. That scene will soon find its rightful place in the book shortly after the weeklong lab.

New scene in Doc's lab follows "Put Your Mind to It." Doc has a thoughtful moment alone in his lab and sings "For the Dreamers." *Glen Ballard's new solo for Doc is given its first slot in the book.*

New scene at school with Biff and his stooges After two days, Biff's guys haven't been able to find Calvin Klein. Has he skipped town in fear?

Biff sings shortened version of "It's What I Do." Scene concludes as they find out Calvin plans to go to the dance. Now Biff will be there, too.

New café scene for Marty's letter, replacing the previous version in Doc's lab. Includes Goldie and Lou. *Doc has a crippling fear of heights. How is he to get the wires strung from the weather vane on top of the courthouse, down to the street, and across the lampposts? Goldie Wilson needs money to further his education. Problem solved. Marty expresses concern about what he's about to do. Marty writes letter in café. Duet with Jennifer is in split set: 1955 café/1985 7-Eleven.*

Parking lot Lorraine kicks the fallen Biff before going with George. They briefly reprise "Pretty Baby" together. (**RULE OF MUSICAL THEATER:** *Having a couple sing together shows they're truly in love.*)

"Johnny B. Goode" Marty does the "history of rock guitar" medley as in the movie (Bob Zemeckis note). At one point, it was considered that Marty would perform "Johnny B. Goode" without the flourishes of other famed guitar performers. Zemeckis disagreed and believed that *not* having a callback to Michael J. Fox's guitar performance and its abrupt ending would be more of a distraction to the *BTTF* fan contingent who would be expecting it and wonder why it would be omitted from the show. Added denouement with George and Lorraine, as in the movie. (BZ note.)

Town square, 1955 Marty sneaks the letter into Doc's pocket, and Doc finds it. (BZ note.)

Hill Valley Celebration Day Lorraine is now a caterer, and she has catered the event. Jennifer's uncle Huey is here to see Marty perform. Replaces Marty being a recording artist.

Direct from the Director

From October 29 to November 2, 2018, Rando put the cast through their paces to sample the new and revised material into which everyone had put so much time and energy.

None of the LA contingent had traveled to London but were sent videos of the work, followed by an assessment of the results by the director:

"The overall work week in London felt extremely useful. So much new material and refined material was generated, created, and tweaked. It was also really helpful to have a cast assembled to test out and help develop the music and scenes.

"Here's my two cents on each of the sections/songs/scenes that we worked on:"

Opening: "A Matter of Time" Great work here. New music, new lyrics, clearer exposition. Can't wait to stage this one.

"Wherever We're Going" Excellent changes to the scene. I think the location change in the 7-11 and adding the character of Joe is a great touch for this. [Joe was a character created by Gale who works behind the counter at the 7-Eleven.]

"Cake" This is really fun and is working! But it still needs some incubation. In the video version, we decided to open it with the "bung bung bungs" of "Mr. Sandman." I also wanted to try doing something like what Glen had originally recorded, and sing a bit of the song and have it turn into "Cake," but we ran out of time. The vocals arrangement is well on its way. And the character stuff for the ensemble is good for them; they won't just be generic people. I didn't really have the chance to mine the comedy with the actors, but there is certainly opportunity. I did wonder if we should maybe not go for applause on this one but let it fade and take us into the diner.

"Something About That Boy" This one has come a long way. I think the addition of Biff singing in this is truly helpful in terms of dramatic action, storytelling, staging/choreography, and comedy. We also added a little "Leader of the Pack" stand-in intro dialogue in the verse opening with Babs and Betty. I think we can do a tiny bit more with this. While everyone is frozen, Babs and Betty are seeing/hearing their friend Lorraine's passion awakening. Maybe Bob can find something. I also can see so much better how we can jump cut between the Lorraine and the girls' infatuation with Marty, and Biff's bubbling anger/jealousness of him. Nick and I kept adding more of Biff and his goons to it. On top of Biff's "Something About That Boy" section, we borrowed his "Teach Him a Lesson" from the Act Two reprise. It all needs more shaping, and it does become hard to understand. It may also be aided by some dance arrangement. BUT it's good stuff, and I can't wait to work more on it.

"This One's for the Dreamers" Hands down the favorite of the week! The actors were completely moved by it when they heard it for the first time. Having the context of the song while Doc watches the video could be really effective. We played with moving the scene in the middle of the song more, as you can see in the video. Not sure about this yet. I think the scene is saying one thing and the song another. There needs to be a line of dialogue that connects them both, where Doc impels Marty not to spoil this dream of his. Maybe we need way less of the dialogue about knowing too much about the future in this scene. Maybe Marty wants to tell Doc the truth, that he is still a crackpot in 1985 and his experiments still fail. Not sure, but I just know we don't have scene and song married yet.

"Deep Diving" The other big hit of the week! Wow. Fun and perfect and does everything we could ever ask in terms of story-telling. Cedric will kill on this one.

"Connections" We have a decidedly mixed response on this one. First off, what we liked about it. The idea of the Act Two opener being in Doc's mind is super fun. The idea that we are in a '50s vision of a futuristic lab is also a real winner. The samba section will be absolutely fun for dance! But the song itself doesn't feel right yet. Nick suggests that we need to have an opening number of Act Two that is in a major key! The minor key just brings the proceedings down. He feels strongly that a major key could lift the whole act off. Colin wasn't keen on the "Connections" lyrics. To be absolutely fair, we did not have Roger Bart in the room to help sell "Connections." We may have had a completely different reaction. That said, though, we have to make a song that isn't actor-reliant. In any case, we need to go back to the drawing board on this one.

Although the song wasn't well received, the points on which Rando gave positive comments would come heavily into play for Ballard and Silvestri in their next composition, resulting in a production number that would surpass everyone's expectations.

The general consensus from all concerned was that the time devoted to the numbers had been well spent, serving as a musical theater "pit stop." The end of the American Church lab work would send the production into an even more intense stage as it prepared for its next critical plateau: the Sadler's Wells workshop.

Let's Dance!

Waiting in the wings was choreographer Chris Bailey, who had first been brought to Ingram's attention as an up-and-coming talent in 2014. Four years later, when John Rando came onto the production, he and Bailey were already well acquainted, having worked together on *Because of Winn-Dixie* and the touring company of *The Wedding Singer*. Bailey was serving as choreographer of Rando's *Puttin' the Band Back Together* while the director was in talks with Ingram and the *BTTF* team. Everyone was happy to have their collaboration continue on *Back to the Future The Musical*.

Bailey first traveled to London to audition members of the ensemble. Once he was satisfied with the selection of talent, he returned to his US home to begin his preliminary work while Rando prepared his cast for the first workshop at the Dominion.

Until he would return to the UK on a full-time basis, Bailey needed someone with whom he could work in New

York and who would also keep an eye on the London workshops. In 2004, as the associate choreographer on a revival of *Guys and Dolls*, Bailey first met Darren Carnall, who already had the reputation as one of the best dancers in the West End. In a 2008 production of *Candide* at the English National Opera, Bailey performed as a swing with Carnall as part of the ensemble. In late 2018, Chris asked Darren to join him as his associate choreographer on *Back to the Future*. Carnall, a huge fan of the film, immediately said yes. Thus, Bailey had found a way to effectively be in two places at once, and not a moment too soon, given what Rando was planning for January's workshop rehearsals.

Step in "Time"

Knowing that the Sadler's Wells workshop would have three times as many people in the audience as the Dominion presentation, Rando wanted to give this performance more

single night, I got home and worked out something for another number," he says with a laugh. "We ended up doing movement/choreography for a fair amount of the big numbers."

"It Works" Even Better!

When first envisioning the choreography for "It Works!" Bart told Rando, "I need some girls behind me, some support. It can't be just me." "First we added them as just a vocal track," Bart said. Suddenly the question was, where are these voices coming from? "We needed girls onstage, but who the heck is hanging out outside Twin Pines Mall at 1:15 A.M.?" mused Bart. "The janitorial staff? That wouldn't be very sexy." So they turned to a musical theater convention by asking the question themselves. Refined after numerous rehearsals, the Marty-Doc exchange became an instant crowd-pleaser:

> MARTY
> Hey, Doc! Who are the girls?
>
> DOC
> I don't know. They just show up every time I start singing!

When performed at Sadler's Wells, the line became an instant audience favorite. This playful wink at the audience would also allow Rando and Bart to devise another crowd-pleasing surprise in a later scene.

flash and movement—it was time for dance to make its first appearance in the show.

Chris Bailey, unavailable to make the trip to London, was still able to contribute. Based in New York, Bailey gathered a number of dancers in a studio and devised some basic yet stylish routines for the workshop numbers, upon which he would later expand.

When he was satisfied with the routines, he forwarded videos of them to Darren Carnall in London, who would then teach them to the ensemble. "Chris also asked that if John needed help with any small bits of choreography, changes, or movement he wanted to put in, could I be in the room for him," says Carnall, who readily agreed to the request. Rando was not shy in asking Carnall to assist him in trying many new ideas. "It seemed like every

Giving It a Little Style . . .

In the first workshop, the team had a chance to "test-drive" Gale's invention of the talking DeLorean. For that performance, Rando had cast a female ensemble member to give voice to the vehicle. "Just to have a person standing there showed that suddenly the 'car' had personality," observed the director. Rando encouraged Gale to write material to push that envelope, and Gale took to the challenge with pleasure, adding a bit of comedy and attitude in the dialogue. The incredibly talented Aisha Jawando (who would go on to play the title role in *Tina: The Tina Turner Musical*) would portray the car at Sadler's Wells, adding her own touches of a fancy silver jacket and sunglasses, and even raising her arms to simulate the gull-wing doors.

ABOVE Carnall runs the ensemble through a new routine in preparation for the Sadler's Wells workshop.

OPPOSITE Rehearsals for Sadler's Wells. Top: "Only a Matter of Time"; bottom: "21st Century."

The guest list for this event was meticulously orchestrated by Ingram and Gale. "Firstly, we invited ticket agents, as we knew they'd be behind us if we got them involved and they were allowed to express an opinion," outlines Ingram. "Secondly, I invited around twenty theater producers, from whom I wanted to get opinions. I've always believed we should work as a 'community of producers,' and I asked for their thoughts after the workshop."

Another very important contingent of this audience would be longtime *Back to the Future* fans. "Without the fans, we wouldn't be here thirty-five years after the film was first released," states Bob Gale. "They deserved to be among the first to see how we were honoring, protecting, and celebrating the film. And we wanted to hear their honest opinions of the material." A representative sampling of the UK fandom was chosen with the aid of BackToTheFuture.com founder Stephen Clark, which included two women who, in the mid-eighties, were the co-presidents of the UK chapter of the Michael J. Fox Fan Club.

Also making their first in-person appearances at the workshop were Zemeckis and Silvestri, whose schedules allowed them to attend. "We also had a number of theater owners and some licensors for foreign productions," adds Colin. "It really was a powerful group of people, like a first night. It showed how important people thought this production was going to be. In that room was the fate of the show."

Ingram welcomed the crowd, gave shout-outs to the "celebrities" in attendance (Zemeckis, Silvestri, Ballard) and a nod of appreciation to the members of the *Back to the Future* fan club in the crowd. He explained the procedure for those uninitiated with the process: "There's going to be a lot of improvisation. I do warn you, there's going to be plenty of air guitar, but I assure you, we'll get real guitars by the time we get to the show!"

Gale also had a few words for the audience, relating a bit of the history of how he and Zemeckis had finished the first draft of the script for the movie thirty-eight years earlier in 1981, and how it had been roundly rejected by every studio and producer in Hollywood. "Back then, if a time traveler from today had come into our office and said that on February 1, 2019, we would be sitting here with all of you, with all these great people behind me [the performers], we would have said, 'What have you been drinking, bozo, and can we have some?'" He explained that a narrator would

Other highlights would include "21st Century," the new curtain-raiser for Act Two, the expanded version of "Something About That Boy" with Biff's new vocals, and Rando and Gale's collaboration in devising the perfect introduction for Doc Brown's inspirational new ballad "For the Dreamers."

All's Wells...

The second exclusive preview of *Back to the Future The Musical* took place on February 1, 2019, at Sadler's Wells Theatre, located on a site in London that has served as home to six theaters since 1683. Invitations went to 180 individuals. Unlike the rehearsal space at the Dominion, this was a real theater with raked seats, and a sound system that would be used for key sound effects.

describe some of the things that couldn't be presented (such as the lightning strike) and further informed the crowd that they were the first people in the space-time continuum to see the version of the show in its current form, and beseeched them *not* to spread the word. "*Please* don't talk about it. Don't put it on Facebook, or Twitter, or Instagram, social media, your web pages. Don't even tell your mom, OK?" Rando came out for a brief hello to the audience and to thank the cast for their incredible work over the previous days.

With no curtain to raise, the show just started . . .

Colin Ingram Productions
CJ E&M, Donovan Mannato, Ricardo Marques
The Araca Group, Hunter Arnold, Augury
Robert Zemeckis & Bob Gale
Present

WORKSHOP PRESENTATION OF

BACK TO THE FUTURE THE MUSICAL

Based on the Universal Pictures/Amblin Entertainment film
written by Robert Zemeckis and Bob Gale

Book by **Robert Zemeckis** and **Bob Gale**
Music and Lyrics by **Alan Silvestri** and **Glen Ballard**

Additional Music includes
"Power of Love", "Johnny B. Goode", "Earth Angel", "Mr Sandman"
by Huey Lewis & The News, Chuck Berry, Pat Ballard and Curtis Williams.

Directed by **John Rando**

Lilian Baylis Studio
Sadler's Wells Theatre, Rosebery Avenue, London EC1R 4TN
Nearest Tube: Angel

Friday 1st Feb 2019
1–3pm

Please enter through the Stage Door on Rosebery Avenue.

"Time" Well Spent

The presentation surpassed everyone's expectations. The actors' performances were infectious, and the audience gave them a lengthy and well-earned ovation as they took their bows. The producers were thrilled with how far the show had come in the several months since the Dominion presentation. Ingram said it had come along further in its abbreviated development time than many of the other shows in which he had been involved.

"Everyone was very positive, though some thought it ran a little long and took too long to get to Doc's entrance," says Ingram of the immediate feedback.

The majority of the fans in attendance wholeheartedly approved of what they had witnessed. "It was our first time meeting them," says Rosie Hyland of the fans. "I remember being more concerned with impressing them than I was the producers and investors. We met them outside the theater after the show, and their response was overwhelming. We were just so relieved and elated to know they had loved the show and the direction in which we were taking it."

"With Bob Zemeckis there for the first time, and the first row of seats being occupied by the *BTTF* fans, it was a high-stakes presentation for sure," notes Hugh Coles. "But both Bob Z. and fan club members pulled me aside afterward to express their excitement for the project, so at that point I knew we were on the right track." Of equal if not greater importance to Rando and his producing team were the impressions of the show from the women who had been the copresidents of the Michael J. Fox Fan Club, and whether two of the actor's most ardent admirers could accept anyone else in the role of Marty McFly.

When Kath Ball-Wood and Lora Colver had received invitations to the event, they knew it had something to do with *Back to the Future*, but little else. The two women were asked to be at an address on a specific date and time. Even though they were given no other details, they were also asked not to discuss with anyone else the iota of information they had been given. On that frigid day in London, the pair arrived at the Lilian Baylis studio at the Sadler's Wells complex to see a sign on the door with the *BTTF* logo and the words "Back to the Future The Musical" printed under it. The secret was out.

They entered the theater and took some open seats, finding themselves right behind Bob Gale and directly in front of Robert Zemeckis and Alan Silvestri. Both women were thrilled to be in such prestigious company, but they were also very much concerned about what they were about to see.

"I must admit," relates Ball-Wood, "when I sat down, I thought, *This is not going to be any good, and I'm not going to like it.* Back to the Future *is my favorite thing. It's sacred.*" Her compatriot was having many of the same thoughts. "Literally the first thing we said to each other was, 'I don't know if it's going to work, because no one else could be Marty except Michael J. Fox. I was very skeptical, and I was convinced I wasn't going to enjoy any of it.'"

5 MINUTES LATER...

Kath Ball-Wood: "I was like, *How could I ever have doubted this?* What made it so good was that it wasn't a word-for-word adaptation. It was so clever because it absolutely got the spirit of *Back to the Future*, the fun and the humor. That's what grabbed me straightaway."

10 MINUTES LATER...

Lora Colver: "I was completely enthralled. I was like, 'Michael J. Who?' I was absolutely riveted. I just couldn't take my eyes off the stage, even though it wasn't a proper production. It was rough, but it felt like *Back to the Future*."

Both women were in total agreement that Olly Dobson had in fact completely inhabited the character of Marty McFly, to their utter delight. "The minute he came out," says Kath, "I thought, *Yes, that is exactly Marty McFly.* Olly totally captures Marty's presence and fun." Adds Lora, "I wouldn't say he's replaced Michael J. Fox, but he's equal to him in his sense of humor, his facial expressions, and his reactions." The pair agreed that Dobson ultimately didn't have to be compared to Michael J. Fox, as Dobson made the character of Marty his own, in the same way that Fox had created his interpretation decades earlier.

At the intermission, Bob Gale was curious to find out if the ladies were enjoying the show so far. And it went exactly like this . . .

INT. LILLIAN BAILEY THEATRE - DAY

BOB GALE approaches LORA and KATH.

>   BOB (to both)
> What do you think?

>   LORA
> When do the tickets go on sale? Can I
> buy one?*

* A FEW YEARS LATER...

As of November 25, 2021, Lora Colver and Kath Ball-Wood had seen the musical six times each. They are far from done . . .

Biff at First You Don't Succeed . . .

Throughout musical theater history, a long list of villains have darkened the stage to celebrate their evil natures or chant about their nefarious plans. Alan Silvestri and Glen Ballard added Biff Tannen to their ranks with an ode to the oppressor when he unapologetically stated to the audience, "It's What I Do."

Bob Gale loved the number, and it remained part of the book for many years, having first been performed at the 2017 song showcase. When John Rando took the helm of the musical, he asked Al and Glen if they could offer an alternate song for the bully. They promptly returned with a new Biff-centric number, "Good at Being Bad," where again, he made no apologies for his actions, but in this version, the song started with a prologue explaining how Biff evolved into the town's teen tormentor:

```
             BIFF
I WAS A GULLIBLE BOY
I HAD A HARD TIME JUST PLAYING WITH
   OTHERS
A DEEPLY IMPRESSIONABLE CHILD
WHO CRIED WHEN HIS BIRD DIED
PREFERRED PASTEL COLORS
I WAS A DELICATE BOY
EVERYONE TREATED ME LIKE A PARIAH
I KEPT MY FEELINGS INSIDE
NURSING THE HURTING
AND DEEP IN DENIAL
LEFT ON MY OWN
THE DAMAGE WAS DONE TO ME
HOW COULD I HAVE KNOWN
SOMEDAY THEY WOULD RUN FROM ME
DAD WASN'T THERE
MOM DIDN'T CARE
LIFE ISN'T FAIR
LIFE ISN'T FAIR

BUT LIFE DOES GO ON...
AND GIVEN THE TIME
LIFE CAN TURN ON A DIME
WHEN I TURNED THIRTEEN
MY FAT WAS ALL GONE
REPLACED BY PURE BRAWN
AND I QUICKLY DISCERNED
THAT THE TABLES HAD TURNED
I HAD A REVELATION
BASED ON MY SITUATION
FOR MY HURT TO BE GONE
I HAD TO JUST PASS IT ON

SO DON'T COMPLAIN
I FELT YOUR PAIN
THAT'S WHY I'M GOOD
AT BEING BAD
I HAVE THE URGE
TO SIMPLY PURGE
THESE NEGATIVE FEELINGS I ONCE HAD
I PASS IT ON
AND THEN IT'S GONE
AND SOMEHOW, I'M NO LONGER SAD
```

After the performance, a member of the audience approached Bob Gale with some negative observations about Biff's ballad. "It was my daughter Samantha," admits Gale. "She made the point that the song kind of made Biff likeable, and she said 'I don't want to like Biff. There is no excuse for being a bully. The song seems to be giving Biff an excuse, and I have a hard time with that.' She was right."

Gale discussed Samantha's concerns with Rando, Silvestri, and Ballard, who all agreed if there was any trace of a redeemable quality within the youth, they would not be faithful to the original character.

So, for the next iteration of the song, the entire prologue was removed. Completely.

Sadler's…and Wiser!

With the audience filing out, Bob Gale was approached by another fan. "He was semi-catatonic, and just stunned at how good the show had been. He was close to speechless, but just able enough to tell me how amazing the show was, and that being there had made it the greatest day of his life." Gale made that day even a little more memorable by posing for a photo with the überfan.

It had been a pretty good day for everyone . . .

Building a New "Future"

Immediately after the Dominion showcase, Ingram received the offer of a West End theater, but didn't deem it the right fit. However, the Ambassador Theatre Group, who had made that offer, did have a theater that Ingram knew would be the perfect place for the show's "out-of-town" tryout engagement.

A longtime theatrical practice, a show slated for Broadway or London's West End would first take to the stage in front of paying audiences in another city as a totally realized professional production, fully choreographed, with costumes, scenery, props, a full orchestra, and special effects. During that time, the creators could tinker with various elements of the show until it was time to move to its intended destination.

Ingram (along with Ballard) was very familiar with ATG's Manchester Opera House, having premiered *Ghost: The Musical* there prior to moving it to the West End. The producer was confident that this would be the perfect home in which to fully realize and present the show to the public. Shortly after Sadler's Wells, he signed a contract that would see the show open with previews on February 20, 2020, and an official "Press Night" premiere on March 11. The show would have a twelve-week engagement before transferring to the West End.

LEFT Gale and Ingram at a BBC interview at the network's headquarters with the proper accessory.

alongside the multi-Tony and Olivier Award–winning design team of Tim Hatley (set and costume design), Hugh Vanstone (lighting), Gareth Owen (sound) and Finn Ross (video), with choreography by Chris Bailey and musical supervision and vocal arrangements by Nick Finlow. Orchestrations will be by Ethan Popp, with dance arrangements by David Chase.

The role of Marty McFly will be played by Olly Dobson, whose previous West End credits include the original cast of *Bat Out of Hell: The Musical* and *Matilda the Musical*. Further casting to be announced.

Back to the Future, the movie, was released in 1985, starring Michael J. Fox as Marty McFly and Christopher Lloyd as Dr. Emmett Brown. The film grossed $360.6 million (£279 million) at the box office worldwide, and the total box office for all three films in the *Back to the Future* franchise was $936.6 million (more than $1.8 billion in today's money).

Marty McFly is a rock 'n' roll teenager who is accidentally transported back to 1955 in a time-traveling DeLorean invented by his friend Dr. Emmett Brown. But before he can return to 1985, Marty must make sure his high school–aged parents fall in love in order to save his own existence.

All members of the original cast of the film are excited about this new musical version. Christopher Lloyd, who played Doc Brown, said, "Ever since Bob Gale told me about this, I've been eagerly anticipating it and, in particular, wondering what it will be like to hear Doc Brown sing. So I'm really looking forward to attending the opening in Manchester to experience our wonderful movie as a musical. I'm only sorry I don't have a real time machine so that I could see it tomorrow!"

Bob Gale, who wrote the film with Robert Zemeckis, and who is writing the book for the musical, said, "Bob Zemeckis and I have been trying to get this project off the ground for years, but good things take time, and finally, the time is right. Our cast is outstanding, the songs are fantastic, and director John Rando is doing an amazing job ensuring the show truly captures the magic of the movie. We're thrilled that we can retell our story onstage in a brand-new way, and we're certain that *Back to the Future* fans all over the world will share our enthusiasm. In the words of Marty McFly, 'Your kids are gonna love it'—and so will you and your parents. There's truly no better way to celebrate the movie's thirty-fifth anniversary, and we're happy to say 'the Future' is coming back!"

FOR IMMEDIATE RELEASE

Finally, on May 17, 2019, a press release was distributed to the global media, providing all of the pertinent details about the Manchester engagement, the most important of which was when the fans, who had been eagerly awaiting even the slightest morsel of information, could finally purchase tickets.

BACK TO THE FUTURE THE MUSICAL TO OPEN AT MANCHESTER OPERA HOUSE ON THURSDAY, 20 FEBRUARY 2020 FOR 12-WEEK SEASON

BOX OFFICE OPENS 10:00 ON FRIDAY, 24 MAY 2019

Producer Colin Ingram (*Ghost: The Musical*) and the creators of the film *Back to the Future*, Robert Zemeckis and Bob Gale, are delighted to announce that **BACK TO THE FUTURE The Musical** will open at the Manchester Opera House on 20 February 2020 for a strictly limited 12-week season, finishing on 17 May, prior to transferring to the West End. The Box Office will open at 10:00 am on Friday, 24 May 2019.

Based on the Universal Pictures/Amblin Entertainment film, the new musical will have a book by Bob Gale and new music and lyrics by Emmy and Grammy Award–winning Alan Silvestri and six-time Grammy Award–winning Glen Ballard, with additional songs from the film, including "The Power of Love" and "Johnny B. Goode."

BACK TO THE FUTURE The Musical will be directed by Tony Award–winning director John Rando (*Urinetown*, *On the Town*),

Four days after the press release went out, the clock tower in Albert Square saw the arrival of the DeLorean time machine along with Bob Gale and Olly Dobson to greet the fans.

Within the first few weeks, the show sold more than £1.2 million in tickets.

"After the success of the Sadler's Wells workshop, my confidence was high," affirms Rando. "With Colin securing the Manchester Opera House, my focus turned to the production. We essentially had one year to go from a pencil sketch idea to a fully realized three-dimensional production." The yearlong effort would include design meetings, more workshops, choreography, "and, of course," adds Rando, "the DeLorean no longer simply being an actress at a music stand in a shiny silver jacket, but a thrilling technological achievement!"

There Are Some Who Call Him...Tim

Although Rando hadn't wanted to get involved in anything apart from the book and music until he was satisfied with the content, producer Ingram had been working behind the scenes to attract the best creative talents to the show, starting with a top-notch production designer. Get the best, and that person would attract other department heads of the highest caliber. For Ingram, there was no one better suited for the job than Tim Hatley.

The Tony and Olivier Award–winning designer was no stranger to transferring a film property to the stage, having done so with popular titles like *Shrek*, *Spamalot* (adapted from *Monty Python and the Holy Grail*), *The Bodyguard*, and *Singin' in the Rain*.

Ingram first contacted him to gauge his interest even before the Dominion workshop. "I remember thinking, *How on earth would you do that show?*" Hatley recalls. According to the designer, it seemed more an impromptu get-together than a formal business offer. "I put it on the back burner of my mind."

TOP "One Day in May": A few days after the show was officially announced to the media, Olly Dobson dropped by the clock tower in Manchester's Albert Square along with his new favorite mode of transportation.

BOTTOM Bob Gale also made the trip to Manchester to greet, mingle with, and take photographs with the fans.

and its continuing popularity was a key consideration in his approach. "This was a very important movie both in the history of filmmaking and for the fans. I think it's on another level, the highest of all that I've ever worked on, and one that has had such an impact on so many people's lives. There were moments in which I imagined the fans saying, 'What have they done to our film?' And that prospect was terrifying."

Ultimately, Hatley came to terms with his apprehension and set off to work. "You can't spend a year working on a musical being scared!" Even though he knew the movie inside out, his first step was to watch it . . . again and again and again. And then he stopped watching it. "I had my list of the key elements, and it was time to start designing," he explains. "The spirit of the musical was in the script and the songs we had, but in terms of what that would look like, it did not exist except in my head.

"In my London studio, which is luckily a big space, I literally took a piece of A4 [8" × 11"] paper for every single moment in the musical, including moments within the scenes. I printed a title for each, a summary of the intention of the scene, the actors who are in it, and what the location needs to be. I laid it out in a great big storyboard all the way around the room. It's a great way to realize the scale of it. You can see the arc, the story, and all the locations. It also points out red flags. If we're going in and out of Doc's lab too often, this isn't good; not for the audience, not for the story. We need to somehow get those two scenes that are saying those two things and put them together so that we don't have to go back and forth scenically. I would feed that information back to John, who then spoke with Bob. And we streamlined the structure, because if the set ever slows down the show, it's my problem. My job is to keep that show moving scenically."

Hatley also had to add physical space limitations into the equation. "We're always limited in theater. Where do you put the set? Where do you put all the scenery? Where do you park the DeLorean? You have to be inventive and as clever backstage when you're storing things as when you're showing them to the audience."

With his room-size storyboard in place, Hatley's next step was to prioritize the most challenging sequences. "Town Square, the clock tower, and the entire end sequence, Doc's Lab, and of course, the DeLorean were all tied for first place."

A casual mention from Ingram to Rando about Hatley found that the director *had* in fact given the matter a little thought and was thrilled to hear that his producer had read his mind. "I had met Tim years earlier," recounts Rando, "and I'd wanted to work with him ever since. We'd had a couple of meetings in New York and talked about various projects. None came to fruition, but Tim had always been on my radar." It was agreed that Hatley would attend the Dominion performance in the hopes he would sign on.

Despite the skeletal nature of the presentation, Hatley saw the possibilities immediately. "I thought it was absolutely brilliant. There were clearly things that were not right, but I thought, *I've got to do this show, because it's really, really good*. It was also terrifying because I thought, *Now I* really *have to do this show, but I don't actually know how to do it*. I left the workshop thinking, *Oh my God, what have I signed on to?*"

In India on another job, Hatley was unavailable to attend the Sadler's Wells workshop, so he had a friend and colleague, lighting designer Hugh Vanstone, call him afterward. Vanstone informed him that this new workshop was even better than the first. A video of the event was forwarded to Hatley, which reinforced his desire to be a part of the production. "That's when I started to sharpen my pencils."

Like Rando, Ingram, and almost everyone else in the production, Hatley was a fervid fan of the classic 1985 film,

Before he chose which to tackle first, he would build one very small but integral tool to greatly aid him in the creative process: a little black box.

Like its namesake in the aerospace industry, Hatley's modest version would offer him countless alternatives on how he might approach the design. "It's a little model theater," he explains. "The proscenium opening is about two feet wide, about a foot high, and inside is the stage."

The "stage" was built to scale from the dimensions of the Manchester Opera House and painted black. Hatley

started populating it with cutout designs of buildings and characters, gauging their proportional sizes to each other, as well as their proximity to the audience.

TOP Having storyboarded the entire musical, Tim Hatley creates a number of 3D models of the sets, the stage, and the action of the characters.

ABOVE Additional Tim Hatley set models.

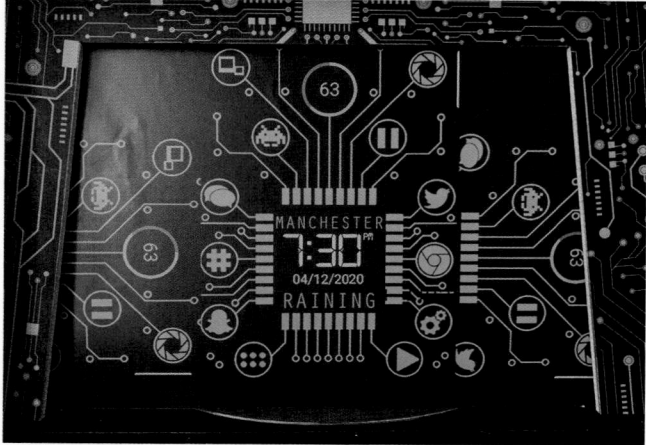

Hatley also knew that technology would ease some of the load. After breaking down the show, he took the list of the sets and backgrounds and delineated which would need to be physically built, and which could be left in the capable hands of video designer Finn Ross.

In designing the sets, Hatley captured the warmth and essence of the film, and each contained a direct link to its cinematic counterpart, to give the audience a sense of comfort with the surroundings. When Doc arrives in the DeLorean at 1:20 A.M. at the parking lot of Twin Pines Mall, in the background stands the familiar JCPenney department store, courtesy of the video and prop designers.

The Circuit Board Proscenium Arch...

Almost as important as the sets that filled the stage was what would frame that space: the proscenium arch. From the beginning, Hatley anticipated devising the proper motif to cover the arch to further enhance the set and serve as more than superficial ornate decoration.

"With a big show in a big auditorium," states Hatley, "if your set can jut out a bit and encompass the people in the front rows, it has a ripple effect on the entire room. You're pulling people into the design, and likewise, the design is being thrown out to the people. It is a fine line, because the focus always has to be the stage."

In most cases, the last thing a designer would want to do is draw the audience's attention away from the main stage, but for *Back to the Future*, there were times when a slight diversion would benefit the stage experience. "We had so many effects to pull off that something in the peripheral vision of the audience would be a clever way to distract them momentarily from what is happening onstage as the lights sparkle or things blow up. It was a great tool to add to our box of tricks."

Hatley still needed to decide what shape the covering would take.

"My first thought was that the design could represent all the wires that connect the DeLorean, or the wires in Doc's lab. From there, it morphed into a circuit board. The image struck me as a good graphic shape, and everyone just got it."

"I thought it was perfect, because I always wanted an immersive show," confirmed Ingram. "You have all the movement in your periphery as well as in front of you, and it feels like it's an extension of the DeLorean." Adds Rando, "I thought it was was spectacular. He had landed on something fun, smart, immersive, and super cool."

This Looks Like a Job For...

As Ingram had hoped, having Tim Hatley attached to the show and the words "Back to the Future" attracted some of the UK's most highly regarded creative talents to the team.

Bright Lights, Hill Valley...

Lighting designer Hugh Vanstone heard about the project from his good friend Tim Hatley, with whom he had worked on *Spamalot* and *Shrek the Musical*. "I thought it was one of the great untapped titles to be taken to the stage. While some people say that good films don't necessarily make good musicals, I thought this one would be an exception. So I signed on."

In the midst of those preparatory months, a sudden health issue befell Vanstone's partner, and it became clear

that the lighting designer would not be able to give 100 percent of his attention to the show. He immediately called the one person whom he could trust to perform the creative duties with consummate skill and aplomb. Tim Lutkin had previously worked as Vanstone's associate lighting designer on many projects and had gone on to a celebrated career on his own. "I was honored to be asked to get involved," Lutkin recalls. It was agreed that Lutkin would take the lead on the lighting design of the show, and Vanstone would function as a key consultant.

"What's great about Tim Hatley designing the set for a musical is that the sets themselves are easy," observes Vanstone. "Here's the town square . . . here's a bedroom . . . they're easy. The hell of musicals is getting from point A to B without having an audience lose their attention because it takes too long for a transition. That's when lighting can create the magic smoke screen that hides some massive piece of scenery trundling offstage or can create the focus that allows something to make a sudden appearance.

"Our lighting also had to connect to the music," he continues. "Music is an emotional response to the story, and lighting is an emotional response design-wise. If a number is up-tempo and rock-and-rolly, you want the lights to be dancing with it. If it's a ballad about love and the stars and dreaming, the lighting has to feel that emotion."

Vanstone and Lutkin would also collaborate with Hatley on one of the designer's signature pieces of the show: the environment for the auditorium. Lighting "tendrils" stretched into the upper levels of the theater, further immersing the audience and providing bursts of luminescence when necessary to enhance some of the special effects and distract from others.

Lighting was also an integral element in the construction of the custom-made DeLorean. Says Lutkin, "We researched exactly how everything looks in the film and then worked out what would actually translate on the stage and made it bigger and bolder." Taking into account the DeLorean's new abilities to speak and accept verbal commands, Lutkin added a few new illuminating flourishes, with components of the car lighting up as Doc programs it for time travel.

However, there was only so much that could be done until the entire production moved onto the stage for rehearsals. "We do very careful and detailed preparation," states Vanstone, "but when the director and the choreographer and the designer get in the theater, it can

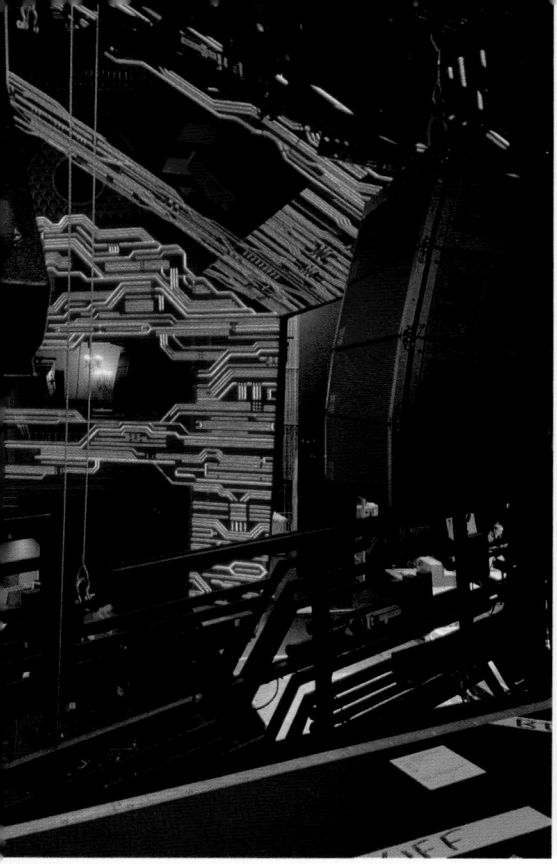

all change because they get a better idea, or because something doesn't work. There's no way of preparing for it. You just have to know that your work isn't going to be fully finished for a while."

What's That Sound?

In 2013, sound designer Gareth Owen noticed an article in a UK publication announcing that *Back to the Future* was going to be adapted for the stage. He promptly sent an email and résumé to Colin Ingram. "I never got a reply, never thought more about it."

Five years later, a rather surprised Owen found an email in his inbox with the subject heading "Re: Back to the Future sound designer," which began "Sorry it's taken me a while to reply. We'd really like to talk to you about the future plans," signed by none other than producer Ingram. One meeting with John Rando later and Owen had the job for which he had unknowingly waited half a decade. "It became quite obvious that we were kindred spirits in our love for the movie," he says of that meeting. "I think it certainly helped that [musical director] Nick Finlow and I had worked together before and had really enjoyed the experience." Over the course of his burgeoning career, Owen

---

ABOVE Lutkin's and Vanstone's lighting included the interior of the theater as well as enhanced lighting for the DeLorean time machine.

had come to understand the relationship between sound design and the music. "Sound and music are completely at each other's mercy," he asserts. "The music can be the best in the world, but if the sound quality is rubbish, it doesn't matter. Likewise, you can be the best sound designer in the world, and if what's coming into your mixing desk is rubbish, there's nothing you can do to improve it. With Nick already involved in the show, John and I getting on really well, and with Alan Silvestri and Glen Ballard doing the music, who could say no to *Back to the Future The Musical*?" The tech-heavy show would count on Owen's expertise for a great number of other sound-related responsibilities.

The sound system: Every single part of the speaker system was designed by and installed in the theater by Owen's team, both in Manchester and later in London, ensuring that every word, every sound effect, and every musical note can be heard with the same quality and clarity from the seats in the orchestra to the last seat in the upper galleries. "If you can't hear the words, then the audience can't hear the jokes. If the cast can't hear the band, they can't sing. If the band can't hear each other, they can't play. If the sound isn't right in the back of the mezzanine, the producer gets very grumpy and has to start refunding tickets."

Owen was also responsible for setting up a communication system for the lighting and video departments. He had video cameras trained on the musical director and broadcast to the other departments who would need to take their

cues from conductor Jim Henson (no relation). And he created click tracks for pieces of the score to enable the orchestra to be able to play the music in sync with the computerized timecode, triggering cues that are sent simultaneously to lighting, video, and automation.

And that was all before lunch . . .

Like many other department heads, Owen's process in creating the sound effects began with going painstakingly through the script and noting every opportunity for an effect. He reviewed the completed list with Rando, who decided which to keep and which he thought extraneous.

Once the technicians programmed the DeLorean for its movements onstage, Owen went to work to provide the sounds that emanate from the vehicle, ranging from the opening of the gull-wing doors to the flux capacitor "fluxing," as well as the fully computer-synthesized "voice" of the car.

For the specific sounds of the car in motion, the designer wrote some original software and utilized a device that was not intended for the theater. "Rather than simply playing back a sound file of a car driving, I wanted to generate that actual sound with a computer-game engine," he reveals. "When you play a driving game, it doesn't play back sound effects. If you're accelerating, it synthesizes the sound of a car accelerating. When you brake, it synthesizes the sound of it braking. So we took a game engine and ran it live on the show. We used the Krotos Audio Igniter car simulation engine, which is loaded with custom DeLorean presets as well as prerecorded samples, and can simulate anything the car does. Not only can the car accelerate, decelerate, change gear, and brake, but the sound of the car changes depending on which way it is facing. For example, when it's facing the audience, they hear less of the engine (because it's a rear engine car); when it's facing away, they hear more.

"As far as I know, taking computer-game sound synthesis and tying it to live events onstage has never been done before. It's pretty cutting edge."

ABOVE Sound designer Gareth Owen.

RIGHT Top: Owen's sound boards in the theater; bottom: A sample of the multitude of sound effects that are triggered manually during each performance.

Other effects came from the designer's gargantuan library of more than 440,000 individual sounds, collated from libraries around the globe, including those of Lucasfilm, Disney, Sony, and many, many others. After Owen joined the production, Bob Gale made sure the designer had access to every sound effect utilized in the original film.

Ultimately, Owen decided to "be as true as possible to the original, but with the benefit of today's technology," offering the best quality sound experience worthy of this new production.

In giving voice to the DeLorean, Owen and his team utilized a computer "text-to-voice" synthesizer, which actually generates the voice of the car live during the performance. This is obvious at the end of the show when the DeLorean announces the future destination time: It's always the exact same time and date of that actual performance.

Push the Button!

Over the course of the performance, a massive network of computers control and trigger approximately 99 percent of the lighting, video, and automation cues that occur onstage. It is the sound department that literally applies the human "touch" in delivering hundreds of sound effects. Starting from the opening, when Marty enters Doc's lab,

an engineer carefully eyes the action, with finger hovering over a button. When Marty adjusts the dials on the giant speaker, that button is pushed, and the sound effects of static and volume and distorted speech are triggered throughout the sound system. Moments later, when Marty puts guitar pick to strings, the button is pressed again, and the audience hears both the chord played and the speaker sparking to life and exploding. The "Go Button," as it was referred to by Reese Kirsh, the sound engineer who pushed it several hundred times each performance, was guaranteed by the equipment supplier to perform to satisfaction for five hundred thousand "pushes." Before the show had reached its one hundredth performance in London, the button had already been replaced once and was due for another replacement shortly thereafter.

One of Owen's great delights is producing subtle effects that an audience might not even notice. One such effect to which he points with pride is when Marty arrives at the clock tower after the dance. As he and Doc remove the tarp from the DeLorean, the sound of raindrops hitting the car cover can be heard. Once they've removed it, the sound changes to that of rain hitting the metal hood of the car!

Clothes Make the Cast

In UK theater, it is not uncommon for a show's production designer to also serve as the costume designer.

"In my training, we were taught to design for the whole show, and there's no discussion about it," Hatley expounds. "You get thrown into the deep end, and it's a great training ground. I learned very quickly about fabrics and costume construction. It's a very different discipline, actually thinking about the drape of a dress. It's also so much easier, in that as a production designer, I've done a fair amount of work with other costume designers, and it's never completely harmonious. This way, I know I'll never have the problem of a red costume against a red wall. It's also satisfying to think about the clothes you want to fit in the spaces you've created."

Hatley acknowledges he had a head start in designing the wardrobe for *Back to the Future*. "There are certain things that are part of the film, and the fan base wants to see them. Marty has to wear an orange puffer vest; if he doesn't, you're going to upset a lot of people. So we've taken the elements of the film that people want to see and added the element of surprise. Yes, Doc looks like Doc,

but no one expects him to leap up onto the DeLorean and perform a fabulous number with six dancing girls who come out of nowhere. I wanted them to look like part of the DeLorean, so I costumed them as 1980s pit girls with big Farrah Fawcett wigs, silver jumpsuits with flames on them, and boots to match. They dance all over the car with Doc, and it becomes like a car showroom fantasy with the DeLorean on a turntable before we're restored to 'reality.'"

With some characters, Hatley chose to clothe them in outfits that "echoed what already exists." When Lorraine is singing "Pretty Baby" to Marty in her bedroom, she's dressed in seemingly the same dress from the film. "I made that dress out of a much lighter fabric, because when she spins and turns, it has to become a dance dress. I used the same print of the actual dress from the movie, but I upped the colors a bit. It's a little more pink, a little more perky, because it is a musical."

As much as he enjoyed re-creating the classic looks of the film characters, Hatley also loved creating outfits for the ensemble, most notably Doc's assistants for the "21st Century" number. "It was completely of my own invention," he discloses. "We didn't have anything to start with. Who are they going to be? What do they look like? I did consult with Chris Bailey to determine what the costumes needed in order to allow the dancers to do the number. From there, I was able to create a fun and inventive look for them, knowing they were figures of Doc's imagination. It was the most fun."

C'S FUTURE LAB
SSISTANTS. ACT 2

DOC'S ASSISTANTSHIPS

Wardrobe/Costume by the Numbers!

- On average, the character of 3-D goes through two pairs of the bicolored glasses every week (eight performances).

- Ninety percent of the laces for the shoes/footwear have been replaced with elastic to expedite the costume change process.

- The record for the highest number of costume changes in one song goes to Katherine "KP" Pearson with four—going from cheerleader to student to teacher and then back to cheerleader for the curtain drop.

- Each member of the ensemble has eleven costumes per show.

- The American football helmets were sourced from the United States and then "retro-fitted" for the 1950s look.

- Each costume worn by one of the DeLorean Girls has two hundred Swarovski crystals attached to the suit and boots. Lots of rocks!

- Waist watchers: three sets of body padding: one for Rosie Hyland as Lorraine in 1985, another for Emma Lloyd as Linda McFly, and a second for Emma to play her maternal grandmother, Stella Baines.

- Doc knows how to accessorize. Most accessories per show include:

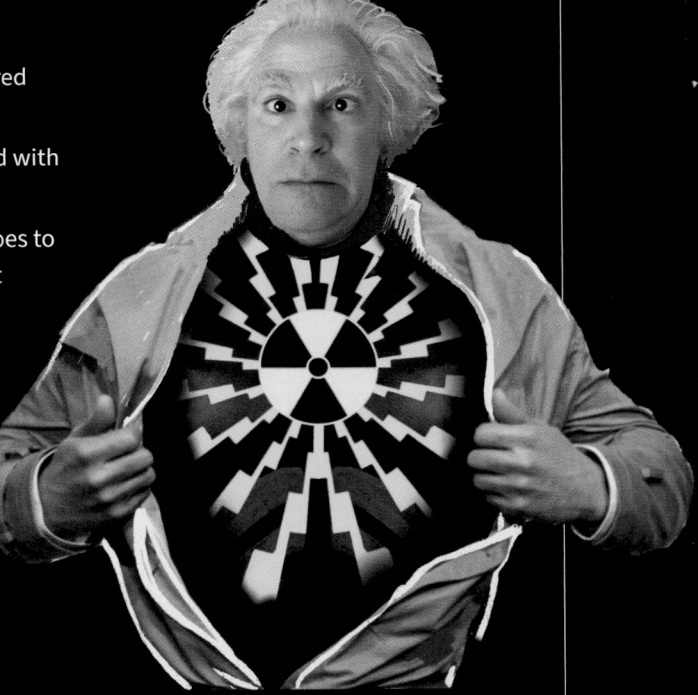

1. Plutonium vest and gloves
2. Stopwatch
3. Toolbelt
4. Goggles
5. *Gremlins* notepad and pencil
6. Watches
7. Brain scanner
8. Radiation suit helmet/hood
9. Telephone area code clipping

71

Video "Games"

Ingram's plan to recruit the top creative talents in the theatrical world scored another coup in the award-winning video designer Finn Ross, who had his own admirable credits in theatrical productions adapted from film, including *Frozen*, *Mean Girls*, *American Psycho*, and *Harry Potter and the Cursed Child*. When he got the call to meet with Rando, "my first thought was, *Wow, someone's being crazy enough to do that*, and it would be brilliant or a disaster, because these things tap dance on the edge so finely." After reading Gale's book and meeting with Rando, he decided it had the potential to be the former, and happily signed on.

"Tim Hatley had a fairly clear idea of what parts of the show would be made from video and some broad reference images for each scene. As we went along, I developed them into a cohesive language to bind the show together. Part of this process involved looking at the physical pieces Tim was designing and taking cues from these to inform the world beyond them so everything always felt like it belonged while being true to the film. There are almost no scenes without video, because the back wall is video, allowing various backgrounds and banners to fly in." For the designer, it was important that the video not call attention to itself. "It's a flow through the show, and because the style of one scene has an impact on another, they have to be part of the same world."

As they storyboarded the show, it became clear to Ross that there would be big, critical moments that would rely on every department's highest level of expertise. "It was always going to be about supporting the DeLorean," Ross affirms. "The appearance, the disappearance, as well as giving the car movement in taking it from 1985 to 1955 and then back again." But Ross also knew there would be many other creative opportunities. "Tim [Hatley] has a real connection to the manic energy of Doc Brown, and there are numbers in the show like 'It Works,' 'Future Boy,' and '21st Century,' where Doc just sort of departs reality and we go into his imagination. With video, you can go into the abstract of reality easily, transforming the stage from someone's backyard garden into outer space."

Getting Up to Speed...

When director Rando finally turned his attention to the physical aspects of the production, one of his first priorities was to work with Hatley on the process that would get the DeLorean to 88 miles per hour and through the space-time continuum.

In the beginning, Rando wasn't sure how they would represent the iconic vehicle. "Tim had already done a lot of research on the DeLorean, and he showed me imagery of DeLoreans drawn in fluorescent colors with various space-age flourishes. For a while, we thought we wouldn't have an actual car. We would have an outline of a car. We went through more crazy ideas until Colin, in his producorial way, told us in no uncertain terms, 'There *has* to be a DeLorean.'" "I was absolutely against any kind of idea that we might just see the inside cabin or something that wasn't literal," confirms Ingram. "I made it clear I wanted to see the whole thing."

All Hands on Deck!

With Ingram's mandate, Hatley ordered a DeLorean model kit from the internet and, after putting a miniature turntable on the bottom of the box, added the assembled model. Other crew members were brought in for their expertise, including lighting directors Lutkin and Vanstone, sound designer Owen, and video designer Ross. It was the video aspect that gave Hatley the germ of the idea that would ultimately provide the answer. Part of what Ross brought to the production was a video wall, used at times to supplant

LEFT Dusk is displayed on the video wall during a rehearsal of "Wherever We're Going."

a backdrop with video, rather than Hatley having to physically build one.

"At times we have full scenery," says Rando, "and other times we have video scenery with a couple of key physical elements in front of it. We can fool the audience like that and entertain them at the same time." "Video was always supposed to be a support," acknowledges Hatley. "I knew we could do the car sequence completely in video, but I had no interest in that option whatsoever. We needed an actual car (as per Colin), but then I realized you could get a sense of speed with video and moving lights."

Ross enhanced the video with more than just lights flying past the windows. Utilizing a 3D software package and reference materials from the film, the designer created his own version of the Twin Pines Mall. Ross would then call on an object to represent the position of the car, attach a camera to that, and copy basic movements from the stage into the 3D world. That camera would mimic the actions of the car. "If it drove forward for five seconds, it would move, accelerate, move forward for another five seconds and then turn. When we took whatever that camera was recording, placed it behind the car, and ran the two in sync, we'd get the world moving with the car. We tried to work it out and do it live but it got too messy, so we put a video into the computer and did some good old animation. It worked really well."

"The illusion is pretty good, I've got to say. I've never done this sort of thing on a stage before, and this was a great solution," comments Hatley. Although everyone was pleased with the results, they would have to wait almost a year before they could test it in the theater. In the meantime, they still had one last "minor" detail to tend to. They had to build an actual DeLorean.

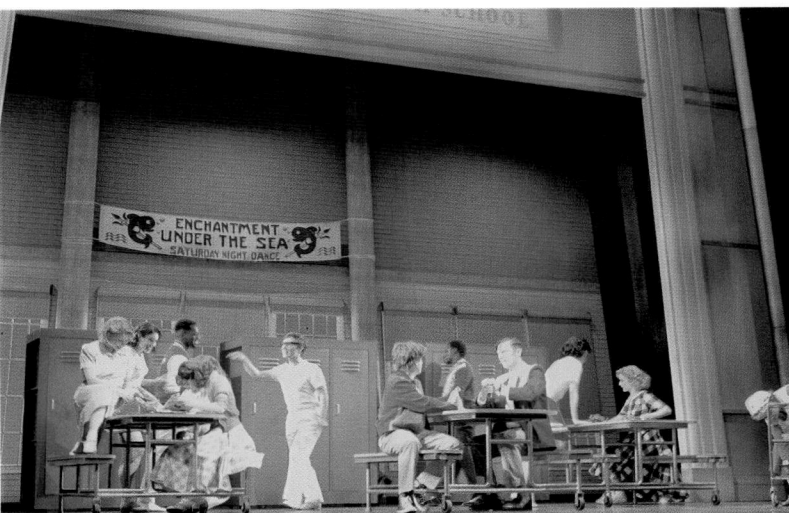

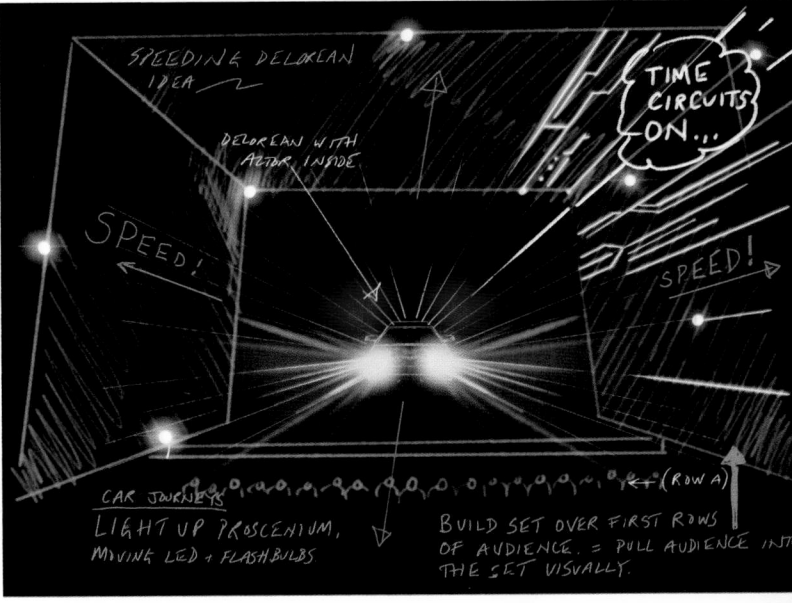

ABOVE Video designer Finn Ross.

TOP The video wall displays the Hill Valley High School wall in the cafeteria.

MIDDLE A backstage passerby cannot find an outlet where she can charge her phone on the rear of the video wall.

BOTTOM Sketch containing lighting details for the DeLorean time travel to 1955 sequence.

If You're Gonna Build a DeLorean for a Musical, You Might as Well Do It with Some Style!

If Tim Hatley thought that devising a way for the DeLorean to "drive" onstage was tough, it was nothing compared with the complexity of building a replica of one of filmdom's most iconic vehicles.

"There were so many questions that needed to be answered," he states. Among them were the following:

Q: The DeLorean appears four or five times. How many are we going to have?

A: I was keen on one car doing everything. There was no space for three, four, five cars. There wasn't even space for just the front of a smashed-up car.

Q: Do we need this DeLorean to fly?

A: Fly? Is it supposed to fly???

Q: Does it have to be strong enough for dancers to dance on it?

A: It's a musical, of course there are going to be dancers on it!

Q: Should we get a real DeLorean and gut it?

A: No, it's already going to be a tight fit and jammed with effects and mechanisms to make it do what it does. (Bob Gale offered the wisdom of a man well acquainted with the workings of a "performance" DeLorean: "If you're building one of these DeLoreans, you'd better build two, so if there's a breakdown, you'll still have a show!")

To facilitate the process and respond to all of those queries and so many more, a "shopping list" was created for what the DeLorean would need to do.

1. The wheels have to rotate (but never touch the ground).
2. Everything has to light up—the lights inside and the time-travel lights outside.
3. It has to shoot CO_2 to create smoke.
4. It has to be on a turntable that can turn 360 degrees.

5. It can tilt sideways, backward, and forward.
6. It has to be strong enough to support dancers.

Among his many other responsibilities, production manager Simon Marlow would be in charge of building the iconic vehicle. In working with the creative team, there were always three questions Marlow needed to address when he received a request for something to be built:

1. Are they asking for something that is physically possible?
2. Can we afford it?
3. Do we have enough time to do it?

"Regarding the DeLorean, the answers to all three were, 'I hope so!'" says Marlow. "The vehicle was absolutely integral to the show, so we had to figure out how to build it, and at the right price. We had a seemingly comfortable eighteen-month lead-up on this show, but it turned out that we needed every moment of it."

Before beginning the work, they needed to determine the scale of the car. "First, we made three different-sized DeLorean mockups out of timber. One was actual size, one was 88 percent, and the third was 65 percent," he details.

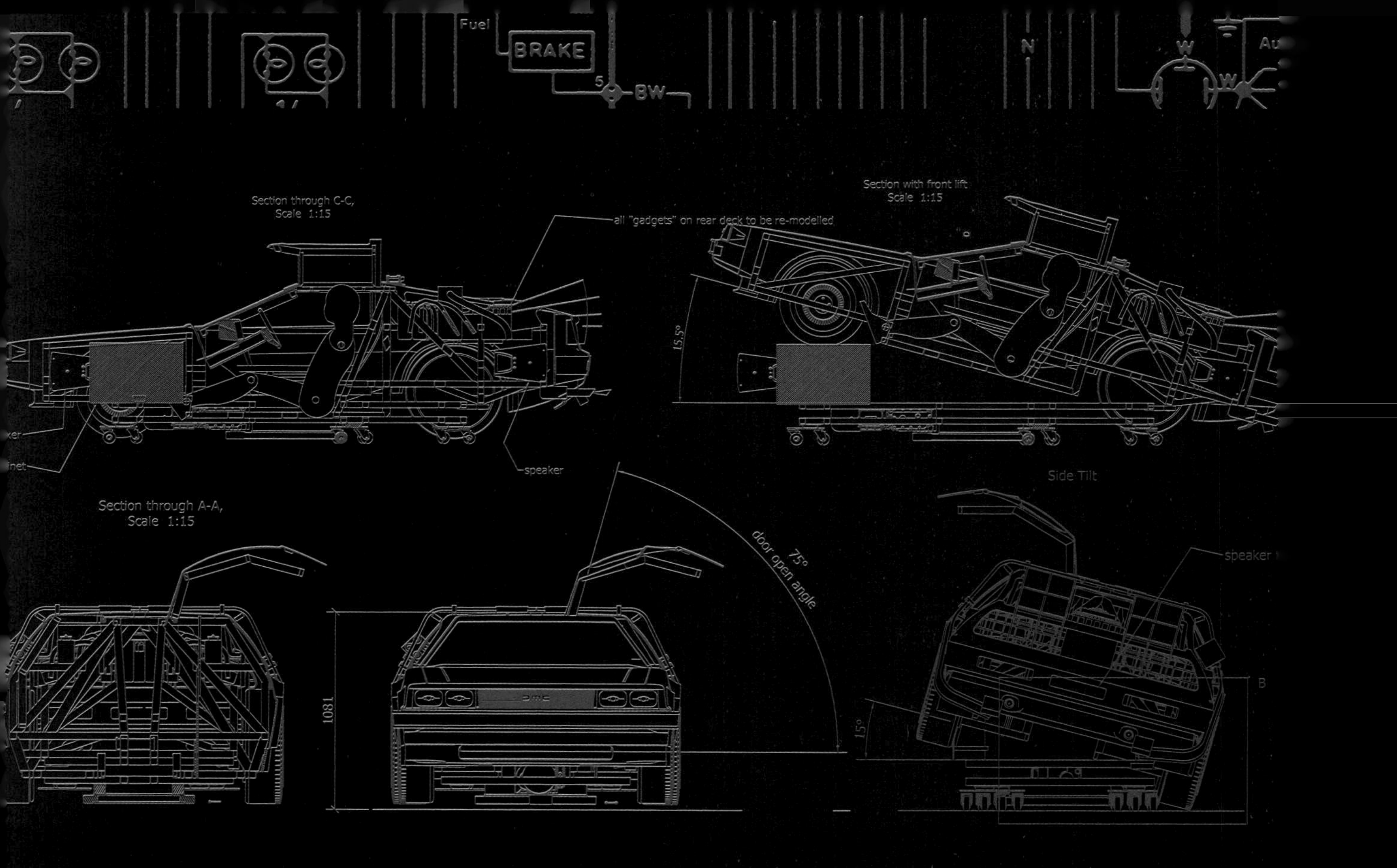

Section through C-C,
Scale 1:15

Section with front lift
Scale 1:15

all "gadgets" on rear deck to be re-modelled

15.5°

speaker

Section through A-A,
Scale 1:15

Side Tilt

door open angle   75°

speaker

1081

15°

B

"Then we hired an empty theater and, after lining the mock-ups up onstage surrounded by lights, it was decided the optimal size was, appropriately, the 88 percent model. If you put a true-size DeLorean on the stage, it looked out of place and didn't work with the perspective of it." Having decided the scale, the scenic shop obtained detailed, 3D versions of the DeLorean's blueprints.

No actual DeLoreans were harmed in the creation of the musical production's offspring, as a time machine replica was loaned to the company by local owner Steven Wickenden, of which they would take numerous scans, photos, measurements, and copious notes to add to the information they had started with. "Everything had to look right, especially to the legions of fans who would be scrutinizing every aspect of it," said Marlow. A mold was made of the car from which they reproduced the body, and then they went to work customizing it. Despite the fact that the audience wouldn't be able to see the interior of the car, Marlow made sure that all of the lights, knobs, switches, and LED displays were exact replicas of the original car. The significant difference between the two was the flux capacitor, which was made removable for both Marty and Doc to display to the crowd in a number of scenes. "There's so much technology in it that I don't think Roger appreciates the slightly shrunk dimensions, because it is very tight," allows Marlow. The addition of all of the machinery enabling it to be put through its paces onstage (built-in turntable, tilt mechanisms, and wireless equipment to communicate with the show's computers) almost doubled the normal weight of the car.

While it was being built, Marlow also had a wooden and metal frame DeLorean constructed for the company to use during rehearsals.

OPPOSITE Building the DeLorean: Months of work went into the development and construction of the car. Top right: Art director Ross Edwards connects the lightning collector to the DeLorean. Bottom: The full-size DMC time machine replica that was scanned extensively for the construction crew sits next to the completed stage version.

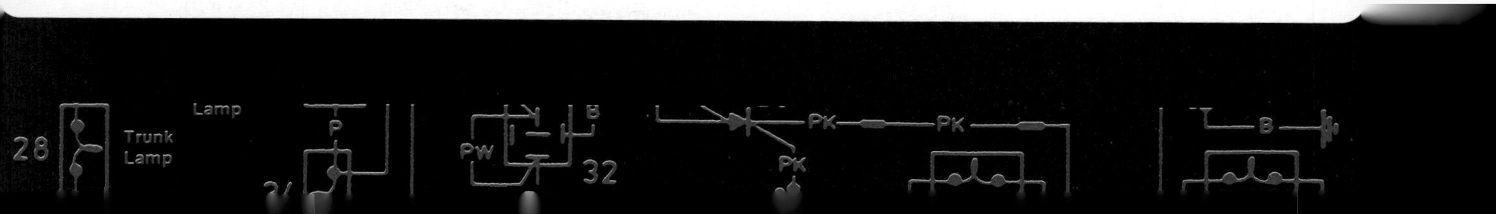

 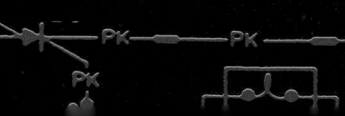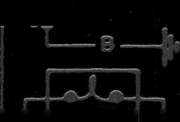

Let There Be Music!

When Glen Ballard and Alan Silvestri completed their work on a musical number, the process was far from complete. Every piece of music written for the show would pass through the hands of additional creative members of the production for further modifications and enhancements.

In 2018, shortly after John Rando signed on to direct the show, Nick Finlow (*The Book of Mormon*, *Mamma Mia!*, *Dreamgirls*) received a call from Colin Ingram asking if he'd like to be the musical supervisor for *Back to the Future*. "Colin and I never actually worked together, but we'd known each other for a long time," says Finlow. "When he asked if I wanted to join the production, I didn't even take a breath. I just said yes."

Finlow's responsibilities within the music department would be multifaceted, overseeing the activities of the department as a whole. He would regularly interact with Silvestri, Ballard, and Rando and was responsible for further populating the music department with some of the foremost talents on both sides of the Atlantic. They would include:

LEFT Glen Ballard and Alan Silvestri.

Orchestrators Ethan Popp and Bryan Crook

Grammy- and Tony-nominated producer, arranger, and orchestrator Ethan Popp wasted no time in accepting the gig for a very personal reason. "I fancy myself probably one of the biggest *Back to the Future* geeks in the world," declares Popp, "and it was Alan Silvestri's work on the original film that was a major influence in why I became a musician and developed an interest in orchestration." In further conversations with Finlow, he learned he would also be integrating pieces of Silvestri's film score into the mix. "After determining the gargantuan task that the orchestration would be, I reached out to Bryan to come on board with me. We have collaborated on numerous projects in theater, film, and television, and we've always had a profound connection in terms of our musical vocabulary." Crook, self-admittedly also an unabashed fan of *Back to the Future*, needed no coercion to join his colleague in this new adventure.

Musical Director Jim Henson

"The music director's primary job," describes Henson, "is to conduct the running of the performance. You're there to lead the orchestra, sometimes conducting with sticks [batons], or, in my case, it's playing and conducting at the same time. Also, I teach all the music to the cast and the band, and then maintain the musical quality for the run of the show. I am essentially the 'keeper of the music,' and on a show like this one, there's an element of development and creativity as well, so I was very lucky that Nick wanted my input and opinions and experience. I was also able to add my two cents' worth on structures, arrangements of

how things might work, or my opinion: Does this work musically or not? I became like a sounding board for him, and we just bounced ideas off each other."

The Way It Worked...

In their writing, Silvestri and Ballard would put forward a fully realized piece, with arrangements. "The bones of most of the tunes remain intact," notes Ballard, "but they were not yet ready for the stage."

Each song would go to Finlow, who would give them a slightly more musical theater arrangement, one that works with the storytelling. Quite often, the songs are interwoven into the script rather than just being a stand-alone song, framed by dialogue. Where there is dialogue in the middle of the song, the music has to keep running. "Part of my job in arranging the song is to tailor the music to fit the dialogue, making sure that the underscore is long enough and malleable enough to accommodate the dialogue and work in the live performance."

A prime example of Finlow's work occurred right before the Dominion workshop with Glen and Alan's new version of Doc Brown's introductory number, "It Works!" "John Rando wanted to put it up on its feet right away," recounts Finlow, "and in the song, Doc is backed by six dancers. I left the room for half an hour, wrote a [background] vocal arrangement for it, and quickly taught it to the ladies." A short piece of dialogue

between Marty and Doc in the midst of the song also required Finlow to add a few bars of music to accommodate that spoken exchange before returning to Doc's vocals.

The song would undergo additional adjustments when the choreography was established by Chris Bailey. "In Manchester," continues Finlow, "the girls are hidden upstage, and the audience can't see them before they enter, when the lights shine on them. Chris Bailey wanted their entrance to be a little bigger musically, so that's part of my remit [responsibilities]—to make sure the choreographer has what he needs from a musical point of view."

Finlow's duties also included working closely with the entire cast, both principals and ensemble, in rehearsals. "I would write the ensemble harmonies, teach them the parts, and make sure everything sounded fantastic."

Play, Orchestra, Play...

When Silvestri recorded the original movie score, there were more than one hundred musicians, dubbed the "Outa-time Orchestra." For *Back to the Future The Musical* (or for any theatrical musical production), an orchestra of that size would be financially and spatially unfeasible. The show would be able to afford and accommodate an orchestra comprised of fourteen musicians.

In August 2019, newly hired orchestrator Ethan Popp flew from New York to attend the laboratory sessions at Jerwood Space in the South Bank of London, where Rando and company were continuing to work on various story points, musical numbers, and choreography.

At the end of the scheduled work, Popp met with Finlow, Silvestri, sound designer Gareth Owen, and keyboard programmer Phij Adams. "The topic," reveals Popp, "was how would we construct an 'economically sized' orchestra that would serve both the more overtly 'theatrical' material composed by Glen and Alan, as well as Silvestri's revered score. Most importantly, how would we re-create the sound of a film score recorded with a one-hundred-piece orchestra with only fourteen?"

Rather than be turned into a "chamber piece" (one designed for a smaller number of instruments), Popp knew that Silvestri's score needed to sound as close as possible to the music that the composer originally conducted in all its splendor. "We were re-creating a score loved the world over, with die-hards such as myself and Bryan able to sing any cue at a moment's notice. Absolute attention to detail in ensuring the score would have equal emotional weight in this medium was our self-imposed moral imperative."

To that end, Popp proposed an intriguing concept that had never been explored for similar situations. "We would not 'reduce' the score to a chamber sound," he discloses, "rather, we would use any means available to include every single nuance."

Ethan's intent was to implore Phij to create a computer server that would "house" high-quality sampled virtual instruments to replicate the remainder of the symphonic orchestra (strings, woodwinds, percussion, brass) unavailable due to budgetary constraints. "These would be created utilizing orchestral sample libraries," he continues, "and two of our keyboardists would be able to access those sounds via their instruments simultaneously via MIDI [Musical Instrument Digital Interface] signals. Bryan and I would often speak of 'rhythmic unisons' within Alan's original score and discovered that two keyboardists could play a great deal of the original orchestration live every night through their four hands and two eighty-eight-key synthesizers. Those 'virtual instruments' living inside this server could then be placed within a virtual soundstage, further replicating a true orchestral sound."

"I'd never pitched anything as challenging as this approach," Popp recollects. "I left the meeting thinking, *We can do this . . . I hope we'll be able to do this . . . PLEASE let us be able to do this!!!*"

Welcome to Jerwood!

Situated in the Southwark section of London, the Jerwood Space rehearsal facilities would host a three-week laboratory.

Boasting a number of spacious rehearsal halls along with several smaller studios, the site had adequate space for full-scale rehearsals in the largest chambers; Chris Bailey and Darren Carnall could devise, teach, and rehearse choreography in a couple of others; there were conference rooms for department meetings, and room left over for costume and wig fittings, all under one voluminous roof. "It was a tremendous location," says Rando. "I would literally be rehearsing a scene and then run out, go see Lorraine in fittings for five minutes, and then go right back to whatever scene or number we were rehearsing."

While not every department could avail themselves of Jerwood Space, they were close enough so the director could make his rounds several times a week to see the progress being made. "On a morning where we were going to do a lot

of choreography, I would get in a car, take a thirty-minute drive to the prop shop where they were also building Doc's lab, then do a side visit where we'd see the bits and pieces of scenery being built, and the DeLorean being put together."

Let's Take It from the Top!

"What was also significant," adds Gale, "was that it was the first time we had our rehearsal space marked off to the dimensions of the Manchester Opera House stage and had some rudimentary props and set dressing."

Unlike the previous workshops, Jerwood was the place where the actors could fully begin the process of getting into their characters. "Sadler's Wells was important," acknowledges Roger Bart, "but there's a certain point for actors where you no longer want to be behind music stands and kind of gesture every once in a while. I'm aware of what my performance does when I can start using my body, I'm off-book [having memorized the script], and I can start to really do what I do physically. I was ready for that."

CLOCKWISE FROM TOP LEFT Jerwood rehearsals of "Gotta Start Somewhere"; Dance captain/ensemble member Laura Mullowney gets a lift; Roger Bart, Olly Dobson, and the DeLorean Girls rehearse "It Works!"; Rosanna Hyland and Aidan Cutler.

at it with a jaundiced eye, looking around and thinking, *This place isn't good enough for me.* Tonally, he wasn't celebrating, [it was] rather more like pure rebellion." What added to the decision to portray Marty in a more disheartened manner was that the book originally began with him being rejected by Mr. Strickland at the band audition before joining the rest of the townspeople in song in the town square:

```
          MARTY
I'VE GOT NO FUTURE
I'M NOT GETTING OUT OF HERE
'CAUSE NO MATTER WHAT THEY SAY
TODAY IS JUST LIKE YESTERDAY
I'VE GOT NO FUTURE
I'M JUST ANOTHER LOSER
AND I'M GETTING NOWHERE FAST
I BLINKED, THE FUTURE PASSED AND WENT
  AWAY...
```

A Matter of Perspective

Jerwood was an opportunity for the entire cast to stretch and grow, both literally and figuratively. The addition of movement and blocking of the dialogue scenes and further choreography work with Bailey saw the show begin to fully take shape under Rando's guidance and expertise. Likewise, there were issues that needed to be addressed in several of the musical numbers, starting with "A Matter of Time."

The first song Ballard and Silvestri had penned was strongly influenced by the opening scenes of the film and its depiction of 1985 Hill Valley. "It's down on its heels," says Glen Ballard of the town when it's first introduced to movie audiences. "The town square is a bit desultory. There's an X-rated movie theater, a homeless man sleeping on the park bench. It feels like it needs a makeover."

In their earliest versions of the song, the audience is first introduced to various citizens of the California hamlet, who decry what has become of their town and their lives:

```
        TOWNSPEOPLE
IT'S ONLY A MATTER OF TIME
AND IT'S SAFE TO SAY WE'RE WAY BEHIND
THIS TOWN ISN'T MOVING
SO MUCH NEEDS IMPROVING
HILL VALLEY IS WAY PAST ITS PRIME
```

"On that level," continues Ballard, "we're just trying to understand how the character of Marty McFly is going to relate to it. Our initial thought was, he's going to be looking

Beginning with the Dominion workshop, Rando, Ingram, and Bailey had all expressed concern about the negative tenor, especially with it being the opening number of the show. "I made notes on that to John," recalls Ingram, "and it actually came from a number of investors that the song was just too depressing. Hearing all this negativity from our leading man was just not what it's about."

"That number had a great journey," recollects the director. "When I first came on to the show, it was quite complicated. One of the things we were wrestling with was how much of Alan's melodies should we put to lyric? Glen and Al had done a great job putting a lot of lyrics to the original melody, but we realized it wasn't really helping us, it wasn't releasing the story, and also, wasn't as danceable as we wanted it to be. Another part of it was that we weren't hearing enough from Marty and hearing too much from the ensemble. And then what we were hearing from Marty was, as Glen described it, 'teenage angst.' I understood but agreed with the others that it wasn't exactly where we wanted to start with our guy. It took us a while to figure out."

When the issue was broached with Ballard and Silvestri, they both took it totally in stride. "There is no ego involved with either of them," observes Gale. "If somebody says they don't like a song, they're of the mind that it can either be replaced with something new or they can work on solving the issue with the original. They've got the same attitude as I do with the book. It's not working? We'll rewrite it. Not a big deal."

"I remember when that happened, it was kind of late in the game," details Silvestri. "As things start to form up and the shape of the show starts to appear, it's time to address this next level of concerns. This one was a very easy adjustment for Glen and me. It was a big tonal change, but we thought it to be a great one. There was no reason to put the audience through that at the very beginning of the show, and it wasn't really necessary for Marty. He's going to have his disappointment soon enough with the audition." "That's my favorite part of theater," adds Ballard. "You start with something on the page and then you get in a room with talented people who are performing it, and then it necessarily grows and changes. We needed Marty to start completely optimistic. He's going to have a big future and take the world by storm. It wouldn't have made much sense if Marty was dancing so hard to 'I've got no future.'" Concludes Rando, "The shift initially was not easy, but it was a great moment of collaboration between people who aren't normally in musical theater. Between Bob, Glen, and Alan, the three of them just banging their heads together, we had a lot of wacky, wonderful lyrics come back at us, and they kept culling it down. We all realized we were onto something for that particular song and that we were definitely going to make it better." Adds Gale, "We all were amazed at how tweaking 'Only a Matter of Time' improved the overall tone."

From those initial steps in the Jerwood lab, the song's journey from the negative to the positive would continue to morph and improve until it was presented onstage in Manchester.

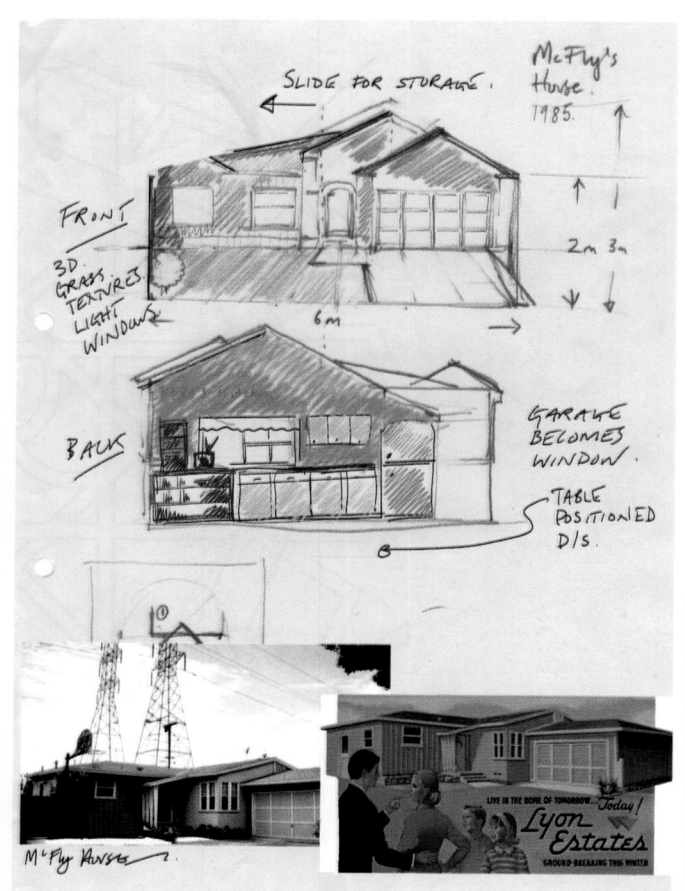

SLIDE FOR STORAGE.

McFly's House.
1985.

FRONT

3D.
GRASS
TEXTURES.
LIGHT
WINDOW.

2m 3m

6m

BACK

GARAGE
BECOMES
WINDOW.

TABLE
POSITIONED
D/S.

B

McFly House

LIVE IN THE HOME OF TOMORROW... Today!
Lyon Estates
GROUND-BREAKING THIS WINTER

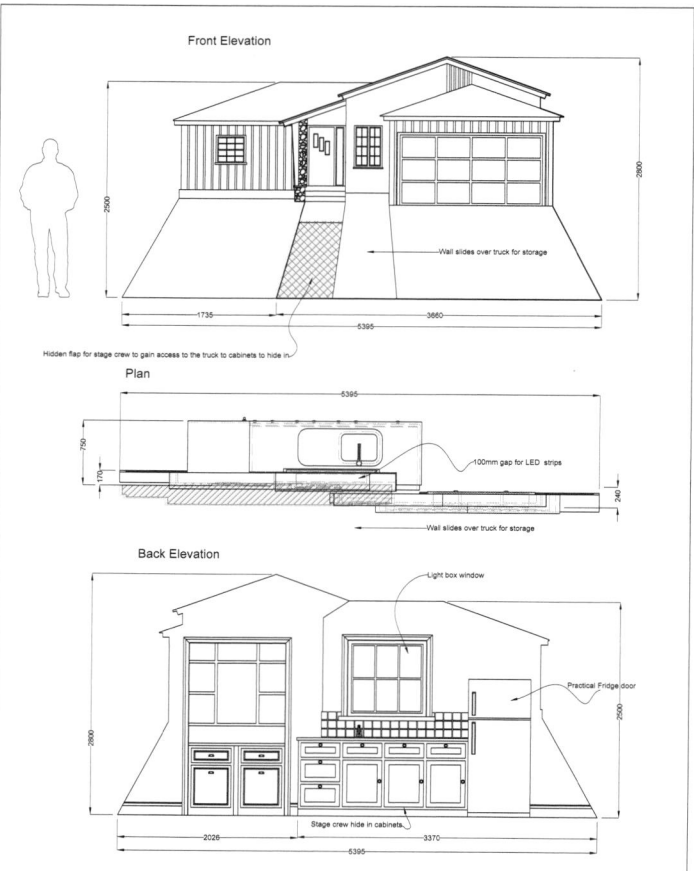

Front Elevation

2500

2800

Wall slides over truck for storage

1735

5395

3860

Hidden flap for stage crew to gain access to the truck to cabinets to hide in

Plan

5395

750

170

100mm gap for LED strips

240

Wall slides over truck for storage

Back Elevation

Light box window

2800

2500

Practical Fridge door

2025

5395

3370

Stage crew hide in cabinets

HEY TO "Z"!

After two full weeks of rehearsal, the schedule for August 6, 2019, had the notation:

FULL COMPANY
Presentation of Act One, Scenes 1–9

Starting at the top of the show, with no stops, breaks, or restarts, the cast and ensemble went through the first forty minutes of the musical, ending with Goldie Wilson's showstopping number, "You Gotta Start Somewhere." Watching the performance that day were a number of marketing and publicity people who had been engaged by Ingram, as well as Hatley and casting director David Grindrod. The most notable attendee of the day was Robert Zemeckis, in London for a scoring session of his latest film, *The Witches*. Zemeckis had been kept up on all the advancements since he had attended the Sadler's Wells workshop, and now he would see how far things had progressed since.

For this lab, a new actor played Biff—a more physically imposing figure than before, as Zemeckis had strongly suggested. Everyone, especially Rando, reacted positively to the bully's more menacing presence. "Ironically, this was cinema," comments Bob Gale. "The picture told the story, as Bob Z. had proven on-screen." While this was a definite step forward, the creatives were hoping that David Grindrod would find an even better fit for the role.

After the rehearsal, Hatley gave Bob Z. a presentation of his black box model and demonstrated how some of the sets would work. One further rehearsal was held on that day of "Future Boy," another number that held promise but was still somewhat lacking. Choreographer Bailey clearly remembers Zemeckis making a simple statement about what he thought might take it to a new and more interesting level. "He said, 'I see tap dancing.'" Those four words would set a new direction and energy to not only elevate the song, but infuse it with the spectacle Zemeckis desired.

It's Magic!

Overall pleased with what he saw that day, Zemeckis reiterated another expectation. "The show had to have spectacular stage illusions and big numbers—it couldn't just be a bunch of dialogue scenes strung together, as Bob and I had seen with other shows based on movies."

Fortunately, the production had already brought someone into the fold who could provide illusions that would fulfill Zemeckis's expectations.

A member of the UK's Magic Circle,* Chris Fisher continues to work worldwide as International Illusions and Magic Associate for *Harry Potter and the Cursed Child*. His other theatrical credits as an illusion consultant include *The Lion, the Witch and the Wardrobe*, *Wicked*, *2:22 A Ghost Story*, *The Prince of Egypt*, *Company*, *Big The Musical*, *Xanadu*, and *Into the Woods*, as well as the UK tour of *Bedknobs and Broomsticks*. Fisher admits he was nervous when he got the call about joining the production. "*Back to the Future*

---

* "An international society of world-class magicians founded in London in 1905, whose purpose is to promote and advance the art of magic" (Wikipedia).

is an imposing title. When you're working on a very big brand name, like we did with *Potter*, you have to stay loyal to what people love about the franchise."

As daunting as the prospects were, so was the promise. Fisher describes the illusions as a team effort. "They utilized not only the talents of the illusion team, but vital contributions from automation, lighting, sound, and video, and cast members who facilitated a number of the effects as well. To create those sequences onstage, we had to think outside the box. And I think we did."

Exactly *how* they all thought outside the box to achieve those astonishing illusions is unfortunately not open to discussion with this author nor you, the reader. The motto of the Magic Circle, "*Indocilis privata loqui*," which roughly translates into "Not gonna tell," is one to which Fisher wholeheartedly subscribes and, despite fervent questioning, clings.

Q: Marty skateboards into the empty lot of the Twin Pines Mall, and suddenly, accompanied by three booms and a flash of light, the DeLorean appears onstage with Doc behind the wheel. How is that done?

A: (Latin) *Non possum tibi dicere!*
(English) I can't tell you that!

Q: When Doc starts to sing "It Works," how do the DeLorean Girls appear from out of nowhere?

A: (Latin) *Non dicam tibi!*
(English) I won't tell you that!

Q: When Doc releases the toy car in the tabletop model of Hill Valley, how does it catch fire?

A: (Latin) *Flamma tape et a wireless transfusor ad accendendum.*†
(English) Flame tape and a wireless transmitter to ignite it.

---

† Not covered anywhere in the motto of the Magic Circle.

ABOVE Illusion designer Chris Fisher.

LEFT Robert Zemeckis pays a visit to the production at the Jerwood rehearsal facilities.

AI Knows the Score...

From the very start of conversations, it was a given that *Back to the Future The Musical* would feature music from the movie. Certainly, the standards from the film ("The Power of Love," "Back in Time," "Johnny B. Goode," and "Earth Angel") would take their place center stage, as well as the new songs created for the show by Ballard and Silvestri. The four creators of the show also envisioned Silvestri's score as an essential presence. "We had an orchestra, we had Alan's score, and what's more, we had Alan!" says Gale. "Why wouldn't we use as much of it as we could?"

"It's one of the few orchestral scores that people actually remember and can identify," adds Ballard. "If you hear three seconds . . . two bars of it . . . you know it's *Back to the Future*."

The thought behind the inclusion of Silvestri's music was much deeper than just trying to placate the fans. As with any classic film score, the music exists as an integral part of that movie's DNA, enhancing every aspect of the story and how it's told on the screen. It can run the gamut from subtle nuance to pulse-pounding excitement and can evoke every emotion in between. Silvestri had brought all of that and more to the entire trilogy, so it was a no-brainer to take advantage of that brilliant asset.

What would ultimately surprise everyone was just how much of it would end up in the finished show. Initial discussions about the underscore identified a number of sequences in the show as obvious points in which to incorporate the music: the DeLorean's first time-travel from 1985 to 1955, and Doc's attempt to reconnect the cable on the clock tower as Marty speeds through the streets of Hill Valley for his rendezvous with the lightning bolt.

But the team learned that what seemed obvious to them was not an ordinary practice on the musical stage. For the most part, other than the intro and coda to an official musical number, stage musicals did not use an underscore to any great degree. As neophytes to the world of theater, it never occurred to Zemeckis, Gale, Silvestri, and Ballard that the music wouldn't work onstage. "Basically," notes Gale, "it was the same when we were starting out in film. We didn't know how to make one. We were learning as we went along. If we wanted something, we asked for it. The same applied in making our first musical. To paraphrase Goldie Wilson, 'We hadda start somewhere!' "

"I was very worried in the beginning," admits musical director Nick Finlow, "about how to meld two very different scores—one with Alan's film music, and the other being Glen and Alan's songs for the show. It was all-encompassing. Not

"The songs were always going to have their musical beginning and ending transitions," acknowledges the composer, "but we always knew we wanted to use the score as well." Rando was happy to have some of Silvestri's score as part of the show, but the veteran director was, at the outset, somewhat taken aback by the enormity of the gift he had been given. "Alan's work is mind-blowing," asserts the director. "But I thought, how is this going to work? This is unheard of in musical theater to have this kind of score. How are we going to get all this musical underscoring in the show? It just doesn't happen!"

just about underscoring dialogue, which is what musical theater underscore is about, but this was also about underscoring *action* on the stage, which is not normally done in musical theater. In the beginning, I wondered how much of Alan's score we would be able to keep, whilst keeping the show in the spirit of a musical theater piece."

One of Finlow's first concerns spoke to the obvious but salient distinctions between film and live musical theater. When a film arrives in movie theaters, it is no longer a fluctuating, unpredictable entity. It becomes a document that will likely never change. It becomes, in the case of *Back to the Future*, for example, a safe haven for the fans. It will always provide them with the exact same elements they've come to love with every viewing. In live musical theater, every show differs from the last. Any number of factors influence the pacing, timing, performances, and emotions of the show that the audience sees each night. At the same time, those differences can have an effect on the music, whether it's being played live by the orchestra or from a prerecorded track. "From a practical point of view," points out Finlow, "I didn't know how we were going to 'tame' Alan's amazing work."

The first priority, as Rando had stressed from his first discussions about the show, were Gale's book, along with the original songs written by Ballard and Silvestri, and those two items were the sole focus of the first (Dominion) workshop. It was only after Sadler's Wells, when Rando acknowledged his satisfaction with the show's progress, that the first discussions of utilizing Silvestri's score began to surface.

Once Rando began to work with the cast on the preliminary blocking of the show, he began to see opportunities in which Silvestri's score would mesh beautifully with the songs, heighten the emotions of the characters, intensify the action sequences, and help propel the musical forward during scene transitions. In other words, Silvestri's musical score would perform the same functions on the stage as it had in the film.

"When I started to introduce the concept of integrating the score into the show during rehearsals," relates Silvestri, "John suddenly had a firsthand experience in real time of what the possibilities could be. He was like, 'Wait a second. You mean I could have score when Biff walks up to the car and drags Marty out? And we can have score after George falls out of the tree and we're transitioning to Lorraine's bedroom?' All of a sudden, it was like a whole new tool kit had entered John's world, and it grew from there."

Nothing demonstrated the power of underscore more to the director than when he was rehearsing the pivotal scene in which George punches Biff and rescues Lorraine. Rando had tried the action in several different ways, but none of them had the "impact" he wanted. Fortunately, Silvestri was on hand that day.

"I was literally sitting there with a MacBook Pro with a Bose speaker tube attached, and the entire score from all three movies with me," he details. "I watched John's blocking for the punch, and I was cutting music from the original score in real time just to give John the flavor. He was able to see possibilities and choices available to him."

Rando was pleased with the new opportunities being presented to him, but there was one person involved who was far more excited than anyone else—actor Hugh Coles. "The way we first rehearsed it was me coming in and singing a few lines of 'Put Your Mind to It,' and then punching him." When they tried the scene with Alan's live, improvised version of the score in it, the effect was immediately evident. "The first time we did the punch with the music," says Coles, "I was like, 'Please keep that in!' because selfishly, as an actor, it gives you everything you need. It's like being in *Back to the Future* [the movie] every night, and it's incredible. It's informing every emotion, and it pays off so well for the audience in terms of a nostalgia moment, but also as one of the peaks of the story. I never, ever get tired of punching Biff in the face!" Adds Rosie Hyland, "Having Alan Silvestri sitting there underscoring me falling to the ground and then having George punch Biff like that was my inner *Back to the Future*. I was really living the dream that day!"

For most film composers (Silvestri included), their process doesn't really begin until the director has completed principal photography and assembled a rough cut of the movie. "If you want to write a convincing score," Alan comments, "you've got to write it to the [completed] movie." As the first rehearsals began, he and Glen would still be refining their songs, and there wouldn't be much that Silvestri could

contribute to the score at that time. "The thing about the musical, not unlike with film, is that it has to be at a certain point in its life cycle before you could even begin to intelligently talk about it. Bob Gale warned me before the workshops that they really wouldn't have anything to show me for some time, but when they did, it was going to come in hot and heavy."

When Silvestri provided the snippet of the score for the "George punches Biff" scene as it was being rehearsed, he would take a cue from Doc Brown and begin to think "fourth dimensionally." A thought occurred to him of how he could start scoring the musical without having to wait for the entire show to be fully blocked and choreographed. "What we wound up doing was a very interesting hybrid cinema/live theater workflow," he reveals. "John Rando would get the scene where he wanted onstage, and we would video it on an iPhone. I'd take that video back to the hotel, where I had my full-on studio. I was playing a 'movie' and either cutting music or writing things on the box, and I was scoring the scene that we had just seen in rehearsal that afternoon. I was back in my wheelhouse! Then I'd send John a Quick-Time file with the scene scored, which could be further refined to address his notes. We wound up doing that for

89

LEFT Silvestri shows Rando, Gale, and others a clip of the show to which he added his score.

which is me getting an idea. But Alan's stuff is both symphonic and emotional. The closest thing to it I've ever heard was *Sweeney Todd* and Leonard Bernstein's *West Side Story*. There's never a false moment in it. Alan knows exactly what the characters are going through. It's an extraordinary score; it challenges me to be dimensional and helps me keep my performance fresh in every show."

The final version of the musical's score is notable for the amount of content that Rando, Finlow, Crook, Popp, and Silvestri were able to seamlessly infuse into the structure of the show. A music cue is defined as a stand-alone section of a musical score, and the average show contains around thirty. *Back to the Future* has 144 separate cues. In 2015, when Silvestri revised his score for the *Back to the Future in Concert* series, it featured a total of 1,863 bars of music, as compared with the 2021 score for the musical, which clocked in at 2,963!

For John Rando, the experience taught him a valuable lesson, which he immediately added to his director's handbook: "Anytime you can add Alan Silvestri underscoring, you just say yes . . ."

Out to Launch

On October 15, 2019, four months prior to the opening night, Bob Gale, Colin Ingram, five of the principal cast, and several members of the ensemble and band traveled from London to Manchester for the official media launch event.

The day began with some photo opportunities at the Science and Industry Museum, including the appearance

the whole show anywhere we considered the possibility of score. This became our modus operandi."

"I don't know of any other show that has the gift that we have," offers Olly Dobson on Silvestri's score. "As soon as you hear the first notes at the beginning, it's like, 'We're here. We're in *Back to the Future.*' It's a special moment, and it happens consistently throughout the show. The little moments, the special moments in the film, we have them in the show from Alan's music. I never could imagine before the show how much of an impact that music would have on me personally, too. On press night in Manchester, when I'm writing the letter to Doc, there was a moment where everything hit me at once—the workshops, the producer telling me I had the role, my family and best friends in the front row. I was reading the letter to that music, and I broke. I was crying so much. It was so profound, and that moment for me was absolutely unparalleled."

"It is the most sophisticated underscoring of anything I've ever done in the theater by a mile," observes Roger Bart. "I'm used to kind of like a 'tinkle, tinkle, tinkle,' and then maybe every once in a while, a 'pling' on high E,

RIGHT The cast perform songs from the musical for an assemblage of invited media.

of the "OD" (Original Doc), Christopher Lloyd, who initiated the proceedings by handing over the keys to the time machine to his successor, Roger Bart. Ingram then formally introduced the rest of the cast.

Dobson then introduced Marty's band, the Pinheads, to the crowd, and the cast performed "Back in Time" (Olly and Roger), "Put Your Mind to It" (Olly and Hugh), "Pretty Baby" (Rosie Hyland), "Gotta Start Somewhere" (Cedric Neal), and "The Power of Love" (Olly and cast).

Speaking to the media later in the day, Christopher Lloyd related, "When I first heard about it [the musical], I thought, this is a whole new concept. It's amazing, and it's very exciting to see something keep going and going

as long as this franchise has. And I get to see myself sing and dance!"

After the interviews were completed, Bart, Dobson, Lloyd, Gale, and Ingram traveled to the Manchester Opera House to film a special trailer for the show that made its global debut online, including on the musical's own website, www.backtothefuturemusical.com, on January 29, 2020, three weeks before the premiere.

ABOVE A visit from a consulting "Doctor": Christopher Lloyd traveled to Manchester to present the keys to the DeLorean to Roger Bart.

Uh, hey, I'm here for the show?

Name?

Marty, Marty McFly.

You're late.

Yeah, uh, you know me: Tardy Marty.

I'm Dr. Emmett L. Brown. I'm a scientist.

You're late.

No, I was just...

GREAT SCOTT! You... You're..

Let's keep it our little secret.

He'll do.

Out from the Shadows...

When *Back to the Future The Musical* was first announced, one of the most oft-asked questions was: Could audiences accept any other actors in the roles other than the actors who created them in the movie?

Roger Bart was already versed in bringing screen characters to the stage. In *The Producers*, he took on the role of Carmen Ghia from the original film and would later take over the costarring role of Leo Bloom from actor Matthew Broderick. He continued with the Broadway incarnation of another of Mel Brooks's beloved comedies, in the title role of *Young Frankenstein*. Bart drew from those experiences in stepping into the

shoes of Dr. Emmett Brown. "Carmen Ghia, in the original movie of *The Producers*, was definitely an impressionable character, but I knew that it was possible to amp it up a hair. I used that wonderful performance by Andreas Voutsinas [in the 1967 film] as a launchpad. Screen time and stage time are very different. When you're out of a shot in a film, you're out of the shot, but in a show, you're still always onstage. There's a lot of fun to be had being there [in character] and just listening."

Two weeks after Bart took over the part of Leo, his friend and acting coach came to the show and suggested

RIGHT Roger Bart as Leo Bloom on Broadway in *The Producers*.

FAR RIGHT "It's pronounced *Fron-kenstien*." Bart starred in the title role of Mel Brooks's Broadway adaptation of *Young Frankenstein*.

that Roger's performance was solid but had some echoes of Broderick's. "I got what he was saying, and I tried to slowly divorce myself from the album playing in my head, which was Matthew doing the show that I listened to for a year.

"With *Young Frankenstein*, I found it very difficult to do a nuanced film performance in a two thousand-seat barn theater. I had a hard time conveying things that you can normally get in a close-up, and since we were dealing with a celebrated movie, it was even harder. What I ultimately learned was that you can be your own version of a character. Rather than coming at it from a place of 'I hope I can be as good as Christopher Lloyd,' I came from a place of 'I'm so lucky that Chris has given me so many wonderful clues of the parameters; here's what you can get away with, and here's some of the things that are iconic and there's no other way to do them.' From that I built it into what worked for me.

"I knew that I would encounter a few 'folded arms,' and I knew that people would think, *He's not exactly talking like him, and he's not as tall as him.* I tried to provide a lot of Doc's qualities, some of the nature of the relationship between him and Marty, and the primary relationship Doc has with the world: science, passion, exploration, the idea that anything is possible, the idea

that you have belief in yourself. Those are inherent in the character and were so vividly drawn by Chris, and I knew, if you hook into those in a genuine way and really play those and you happen to be funny, you're going to make the audience come your way."

In the casting process, John Rando cited Olly Dobson's look and his "superb" American accent as key elements that led to him being chosen for Marty McFly. As they went through the workshops and rehearsals, Rando noted that "you could see the development and growth in the ownership of the role, and at the same time, loving and respecting the original performance."

Dobson readily admits that the shadow of Michael J. Fox loomed large in how he approached the role, and that

by embracing it from the start, he was able to pay homage without trying to be a carbon copy of his predecessor.

"I've always had such a connection to his performance, and I put so much effort and work into trying to bring what people remember from his performance into mine. The pressure for me was if the audience was going to enjoy that and embrace it. I know I did, and the other actors and I are all having fun doing it. I love the role so much that I eventually stopped thinking about it a lot." Dobson credits the book as inspiring him to go above and beyond in his characterization of the time-traveling youth. "It is written amazingly, and the characters all come together and it's wonderful. Something that John Rando really focused on in telling our story was trying to get out of everybody's heads that this is already alive in the world."

and where I want to take my emotions, whether it's to comfort Lorraine or to intimidate Biff, and still remind people that this is from a source of something that is spectacular. I felt if the audience could see that an actor is actually able to replicate the voice of Michael J. Fox (which is definitely a hard thing to do), I knew that people were going to feel safe. When I heard Hugh Coles talk like Crispin Glover, I knew my choice was a good one."

His characterization also extended to some of Fox's physical aspects, down to the way he walks in some of the scenes, which made him even more comfortable onstage. "As an actor, when you get a walk right that's different to yours, you get an easy sense of where you are onstage, who's with you and the lines that are coming that you don't even think about coming. And you know what? People in the crowd might not even notice it, but it's part of seriously respecting the role and the words and the story. If I didn't do a respectful job, people would have my head!"

Of accepting the role of Lorraine Baines McFly, Rosie Hyland admits, "There's always the worry of 'OK, if I say yes to this, I've got to get it right. This is something you don't want to mess up, but I wasn't about to turn it down because of that fear. It's a dream show and a dream role." Though she also admits to feeling a little pressure of taking on the seminal role of Lorraine, she stresses it was self-inflicted. "Yeah, I did that to myself. Never, ever from Bob Gale or John Rando or anyone on the creative team was there a moment in which they said, 'Can you do it more like in the film?' I would like to pay a little bit of an homage to Lea Thompson. I think you have to, but without being a carbon copy. Yes, we need to be those familiar characters, but they have to be living, breathing characters in their own right. Otherwise, an audience isn't going to be invested in the story if we're just going through the motions."

"Crispin Glover's George McFly is indelible. The outline of George is firmly stamped in people's minds," observes Hugh Coles of his onstage persona, "but we don't get to see much of George's inner life in the film. We see *how* he behaves, but we don't really know *why*. He just is . . .

At the same time, rather than trying to give the character a different vocal style, he took great pains to give the fans an immediate comfort with the 2020 incarnation of Marty. "I spent so much time getting the voice right from the intonations," he admits, paying particular attention to one of the most iconic lines in the script.

"We were in the rehearsal room, doing the scene in the parking lot, and I say to Doc, 'A DeLorean? You mean to tell me that you built a time machine . . . out of a DeLorean?!' Rando said, 'You would not pause that way. You simply would not pause.' And I tried it many times, but it was the only line I felt uncomfortable doing differently. The only one. With every other line in the show, I could keep that lovely inflection while still holding the immediate action

"During the rehearsal process, I noticed how the musical as a whole happened *to* George. He wasn't taking part in it . . . he didn't get it. In the number 'You Gotta Start Somewhere,' George finds himself front and center in a show-stopping Broadway musical number. Everybody dances *at* George, all of their attention on him. In fact, there's an off-mic line that I say to Cedric in the diner every night: 'Why are they all singing?'"

Coles first begins to reveal more about George with the song "My Myopia," which was not an option in the movie. But for the actor, the key moment is where Marty and George truly connect for the first time in the number "Put Your Mind to It." "That's where George really joins the musical," states Hugh. "For me, it's tracking the journey of George that sustains the performance. These are the rehearsal discoveries I'm playing out each time I grasp the notebook and walk out onstage with that classic haircut.

"Hopefully in the end the audience gets a George that is faithful to the film but also a George that you feel you know much better, and as a result, you want to root for him to get the girl, stand up to the bully, and finally come out of himself."

Biff Tannen portrayer Aidan Cutler credits Gale for giving good advice to the cast. "Bob Gale put it perfectly to all of us in rehearsals. He said, 'What you guys are bringing to the table is a reflection of the film and their stereotypes—what the actors created in the original film, what the audience members will know and love. But you're also bringing your own twist that allows you to put your own mark on it.' I have to credit a lot of what I bring to Tom Wilson. I feel it would be completely disrespectful not only to the writing but to the films and Tom himself to not honor him. Keep what everybody knows about and what everybody hates about the character, but also to be able to say there's a line that is drawn."

Gale's words were made all the more gratifying later, when in the middle of the previews in Manchester, he called the cast together to address them again. "He actually said he didn't want us to watch the films again until the show closed," says Cutler. "He said what we all had was the perfect balance."

Recollects Gale, "I told the cast they came across with new confidence the night before, as if all of them knew that the musical was its own entity, that the roles were theirs, that I was very proud of them, and they no longer needed the crutch of leaning on the movie. Then I did an evangelist imitation: 'Throw away those crutches, you don't need them anymore!'"

Taking a Test Drive— November 2019

One thing that needed the special attention of everyone was the completed stage DeLorean. "In November we took a big studio space," says Simon Marlow. "We laid the floor, the tracks, the turntable, the automation, and we went through a lot of the car moves. We wanted to give John Rando a really good chance to see what the car could do, because we wouldn't have had the time to do it when we hit the stage in Manchester."

"It was the most joyous day," says Ingram of the test results, "and honestly, it could have been just so bad. In

FAR LEFT John Rando watches the stage DeLorean being put through its paces for the first time, while sending his reactions to the creative teams telepathically.

LEFT The stage DeLorean is put to the test by technicians at a studio outside London.

the end, we didn't touch it." Rando was pleased because the success meant he would have the real car to work with onstage when rehearsals started in Manchester. For Marlow, it meant "we could all have a happy Christmas without losing any sleep, at least not because of this."

Lanterns Studio Theatre January 2020

As the new year dawned, it was time for the final month of rehearsals in London before making the move to Manchester. The Lanterns Studio Theatre in London's Canary Wharf was the choice of location.

Again, a full-size mock-up of the Manchester Opera House stage awaited the production, using the precise dimensions taken directly from the venue. Both on- and offstage areas were clearly defined with multicolored tape, which informed the cast where they could move freely or where they would be blocked by a piece of the scenery, props, machinery, or, at times, the DeLorean. Tape

also marked the placement of the automated tracks on which pieces of the set would be attached and be moved on- and offstage during the actual performances. On the edge of the "stage" was a series of numbers spaced two feet apart. These digits gave the members of the ensemble their starting places in the musical numbers and could be referred to by the choreographer when giving notes about a routine. In Manchester, those numbers would be replaced by LED lights.

"We had plyboard mock-ups of all the big scenic elements," imparts stage manager Graham Hookham, "the McFly and Baines houses, the diner, basically every piece of the show. We had a crew of eight people who were there just to move the scenery and push the makeshift version of the DeLorean around, and we built our own functional turntable."

The furniture purchased for the sets was utilized as well. "Normally you would work with rehearsal versions,

RIGHT Lanterns Studio Theatre was the last rehearsal space used by the production before leaving London for Manchester.

and when you get to the theater, you'll have the actual furniture," continues Hookham. "In the number 'Hello, Is Anybody Home?' Marty climbs the chairs onto the dining table and later jumps off. We figured it just made sense to have the actual ones in the rehearsal room so that the actors get comfortable with it all. One less distraction for them when we make the move."

Please Excuse the Crudity of <u>This</u> Model...

The memorable "Doc explains his plan to Marty" scene, featuring the scientist's detailed "homemade" model of Hill Valley's town square, had been a topic of discussion throughout the development process. Says Gale, "The question was how the model itself would exist. As a physical piece? Virtually? Or as a diagram projected using video?"

"Video felt lame in this case," comments Hatley. "The model of the town square was such a memorable moment from the movie for me—the invention of using everyday objects painted white to resemble the buildings. I think it had always struck a chord with my inventive theater mind. I pushed for there to be an actual model. I knew it would have to be replicated as a large prop so that everyone in the theater could clearly see it, but the challenge was how to get it onstage in a way that it could then be revealed to both Marty and the audience in a 'Ta-dah!' moment."

A simple piece of furniture that any self-respecting scientist would have on hand provided Hatley with the answer. A double-sided pivoting blackboard could show off Doc's mathematical equations on one side; when in a vertical position, it would take up minimal space to slide onto the stage, and when flipped ninety degrees, it became

TOP RIGHT Tim Hatley's sketch that solved the problem of how to build and store the Hill Valley Town Square model for the stage.

RIGHT One-minute photo! Each understudy for the roles of Marty, Linda, and Dave was photographed so the disappearing photo could be tailored for each performance by computer.

a tabletop on which the model of the town square was constructed by Chris Marcus and his team.

"Obviously we looked at a lot of photos from the movie," he says of the process. We had to slightly change its orientation because of how we were going to use it in the space. And we had to make something that could survive eight times a week, and not burst into flame. We got a load of vintage Coke bottles and milk cartons, and cast them all in silicone, and made them in a hard frame of foam so that we could screw it all together really well, since we were going to be flipping it and couldn't have things flying off. We've got as much small detail on it as there is in the film, because I don't think you want to feel like you're shortchanging people. It was a fun piece to make."

Let's *Look* at the Photo!

It was essential for the audience to see the notorious photograph that showed the gradual disappearance of the McFly siblings from existence. "It didn't seem right to just show the photo on a wall like a POV," says Gale, "so I thought of the opaque projector." First created in the mid-1700s, it's a device that displays the images of an object by shining a bright lamp on it from above. A system of mirrors, prisms, or lenses is used to focus and project an image of that object onto a viewing screen or blank surface. It was widely used in the classroom in the first half of the twentieth century

for educators to display charts, photos, graphs, and other educational materials. Low-cost, portable versions of the device were even marketed as a toy. "I had one of them called the Magnajector, when I was nine," admits Gale. "I remember projecting Superman comics on the wall in the basement. It felt right that Doc would have one in his lab."

Let's *Take* the Photo!

With prop supervisor Chris Marcus having procured just the right model of projector, it would be up to Finn Ross to create the photo, suitable for each performance. Since the entire audience would be able to see the image, there would have to be different versions of it, and a number of configurations depending on who would be playing each one of the three young McFlys. Ross had Olly Dobson

LEFT Doc examines the photo of Marty and his siblings.

(Marty), Emma Lloyd (Linda), and Will Haswell (Dave) photographed separately in front of a green screen, as well as each actor's understudy. Everyone's images were loaded into Ross's computer database, and just prior to the performance, he punches in the file for the actor who will be portraying the character, and the photograph for that performance is created. "I think there are sixteen potential different combinations," explains Ross, "so doing them as individuals makes it a lot simpler, and quite future-proof."

The background for each photo variation remains a majestic vista in Monument Valley, Arizona, familiar to film buffs as a location featured in legendary director John Ford's classic Westerns, including *Stagecoach*, *My Darling Clementine*, and *The Searchers*. Monument Valley also remains recognizable to fans of *Back to the Future Part III*, with a key scene of Doc and Marty driving a team of horses pulling the DeLorean through the magnificent terrain. Using this background was Gale's idea. "I thought it would be a nice Easter egg for our fans, and it made sense as a family vacation photo."

Barnstorming

As Tim Hatley and Finn Ross continued work on the first time-travel sequence, there was one crucial piece of information missing: where the DeLorean would appear and come to a stop in 1955.

Since the very early drafts of his book, Bob Gale had consciously avoided having the DeLorean crashing into a barn, as it had in the film. He felt if he placed the same setting as in the movie, audiences would also expect the arrival of farmer Peabody and family to confront the time-traveling McFly. The Peabodys had been one of the very first excisions from the book. "I knew there was no way to do a decent version of the Peabody gags onstage, so I wanted to nip those expectations in the bud."

Gale proposed that the car crash into a billboard for a "giant 16-inch television," with the front end partially exposed, looking like a 3D advertising stunt. "I was after a 'hide in plain sight' gag, which would clearly tell us we were in 1955, because I felt we needed a stronger punch line to the first time-travel sequence. But John convinced me to

go with the barn as a practical matter. Constructing the car-in-the-billboard for one visual gag wasn't cost-effective, while the barn could be used twice, and allowed for better staging when 1955 Doc sees the car for the first time."

Gale relented, with the proviso that Finn Ross add a piece of video scrawling on the barn door reading "Property condemned." "Even though it's only seen briefly, it explains why no one else had wandered into the barn, and tells the audience not to expect Farmer Peabody."

One Car to Rule Over Them All...

After Colin Ingram had made it clear that the DeLorean was going to be a real, physical vehicle onstage, Rando then decreed it would be the *only* vehicle onstage for the entire show.

No other cars meant:

No Libyans to chase Marty, but that's OK. Doc would now need medical help due to radiation poisoning.

No McFly car was totaled by Biff at the beginning of the show. That plot point had already been dispensed with by Bob Gale. Marty didn't need George's car.

No car to hit Marty in the street outside of Lorraine's house in 1955. It became George and the tree branch falling on him that knocks him unconscious in the street so that Sam Baines could take him into the house.

No car with Biff and his gang chasing Marty through the town square? No manure to clean up onstage!

No car trunk in which Biff's goons can lock Marty? That garbage bin in the corner looks like it can hold him!

Not even a real car in which Marty and Lorraine can park outside of the school. Just a bench seat. That is going to be a hell of a lighting job . . .

This was one of the few issues on which Robert Zemeckis questioned the director. "Cars were part of the culture," he explains. "I think the scene with Marty and Lorraine could

---

ABOVE After much discussion, it was decided that the DeLorean would crash through and come to a stop in a condemned barn, providing a temporary hiding place for the vehicle, and a set that could be multipurposed.

have been put in a stylized car. Just my thoughts." Ultimately, Zemeckis ceded to his theatrical counterpart, later admitting that Rando's decision served the show well, and that the audience never raised the question of the absence of any car other than the DeLorean. Gale took the changes in stride. "From my perspective, it was just pragmatism to not put a car onstage if you don't have to. There's always another way to do it; it shouldn't be a problem."

Speaker of the House

Finding the right way to adapt the opening "Giant speaker gag" for the stage had been a conundrum.

"We always knew it was important to have some version of the scene, just so we hear Doc's voice on the recording, telling Marty to be at the mall later that night. It seemed forced if Marty had to explain the situation to Jennifer," states Gale. "In the early, early drafts, Bob Zemeckis and I had this fantasy about literally blowing a stunt guy into the audience, and then having actor Marty come running down the center aisle and jump up on the stage for the next number. But that was before reality set in." For both the Dominion and Sadler's Wells showcases, the speaker bit was not included, since the focus was on the script and songs.

A number of approaches were attempted and explored, with fight coordinator/stunt supervisor Maurice Chan

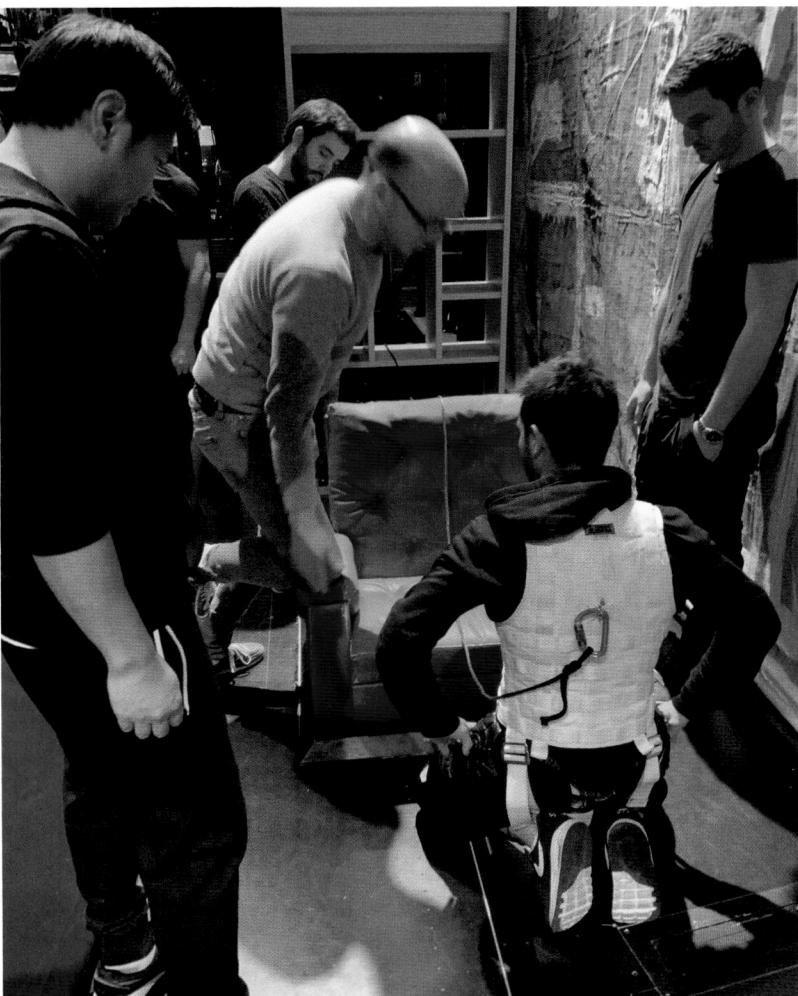

coming from France to lend his expertise. Olly Dobson was keen to try to make it work, allowing himself to be strapped into a harness and bungee rig and get yanked backward off his feet into a waiting chair. The problem with that, says the actor, was: "Even with the chair modified, there was still about a fifty, sixty percent chance I was going to get whiplash every time. Not a good way to start a show." Everyone was in total agreement with his conclusion. "We were absolutely insistent that Olly could not do that eight times a week," agrees Ingram. When the curtain rose in Manchester, and the speaker exploded, the actor carefully propelled himself backward into the chair without any wires, and light objects from a shelving unit behind him fell around him. The audience loved it. Every time.

FLASH FORWARD TO LONDON At the Adelphi Theatre, a new approach found Marty standing proudly next to the speaker, guitar pick at the ready. One strum of the instrument triggered an explosion all around the youth, leaving him unscathed and ready to "rock and roll!"

How's the Weather Up There?

Before the company moved to Manchester, sound designer Gareth Owen needed to record a weather report for the radio in Lou's Café, contradicting Marty's information that a fierce storm was on the way to Hill Valley.

> RADIO ANNOUNCER (V.O.)
> Weather forecast for tonight, mostly clear with some scattered clouds, temperatures going down to about fifty degrees...

ABOVE Fight director Maurice Chan (back to camera) and prop supervisor Chris Marcus (center) check the cable designed to yank Marty backward as the speaker explodes. After testing of the gag, it was deemed too dangerous for Dobson to endure eight times a week.

It wouldn't be necessary to audition an actor to do the voice over; nor did Owen need to "create" a voice. Instead, the weather forecast was delivered by the man who wrote it and every other line in the show. Bob Gale thought it would be something fun to do, as long as no one had any objections. No one did. "When my wife and daughter came to the Manchester opening, they had no idea I'd done this. They both almost fell out of their seats when they heard my voice!"

"Back" Where It Belongs

With just days before the company moved to Manchester, John Rando had a big decision to make. After months of rewriting, reconfiguring, inventing new action, and untold numbers of rehearsals, he had turned "Something About That Boy" from a ninety-second song into a crowd-pleasing, high-energy five-minute extravaganza upon which to bring down the curtain on the first act.

There was one problem: The act wasn't over. Since the very first workshop, after "Something About That Boy," Marty had been running back to Doc's lab to plead with the scientist to get him "Back in Time." It had been effective in exciting the test audiences, but as "Something" kept evolving, the director became less enthusiastic about keeping the status quo.

"We were rehearsing 'Back in Time,' and Roger and Olly were doing their dances," continues the director, "and I started to realize their hearts weren't in it for some reason, and neither was mine, despite the fact I was the one who came up with it and had been championing the idea. I went home and did some soul searching, and I walked in the next day and announced 'Back in Time' was cut as the act closer, and we were going to end it with Biff in the laundry basket. Twenty minutes later, my cell phone rang, and it was Colin asking, 'What the hell are you telling me?'"

The producer had seen growth in the number over the course of rehearsals and had been duly impressed with the changes, but strongly expressed his concerns with moving the stalwart fan favorite to the end of the show. "Bob [Gale] and Glen and Alan were all on board," says Rando about the change. "I told Colin everything I believed about this number being the perfect place to take the intermission, and offered to do one run-through with it, and one without

it. When we did the one where Biff fell into the basket to end the act, our little invited audience loved it. Ingram agreed that Rando had made his case.

On January 30, 2019, after the next-to-last rehearsal in London, "Back in Time" was moved to the end of the show, and "Something About That Boy" took its place as the official Act One closer. Ironically, this was exactly the structure Gale had originally scripted before the very first workshop at the Dominion in 2018.

Move 'Em Out!

Strictly following the advised precautions of health officials due to the emergence of COVID-19, the company loaded the trucks and began its move to the north. Graham Hookham and associate director Richard Fitch went along and oversaw the load-in of the sets, props, costumes, and technical equipment into the theater. After everything was properly installed to everyone's satisfaction, they ran initial dry-tech rehearsals of the technical aspects of the

show—sound, lighting, and automation—while John Rando and the cast remained behind for their last rehearsals at the Lanterns studio.

On January 31, 2020, the final London rehearsal was held. "We did a full run-through that day," notes Gale, "and the one area that wasn't working was 'Earth Angel.' We had a long discussion about that one. Bob Zemeckis, who was in town looping another film, talked it through with John about how he thought it could work better onstage. And then, we walked out the door and switched off the light behind us!" Next stop, Manchester.

Manchester England, England

Puttin' on the Sitz...

For the first week in Manchester, no two men were as busy as Nick Finlow and Jim Henson. In the mornings, they would rehearse various numbers with the newly assembled full orchestra in a studio on the outskirts of town. From there, it was on to the Manchester Opera House, where they would join John Rando and the cast for the actors' blocking and rehearsals. On Saturday, February 8, 2020, the two groups would converge for what was one of the absolute highlights of the process to date—the *sitzprobe*.

In opera and musical theater, a *sitzprobe* (from the German for "seated rehearsal") is a rehearsal where the cast sings with the orchestra for the first time. "It's one of the most exciting parts of the preshow process," explains Glen Ballard. "The actors and orchestra have been rehearsing separately, and this is when they all come together. The music is really loud and exciting and literally enveloping and embracing everyone."

Henson wanted to make sure it was an unforgettable experience for everyone in attendance. Of course the orchestra would play all the songs that the actors would perform, but there was one instrumental piece that Henson

LEFT The cast perform the songs for the first time with full orchestral accompaniment.

such gusto, it really blows the roof off. That first experience of hearing it live is a cherished memory."

Cast a Giant Shadow

Before bringing in the cast for onstage rehearsals, the technical departments had their own dry-tech period. This included Tim Lutkin, who finally could begin the actual in-theater lighting based on the designs he had created over the past months in consultation with Hugh Vanstone. When Marty and Lorraine arrived to park at the high school just prior to the dance, one of Rando's choices for the show produced a very unexpected dramatic enhancement of the scene.

Rando's "no vehicles" decree meant that Rosie Hyland and Olly Dobson would make their entrance on nothing more than a car bench seat, gliding into place on an automated track. Lutkin's first approach was based on a time-honored practice. "When somebody is in a car and it's nighttime, we replicate the angle of light on the dashboard with an uplighter," he explains. "It always looks fun, people

chose to begin the evening. "I told Nick Finlow that we needed to knock their socks off," says Henson, "and we're not going to tell them what we're playing. We're just going to start. They're not going to know what hit them."

Quite fittingly, Henson began with Alan Silvestri's exhilarating overture. Recalls the conductor, "The looks on their faces were priceless."

"None of us will ever forget the jolt of excitement from hearing Alan Silvestri's iconic overture blasting out for the first time," says Rosie Hyland, "and getting to hear the songs fleshed out finally was so satisfying and exciting. There wasn't a single dry eye in the house. The *sitzprobe* is always a highly anticipated day for any show; it's always exciting, but *Back to the Future* dwarfed every other *sitzprobe* I've ever been part of." Adds Aidan Cutler, "That moment we heard that iconic cymbal crash for the first time! The orchestra flared and took us all by surprise. I was absolutely blown away. The hairs on the back of my neck were standing to attention the entire time. Alan Silvestri's score really is a marvel, and when played with

RIGHT The lack of a real car, and the specialized lighting, results in a dramatic effect for George confronting Biff.

recognize it, and it's a quick way of putting the audience in that space." What became immediately evident was that without a physical car around them, the light from the "dashboard" exaggerated Marty's and Lorraine's figures to produce enormous shadows. "Those two big shadow puppets on the upstage wall looked great," he recalls. "It gave the scene a whole new look and a new energy."

The initial positive results of this new visual perspective inspired Lutkin to continue the motif as the scene progressed. "I added another unit [light] for George, and that became even a bigger moment, because George, who we've seen as somebody who struggles with his confidence, is suddenly this huge image on the back wall. It's both a metaphor and a prediction for the man he's going to be. Everything the scene became was inspired by the dashboard lighting, then adding it onto that other world, where it supports this idea of him finally growing up and facing his demons."

Rando *loved* it. "Tim lit it all like a noir movie, and I thought it was magnificent!"

And He Writes Music, Too!

One Sunday evening, John Rando, Bob Gale, Alan and Sandra Silvestri, and Glen Ballard got together for a traditional Sunday roast at a Manchester restaurant. When the food arrived, each plate included a side order of kale, much to the irritation of a certain composer. Alan Silvestri does not like kale. Alan Silvestri has never liked kale, and he went into a several-minute diatribe about the evils of what he didn't even consider a legitimate vegetable, to the amusement of his dinner companions.

A day or so later, Roger Bart received a revision in his dialogue after he wakes up from his "21st Century" dream:

> DOC
>
> I dreamt I was in the year 2020. Although the sartorial aspect was questionable, it was a fascinating place. There was no war, no crime, no traffic. **And everyone ate this weird green tissue paper called "kale."**

From the audience's amused reaction, Silvestri was not alone in his disdain for the "edible leaves." It became a permanent addition to the script, much to the chagrin of the World Association of Kale Growers.*

---

* No such organization exists, but if it did, they would not be happy.

The Night Before . . . February 19, 2020

In the workshops and labs of the prior months, the care, work, and dedication from every member of the team saw the show firing solidly on all six cylinders of the DeLorean's V6 engine as it approached the starting line of the Manchester stage. On the night before the world premiere, Rando put the cast through their first dress rehearsal with a small audience: ushers and theater employees of the Opera House.

And for Ingram, everything came to a screeching halt. There was precious little response from the audience. No laughs, no enthusiasm, and only a smattering of polite applause at the end. "I was really worried," he laughs. "We'd gotten more enthusiasm at the first Dominion workshop. I called for everyone to come the next morning to a meeting on the basis that we had a crisis on our hands."

As he had requested, everyone showed up for the meeting, all of them sharing his concern about the night before. "Except for John Rando," he clarifies. "He was the only one not concerned, as the rest of us were looking at each other and going, 'Why is it not working?' It ultimately came down to the fact that it was a terrible audience." That afternoon there was another dress rehearsal. "It was twice as good, and I felt better, but I still was quite anxious." He needn't have been.

Time Circuits On!

On February 20, 2021, at 7:30 P.M. GMT, on the stage of the Manchester Opera House, musical theater history was made with the world's first official performance of *Back to the Future The Musical*.

Every one of the 1,920 seats in the theater was spoken for. A throng of humanity dressed in orange puffy vests and white lab coats milled eagerly about, to the amazement and excitement of the cast and crew members peeking through the curtains.

When the first notes of Silvestri's renowned fanfare trumpeted through the auditorium, the audience erupted in delight. It never stopped.

The fans applauded the entrance of every character. They laughed at all the lines. The DeLorean's entrance, as noted in stage manager Graham Hookham's postshow report, stopped the show (in a good way). The audience was one with the show for every second of the almost three-hour journey. Signature *Back to the Future* moments were met with cheers of joy and satisfaction.

"Their reaction was totally off the charts, and lots of them had tears in their eyes," relates Bob Gale. "But the reactions I enjoyed most were from our company and from the staff at the theater, who were totally unprepared for the experience." Having seen the movie play to packed houses of enthusiastic fans at film premieres, and at events such as *Back to the Future in Concert* and 2014's Secret Cinema (which saw crowds of three thousand people per show), Gale knew the potential for the overwhelming adulation they could expect if the show played as well as everyone hoped it would (and did), and he shared those stories over the days leading up to the premiere. "I had told everyone that it was going to be crazy-great bedlam like they had never seen. They all thought I was just excited and overhyping things, but by the time Doc Brown made his entrance, no one thought that anymore!"

Hugh Coles (who got a thunderous reception in his first moments onstage as George) recalls, "It was mad. It was crazy. And it was the most fun! By this point in our process, the characters had come to mean so much to us, and obviously they mean *so much* to these people, and it was the first time they got to be in a room with them." Coles loved that at times, audience members expressed aloud their appreciation to the actors during the show. "In the lunchroom scene, when I go to tell Lorraine she's my density, I did my chocolate milk gag and turned toward her. From out of the rafters, someone suddenly screamed 'Go, George!'"

Another memorable moment for Coles occurred with Olly Dobson center stage, having just finished the last few notes of his "Johnny B. Goode" guitar solo and realizing everyone was staring at him. Before he could deliver his next line, "a woman in the front row," continues Hugh, "so very quietly went, 'I love you . . .' and *everyone* in the theater heard it. Olly looked at her and gave her a wink."

"I've played some very big theaters in my life and know what a big audience sound can be like," says Rosie Hyland of the experience. "I've never heard anything like I did in Manchester. The combination of hearing that overture and the sound that erupted from the audience when it started was overwhelming, to the point where I told myself I was going to

---

have to block it out if I was going to get through the show. In the parking lot scene when George punched Biff, the roof came off! As Hugh and I exited the stage together, holding on to each other, I gripped him for dear life. It was just so much more than I ever hoped it could have been."

They came for *Back to the Future*, and they got everything they had hoped for and more. At the end of the show, every person in that theater was on their feet dancing, cheering, applauding, and letting everyone on the stage know how much they had adored the performance they had just experienced.

"That first night was f–ing crazy," says Roger Bart, grinning. "John Rando came into my dressing room, and I was sopping wet from sweating through everything. I got my costume off and he just bellowed and cried with joy. It was an extraordinary journey to arrive there. You think something is special, but you don't really, really know. And then suddenly you're in front of two thousand paying customers. We were all just blown away."

"There was this big sense of relief," admits Rando. "What was really fun about that night was there were a couple of American producers there that rarely give compliments. They basically tell you what they think. To hear them glow about the show was stunning."

"I've never, ever, in my career seen an audience like that," admits Colin Ingram. Despite having been prepared for the potential response of the audience, Gale reveled in the entire evening. "It was truly one of the greatest nights of my life. As the saying goes, you had to be there!"

Applause Notes:
- Rounds for all of the principals first entrances
- Whoops and cheers for the guitar explosion
- Show stopping reaction for the first car reveal
- Laughter and applause of Doc's "serious shift" line
- Applause and whoops for the model reveal in Doc's Lab
- Audience chanting "come on George" before the punch
- Show stopping reaction for George punching Biff

The media would not be allowed to formally review the show until the official opening, but the fans were under no such restriction, taking to the internet in force to report to the millions waiting to hear if Gale, Zemeckis, and company had made good their promise to deliver a fresh and new iteration of their beloved movie.

Adam Gradwell (host and producer of the *Geeky Retro Nerds Show* podcast): "When it was first announced, I wondered, like so many other fellow fans, how would the

greatest movie of all time translate to the stage? It was amazing! The cast was brilliant, the songs were catchy, funny, and fresh. I'm still trying to figure out how they did the visual effects! It was like nothing I've seen or heard onstage before or will again." (He has seen and heard it again, more than once.)

Dedicated *BTTF* fans and Manchester residents Tony Ruscoe, Angela Smith, and Darren "Daz" Chadderton met one another at a local publicity event for the show, where Ruscoe asked the other two to join him as partners in the "Back to the Future The Musical Fans" page on Facebook he had started two days after the show's premiere.

Ruscoe: "I don't think I stopped grinning from the first moment I saw Doc's lab until the mind-blowing finale. I was thrilled to hear so much of the iconic dialogue and original score being reused. It simultaneously felt very familiar and yet it was brand-new."

Smith: "Nothing could have prepared me for what I saw that evening. I went through every emotion possible, and from the opening act, I knew I was witnessing something incredibly special."

Chadderton (asked for an on-camera reaction to the show): "We don't want a sequel. We don't want a remake. We just want this musical!"

By the time the show premiered in London, their Facebook page had amassed several thousand fans, and it has continued to grow every day since.

Those who filled the Manchester Opera House on the first two nights of the engagement wanted to make sure they took home a piece of history. "The theater sold out nearly all their merchandise in those two nights, and they were supposed to have enough to last the first full week or two," says Gale, laughing.

The only thing that had been missing from opening night was the cast performing "Back in Time," as it had only recently been removed from the end of Act One. It wouldn't be gone long, because, as Colin pointed out, (1) The song had been paid for to use in the production, and (2) It had been promoted over and over to the public that the song was featured in the show.

On February 21, for the second show, "Back in Time" took its rightful place at the end of the show for the cast's final bows. It has remained there ever since.

Miles to Go . . .

Although the opening of the show had allowed everyone to take a big "exhale," there was no time to bask in the newfound glory. It was always expected that the preview period would concentrate on polishing the show and making it better and better, as press night was coming up quickly in the DeLorean's rearview mirror. There was still work to be done, and the words "It's good enough" were never an option.

Hickory Dickory Doc!

When you asked anyone involved in the company what they considered to be the most ambitious, challenging, formidable, and demanding scene of the show, the answer was unanimous: the clock tower scene. For a scene that

ABOVE Marty rocks the opening-night audience with "My Future."

Doc on a clock.

was difficult enough to create for the motion picture, it would take the combined knowledge, imagination, and creativity of every department to bring the breathtaking action before a live audience. Whatever form it was going to take, there was one thing about which Tim Hatley was adamant: There would be no "shortcut" taken, such as resorting to a video clip. The audience had paid to see a live version of *Back to the Future*, and Hatley would give them their money's worth.

First it had to be established exactly where that edifice would be located, what form it would take, and how Doc would get on and off that ledge. "I storyboarded this scene within an inch of its life," states Hatley. "I knew we had to be really dynamic with the staging of it." "Tim was like a mad scientist," adds Rando. "To my mind, this scene is the most 'cinematic' of the show, and we were all committed to doing it justice."

"One of the very early ideas," recalls Lutkin, "was that the clock itself would be attached on top of the first lighting bar, and we would fly the clock in on it. We decided against that for safety reasons."

The height, size, and placement of the clock required a great deal of consideration. At times, it was more helpful to the team to start by ruling out what *wouldn't* work, which would lead them to a viable solution.

"I knew we couldn't have Doc at the top of the clock tower at the very back of the stage," offers Hatley. "A great deal of the audience seated in the stalls wouldn't be able to see any of the action, as their viewpoint would be cut off by the balcony that's directly above them. Those people couldn't see any higher than ten feet, and we certainly couldn't have a big chunk of the audience unable to see one of the most important scenes in the show. The clock had to be front and center, and large enough for Doc to be able to hang from it. That negated the idea to fly it in on a wire, as it would be too unstable."

Over the course of months of research, analysis, and testing, the solution still remained a conundrum.

Ultimately, Hatley hit on an idea that would heavily rely on the video talents of Finn Ross. The clock would indeed be full-size, attached to a large metal climbing frame, sitting behind the theatrical gauze on which Ross could project the courthouse frame as well as the inclement weather. The piece would come out on a truck and stop center stage, where Roger Bart would brave the "elements" to attempt to connect the wire to the circuit box. The lights would go down as the frame moved out, and then come up again on Olly driving the DeLorean.

Step in Time

Ross would also provide a clever solution for getting Doc up the stairs to the ledge. There were no long flights of stairs for Roger Bart to ascend to the clock face, but video, combined with Bart's brilliant pantomime skills, would provide a huge laugh as the scientist climbed dozens of stairs without actually moving an inch. "We started with a little stairstep device," says Hatley, "as we thought it might make it easier for Roger to begin that climb, but it was too static and caused problems." Once again, Ross and his traveling gauze facilitated the scene. Roger puts his hand on a video bannister and climbs in place, as the video stairs disappear under him.

"We first tried that in a video workshop with a student actor doing the movements," notes Ingram. "We could see the potential. Then, when Roger did it, it was just hilarious,

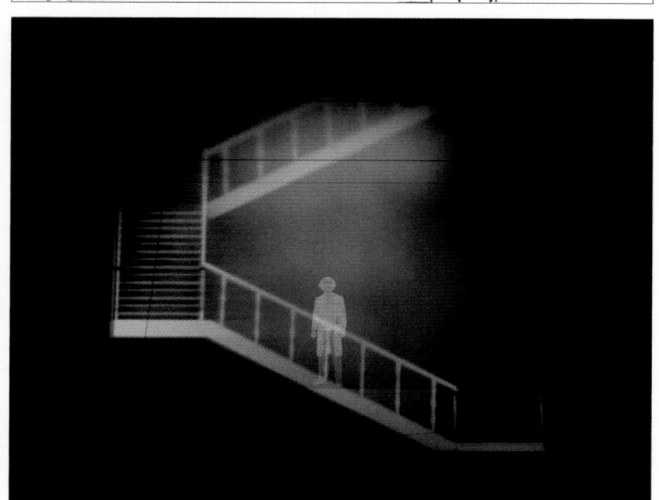

and it still gets a laugh every night." Says Gale, "It's the goofiest thing in the show. At the first preview, I wasn't sure whether the audience would embrace it or throw things at the stage. But they loved it, and it often gets applause."

As they began the previews in Manchester, everyone was thrilled with the way the sequence had come together, but it wasn't yet perfected. Hatley points out, "When you're in front of an audience and you're in the arc of the show, you realize you can really outstay your welcome. You think you're being so clever in that everyone *has* to see Doc go all the way up the staircase, or see him scaling down the building. People actually lose interest. You've got to keep pace, so we cut it in half." When it first debuted in Manchester, the sequence was almost eleven minutes long, but after a number of judicious cuts, it was trimmed to a tight five and a half.

Sound, video, automation, music, and book changes would all come into play until Rando and company gave their blessing on the completed version. "When you're in the theater watching it," sums up producer Ingram, you're exhausted from all the excitement, and it's such an exhilarating moment when Doc sees the flame trails on the stage and proclaims, 'It worked!' I think it's really an amazing achievement." "It's our finest hour," exclaims Hatley proudly.

March 4, 2020
The Most Unkindest Cut of All...

There was absolutely nothing wrong with it. Glen Ballard loved it, as did Silvestri, Rando, Ingram, and Gale. Young Aidan Cutler, in his first major theatrical role, had been killing with it. But ultimately, it had to go.

From the time it had started its life as "It's What I Do" in the 2017 song showcase, through its metamorphosis into "Good at Being Bad," there had been some uncertainty about its place in the show. "It's a really good song," declared Rando, "and the actor we had in the first workshop just rocked it. As time wore on, we shortened it, focused it, and when we cast Aidan Cutler as Biff, he was really funny in it. We knew we had it all. But it still had to go."

There was more than one reason for its impending extraction. The running time of the show was three hours, and it was essential that it be pared down wherever possible.

THIS PAGE Sketches and computer animation illustrate the "steps" it took to get Doc from the stage to the ledge of the clock tower.

LEFT Biff explains in song how he came to be Hill Valley's bully extraordinaire.

Another consideration was its placement, coming as the teenage Biff enters Lou's Café to torment young George, mere moments after the big musical number "Cake," in which Marty arrives in the 1955 Hill Valley town square.

Immediately after Biff was finished with his ode to oppression, Goldie Wilson would take center stage with his tour-de-force number, "You've Gotta Start Somewhere." An unwritten rule of musical theater is that there should never be two major musical numbers following each other in the same setting. The audience needed a chance to breathe.

The song remained in the show for the first two weeks, and people were starting to question Rando as to when he was planning to make the cut. "Glen was working on his Netflix show, *The Eddy*, in Paris at the time, and I didn't want to cut it without him being there," responded the director. "When he got back, I told him I was going to do it, and he said, 'Let's see it. That's why we're doing previews.'"

"John was worried that Glen would take it hard, but I assured him Glen would support anything that made the show better—and he did," says Gale. "I was more concerned about how Aidan and Hugh [Coles] would react—Hugh because I thought he enjoyed the shtick of how Biff abused him in the number. We told them together."

"It was the morning of the fourteenth preview of the show," pinpoints Cutler. "I got a call from John asking if I could get down to the theater because we needed to have a chat. John and Bob said, 'We think the song has to go, and we want to try it without the song tonight if that's OK.'" "We assured both of them that if the show didn't play as well without the number, we'd restore it," adds Gale. Along with the other reasons for cutting the song, John mentioned to Aidan there was still a slight concern that the number was serving to somewhat humanize the character.

That was more than enough for Aidan to understand why the song had to go. "First and foremost, I don't want audience members to look at Biff and say he's a cool guy, or little kids thinking that the decisions Biff makes are the right ones to make in life. I know I've done my job right if the audience leave at the end of the night and nobody wants my autograph or wants to talk to me. I'd be happy knowing that I've pissed off that many people because they just think of Biff as an awful human being."

The song was dropped from the performance that night. "It played great, the pace improved, and no one missed it," reported Gale. Immediately after, Cutler praised Rando for his actions. "He completely changed the angle of the show for me, as well as my perspective on the character, even though I'd just spent months getting so in the head of this guy. Within just the space of one night, it completely added this extra layer of evil."

Your Call Cannot Be Completed...

During the second week of previews, another popular moment from the film would be sacrificed. It had been in the show from the very first drafts, during Marty's performance of "Johnny B. Goode" when Marvin Berry rushed to the phone to share this exciting new style of music with his cousin Chuck.

In repeated viewings during the previews, it had become apparent to everyone that this was one of those instances where the film scene simply couldn't be re-created onstage in an organic way. "There was already so much going on in this scene that needed the audience's attention: Marty playing the song, with the ensemble dancing to Chris Bailey's high-spirited choreography," explains John Rando, "and in the middle of all that, Cedric had to cross over to the side of the stage, holding a phone handed to him from the wings, and yelling the dialogue into it over the music. I thought that I really couldn't make it any better than that, so maybe we should lose it."

"Bob Z. recognized this pretty early on," recounts Gale. "It was really easy to intercut to it in the movie. We had the band riffing in the background with the volume of the

No! The cable will get in the way. We're
doing incredible lifts and spins. It's too
dangerous. What if a dancer steps on the
cable and trips and accidentally drops
the girl?

RANDO

I don't care! It should be plugged in!

He thinks and hesitates for a moment.

RANDO (cont'd)
OK, OK, we won't plug it in. We'll just see.

At the first preview, Bailey sat directly in front of the director. Recounts Rando, "Olly goes through the guitar riff, and the audience is screaming. They're just delighted. And then he finishes it to big, big applause. I leaned over and said, 'I guess we won't be putting the cable back.'"

Months after the fact, the director acknowledged a certain irony in the situation. "Theater is theater," he concedes. "I was so adamant about plugging in the guitar for the sake of authenticity, but at the same time, I had no problem with Lorraine and Marty sitting on an open, bare bench seat for the scene that takes place in the car!"

music lowered, cut to a close-up of Marvin delivering the joke, and then cut back to the action of the dance. Onstage, trying to keep that moment in the show broke another musical theater rule: Don't interrupt the music. Especially if it's one of the greatest rock-and-roll songs of all time. The real moment that the audience wanted to see was Marty going through the history of rock-and-roll guitar moves, ending with the payoff of, 'I guess you guys aren't ready for that yet, but your kids are gonna love it.'" With everyone in agreement, a preview was done without Marvin making the call, "and it worked so much better," says Gale. As Aidan Cutler had understood the need to sacrifice his song as Biff, so did Cedric Neal in the interest of making the show even tighter and more polished.

Cable for John Rando...

Satisfied with the resolution of the Marvin/Chuck Berry phone call, Rando still had one issue he felt needed to be dealt with in the "Johnny B. Goode" number. It had nothing to do his actor's performance, but rather, with the incongruity of the instrument in his hands. "I was very upset that we were in the fifties, and the guitar itself wasn't plugged into the amp." Rando made his objections clear but was challenged strongly by his choreographer. "Chris Bailey and I got into big arguments about it."

RANDO

It needs to be plugged in! The audience
isn't going to believe that he's playing it!

ABOVE Marvin Berry tries to share a new musical style with his cousin Chuck by phone.

RIGHT Marty gives the kids at the Enchantment Under the Sea dance their first taste of rock-and-roll, ending in a McFly flourish.

March 5–6, 2020
Where There's a Will…

As the show crept closer to the official opening night, rehearsals and performances forged ahead, yet there was escalating concern in the outside world due to the growing threat of coronavirus. When Olly Dobson began to display some cold symptoms, it was decided he should immediately be checked out by a physician. "No one really thought it was COVID, or pneumonia, or even the flu," says Gale, "but we didn't want to risk it turning into something worse." The examination yielded a classic good news/bad news scenario for Dobson and the show.

"The ENT told me, 'There's nothing wrong with you. Your vocal folds [cords] and your instrument are in perfect nick [condition].' The problem was that I was just overworked and really tired. We found it necessary for me to go on voice rest for forty-eight hours." "There was no choice," says Gale. "It was better that Olly miss two days and get healthy than to risk him getting sicker and not being onstage for press night."

In the limited number of previews the company had performed since the opening night, there had been a few times that a couple of members of the ensemble had to be covered, and the swings had done their jobs flawlessly, never missing a step. Normally, all the understudies would have had a number of their own rehearsals by the time the show had opened to the public, but due to the expedited schedule in making the March 11 press night opening, that had yet to occur.

Late that morning, Will Haswell had already arrived at the Opera House to get ready for the daily preshow rehearsal when he got a call from company manager David Massey. "He asked, could I come down to the auditorium." Massey, John Rando, and the producers explained the situation. "They said, 'We know you haven't had a rehearsal [as Marty], but how would you feel about going on?' I was like, yeah … let's give it a go! So in an afternoon, we managed to get the show up and running, which was amazing."

The actor had already experienced replacing the star of a musical on two separate occasions. He took over the lead role of singer Frankie Valli in a West End production of *Jersey Boys*, and headlined as Danny Zuko in a production of *Grease* that had been produced by Colin Ingram. "Will is a really special guy," says Ingram. "He's one of those incredible triple threats. I had no doubt he would pull it off."

A key thing that helped Haswell through the process was the fact he had been with the show since the very first workshop in 2018. As Olly's understudy, the actor had already committed to memory all of Marty's dialogue, as well as the song lyrics. The primary focus of the intensive afternoon rehearsal would be on movement and blocking. "Knowing the scripts and the songs, I was able to throw myself one hundred percent into where he [Marty] goes," he explains. "I got this rush of adrenaline and got into a mode of 'let's try this' and I'll retain as much as I can."

For those intense hours, every department was on alert to provide any help they could until that curtain went up, and even after. "I couldn't have gotten through it without the cast. There are certain numbers where there was so much information, I said to them 'just shove with love,'" trusting the cast members to gently guide him to where he needed to be if necessary. The cast took him at his word. "In 'Cake,' when Marty arrives in the fifties, there's a big 'Welcome to Hill Valley' sign across the stage as I enter. I was over on the far side of the stage when I was supposed to be in the middle. Katie [Pearson] as the young Clock Tower Lady] came over to me, took me by the hand, and walked me into the middle around everyone and was just holding me. Everyone on that stage had my back."

Despite the tremendous amount of pressure he was under, there were moments when the actor was able to appreciate the enormity of the situation in which he found himself. The most stirring of those moments came in the second act, as he stood and watched Doc sing "For the Dreamers." "I'd obviously seen and heard Roger perform the song before," Will reflects, "but standing there onstage as Marty, and to really listen to what Doc was expressing about his life, his work, and for all the other dreamers who came before him, as corny as it sounds, the small kid in me was thinking, *I'm living the dream*. It was such a surreal, wonderful moment that will stay with me for the rest of my life."

RIGHT Will Haswell prepares to take the stage for his first performance as Marty McFly to cover for an ailing Olly Dobson.

On that night as well as the next, Will handily won over the audiences (which included his parents and girlfriend) to the delight of the whole production. Popular UK comedian and television presenter Keith Lemon (Leigh Francis) was in the audience for Will's first performance. "Keith had seen Olly at the Sadler's Wells workshop," notes Bob Gale. "He was aware that he was seeing a different actor that night in Manchester, but it didn't detract from his enjoyment one iota. In addition, he also brought his mom, who declared, 'It's the best thing I've ever seen!'"

"He was a rock star that night," says Roger Bart of Haswell's performance. "There's something beautiful to be discovered whenever something is really, really different. You are always in a learning place. The audience is seeing it for the first time, so they don't know anything is unusual or amiss. I always want the actor in that situation to have as much fun despite the acid trip experience that it is. Will is super talented, and it was genius what he did. It was really astounding."

No one was happier for Will's success in those two nights than the man for whom he was substituting. "Kudos to Will," says Olly, smiling. "I had two years to learn the entire show, and he did it in four hours. Everyone was so happy

for him. I love it when covers go on. I'm fully in support of that. My philosophy is, if I'm off, take good care of him [my character] and make sure you do *you* and have your personality in this. Have fun with it for a couple of days. Look after him! But only for a couple of days!"

The entire episode, the results, and everyone's contribution to it were summed up perfectly in Graham Hookham's performance report for that evening:

"After a very long and relentless day, this evening's show was a true testament to the dedication of everyone involved with this production. The camaraderie from everyone, rallying behind our incredible understudies and swings, was humbling, and everyone focused down and got on with the job in hand. Tonight's house would never have known that we had debut performances, it was seamless and impressive. There was a standing ovation from the top of the bows, and dancing along to 'Back in Time.'"

March 11, 2020
Press Night

After twenty preview performances, it was time for the "official" opening of the show, referred to in the UK as press night. Members of the media were invited, and they would be free to review the musical for their various outlets. As it had been every night since the first preview, the Manchester Opera House was filled to capacity, and again,

ABOVE Left: Haswell and Roger Bart take their bows at the end of Will's first (but not last) turn as Marty. Right: Popular UK entertainer and *Back to the Future* superfan Keith Lemon takes a post-show photo with Bob Gale, Roger Bart, and Will Haswell.

the fans turned out in force (and in costume).

From the opening fanfare to the curtain call, a love affair between the cast and the audience flourished, each entity feeding off the other's excitement and appreciation in a way that can only exist in the immediacy, intimacy, and immersion of live theater.

When they first decided to undertake the creation of the musical, the mandate for Zemeckis, Gale, Silvestri, and Ballard had always been to give the fans a new rendition of *Back to the Future* that honored and celebrated the film but offered a fresh and entertaining recounting. Gale had come to realize the fans didn't want a sequel or reboot of the franchise as much as they wanted to recapture the feelings that had caused them to fall in love with these characters upon the first of what would be countless viewings of the films. On that night in Manchester, Bob Gale, Robert Zemeckis, Alan Silvestri, and Glen Ballard stood onstage with the cast and took their well-deserved bows, and they were overcome by the reaction that their work, and the work of countless others on the team, had engendered. "It delighted the audience," reflected Glen Ballard, "and it delighted us that it delighted the audience."

It had always been stressed from the beginning that the musical had to be accessible to people who had never seen the films. On press night, there was at least one person in the audience who exemplified that very demographic. She had never watched any of the movies and had little, if any, awareness of the franchise in general.

Lady Madeleine Lloyd Webber (wife of Sir Andrew Lloyd Webber) traveled from London to Manchester at the behest of two people, the first being Rebecca Kane Burton, at the time the CEO of the LW Theatres. Ms. Burton was already a fan of the musical, having been invited by Ingram to a number of the workshops. Her second invitation came from a dear and longtime friend, David Grindrod, the casting director. "We literally had to drag her up there," says Grindrod, "but when she mentioned to two of her [twentysomething] children that she was going to see *Back to the Future The Musical,* they both got very excited, and she was surprised they knew about it." As the show progressed, Lady Lloyd Webber was totally struck by the audience response, as well as the show itself, both in performance and in execution.

"Manchester was a fully realized show, indistinguishable from any professional production," states Gale. "Or even better," adds Zemeckis. At the end of the evening, Madeleine Lloyd Webber declared the show "West End ready," and that one of the LW Theatres had to have it. With that pronouncement, an enormous burden was lifted from the shoulders of Ingram and the entire company. With COVID almost sure to be closing down the theater industry (along with the rest of the world), when it ultimately did reopen, *Back to the Future The Musical* would have a home at the Adelphi Theatre in London's West End.

YOU ARE INVITED TO ATTEND
THE OPENING NIGHT OF

BACK TO THE FUTURE
THE MUSICAL

WEDNESDAY II MARCH 2020
AT 7.30PM
RED CARPET ARRIVALS AT 6.30PM

OPERA HOUSE
MANCHESTER

**QUAY STREET
MANCHESTER, M3 3HP**

PLEASE JOIN US AFTER
THE PERFORMANCE FOR THE
POST SHOW PARTY AT

**SCIENCE AND INDUSTRY MUSEUM
LIVERPOOL ROAD,
MANCHESTER, M3 4FP**

CARRIAGES AT IAM | DRESS CODE: SMART

BACK TO THE FUTURE
Coutts
American Airlines
BACK TO THE FUTURE
Coutts
American Airlines
BACK TO THE FUTURE
Coutts
American Airlines
BACK TO THE FUTURE
Coutts
American Airlines
BACK TO THE FUTURE
Coutts
BACK TO THE FUTURE THE MUSICAL
Coutts
American Airlines
BACK TO THE FUTURE THE MUSICAL
Coutts
American Airlines
BACK TO THE FUTURE THE MUSICAL
Coutts
American Airlines
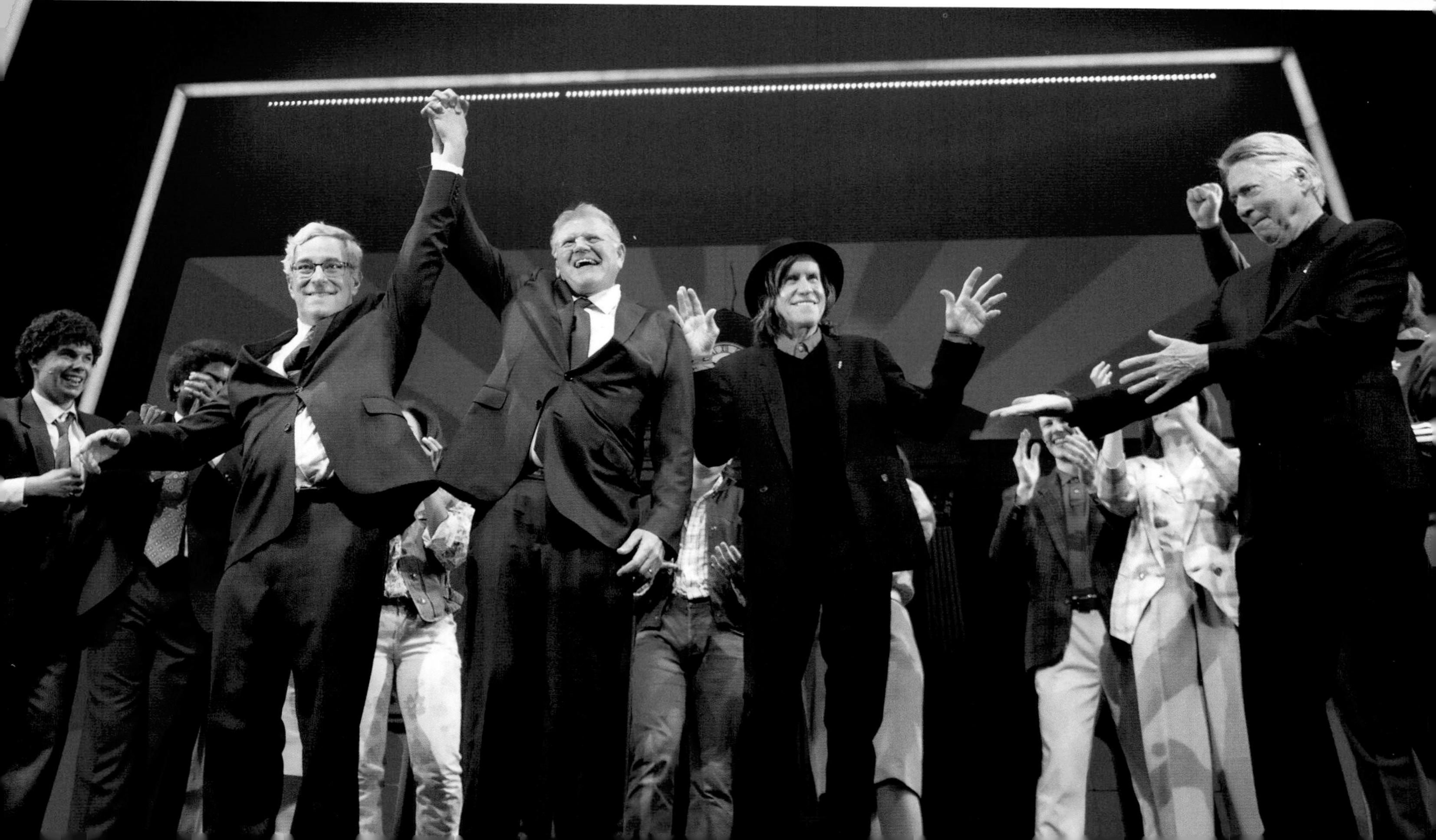

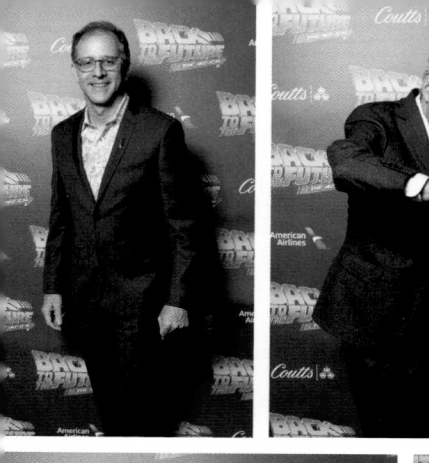

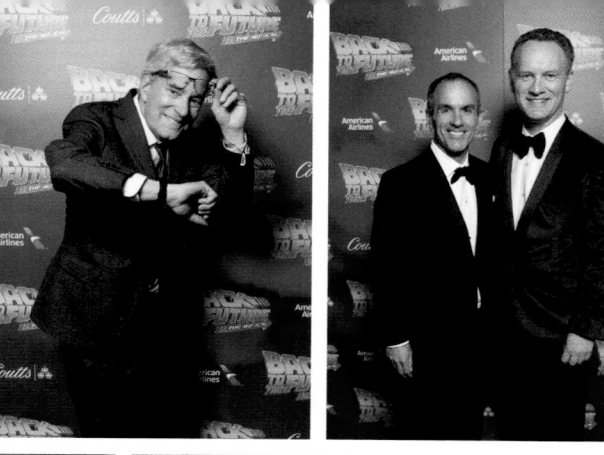

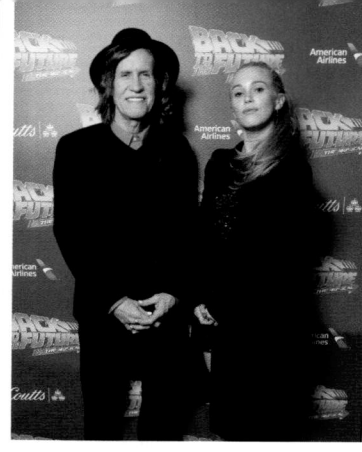

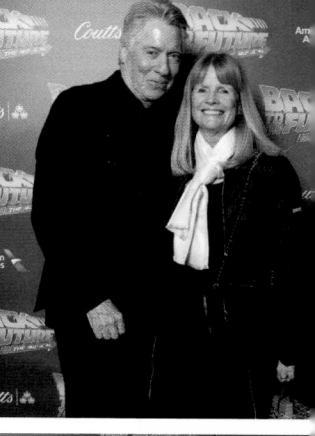

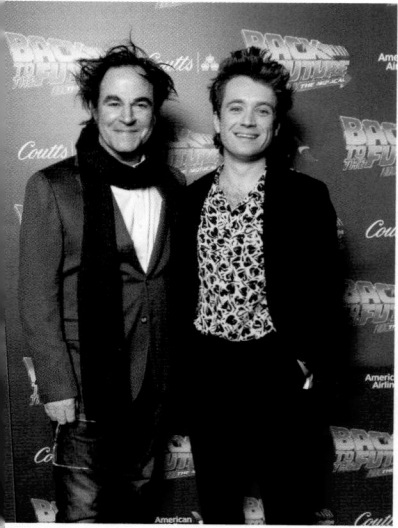

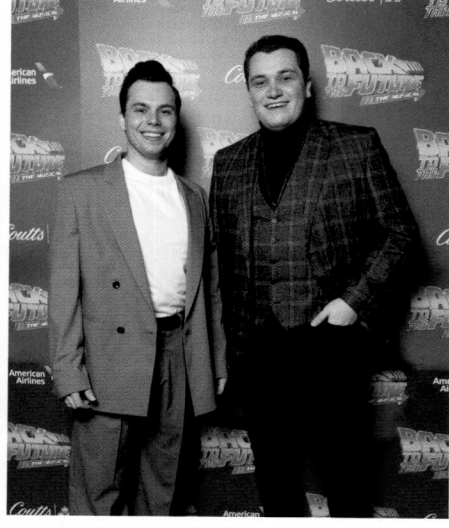

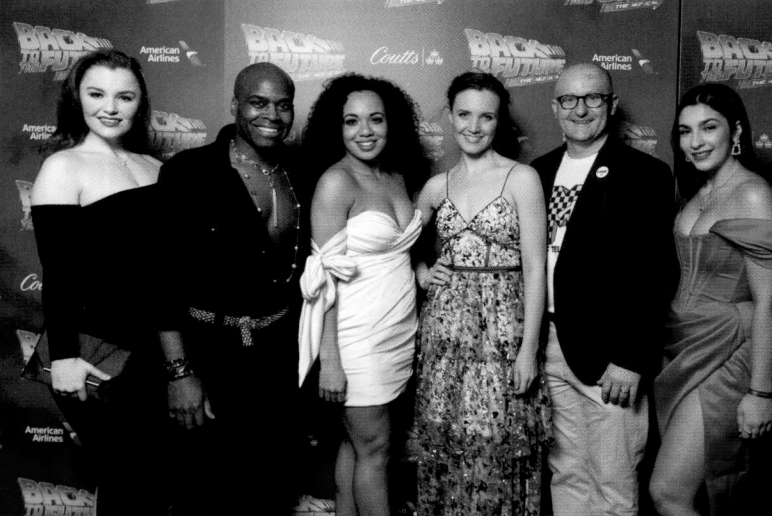

"It was a massive night," says Rando. "Since it was so close to the start of the COVID crisis, it was a miracle that we even got the show open. It had been such incredible hard work getting the show through tech and previews and then through press night, not to mention the years of development. Everyone in the cast had such a great night. After the show, we went to the party at Manchester's Science and Industry Museum and closed the place down. Then we went to a late-night pub, crowded in there and drank beer and ate pizza till three A.M. We partied like it was 1985!"

March 12, 2020
The Day After…

The press night performance was met by raves from the media, with every aspect of the show, from performances and script to music and special effects, unanimously praised. No department's contributions went unnoticed.

"*Back to the Future* just became the new must-see musical hit." —London Theatre Direct

"The quality of the new music, alongside the faultless casting, show how this musical stands on its own two feet and is much more than just a mere extension of the film series. ★★★★★" —*Manchester Evening News*

"*Back to the Future* is a must-see, whether you're a fan of the film or not. First stop, Manchester. Next stop? World domination. ★★★★★" —BroadwayWorld.com

"An impressive and exhilarating musical adventure, faithfully reinvigorating a classic of cinema history while leaving its own dazzling impression, sure to last long into the future." —WhatsOnStage.com

A Bit of "Relief"

Less than twelve hours after the press night celebrations had concluded, the entire cast was back in costume at the BBC Television facilities in Manchester, where they performed two numbers from the show for the benefit of Sport Relief, a long-standing UK charity telethon.

Doc and Marty (Roger and Olly) arrived at the television studio by DeLorean and took the audience back to 1955, where they observed George (Hugh) being harassed by Biff Tannen (Aidan), after which Goldie Wilson (Cedric) offered his musical advice, "Gotta Start Somewhere," to the beleaguered youth. Following that, Marty helped Doc recharge the time machine's flux capacitor with a 1.21-gigawatt performance of "The Power of Love," backed up by the entire company.

OPPOSITE The press night reception following a momentous performance. Top row, left to right: John Rando; Bob Gale; producer Donovan Mannato and lead producer Colin Ingram; Glen Ballard and Steph Whittier; Alan and Sandra Silvestri. Center row, left to right: Roger Bart and Olly Dobson; Will Haswell and Aidan Cutler; Emma Lloyd, Cedric Neal, Courtney-Mae Briggs, Rosanna Hyland, Mark Oxtoby, Bethany Lythgoe. Bottom: Bob Gale, Robert Zemeckis, Glen Ballard, and Alan Silvestri take a well-earned bow as a sold-out audience express their love for this new incarnation of their beloved *Back to the Future*.

RIGHT Olly (left) and Roger (right) with Sport Relief presenter Oti Mabuse.

Safely back in 2020, it was show business as usual in Manchester as another sold-out crowd awaited the curtain to rise on the second night's performance. However, few people either onstage or in the audience were aware that several hours earlier, New York City had instituted a total theater shutdown. Broadway had gone dark.

Shows continued over the next two days, with one performance on Friday night and a matinee and evening performance on Saturday, March 14, marking the end of a frenetic week during which the entire company had more than earned a well-deserved day of rest.

As they relaxed and spent a recuperative day with spouses, friends, and family, Colin Ingram was closely monitoring the news. "The prime minister went on TV that Sunday at five P.M. and rather unhelpfully told people to stay at home but didn't declare a formal shutdown. We were lucky, because that was our rest day, so cast members were either in Manchester relaxing or in London with family," he recalls. "There was a lot of confusion and discussion between producers. At six P.M., the Society of London

Theatre [our industry body] declared that all theaters should shut on the government advice."

Ingram sat in his office and conferred with other producers to get their thoughts on their next steps. On Monday, March 16, the following email went to every member of the production:

> Dear all,
>
> I regret to inform you that the production of *Back to the Future* will be suspended as a result of force majeure. Over the next few days, I will have further information once we have discussed the situation with the insurers and our trade organization.
>
> So sorry for all of us.
>
> Best,
> Colin

He further communicated with everyone that they would get paid for the next two weeks but that it was doubtful the show would continue any part of its run in Manchester.

As Bob Gale was used to saying in situations regarding *Back to the Future*, "there's good news and then there's bad news." The bad news, of course, was that the show was shutting down. The good news was that when the world reopened, the show would have a home in the West End at the Adelphi Theatre.

When would that be? No one knew for sure, but it was only a matter of time . . .

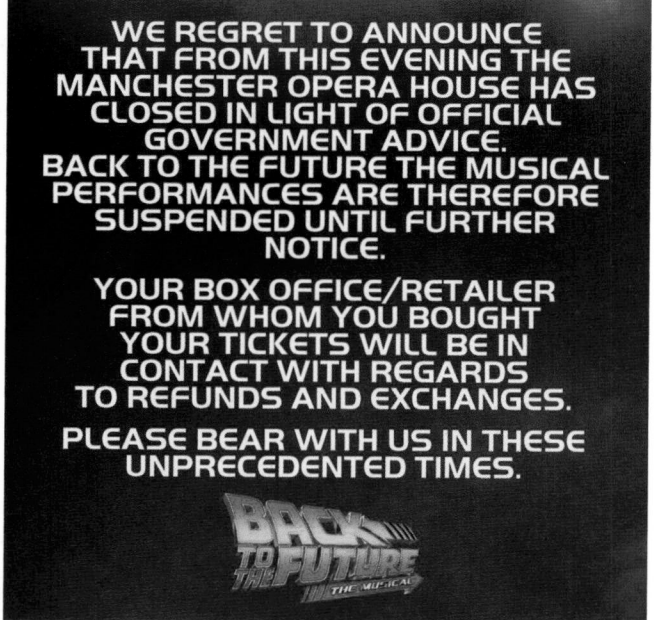

WE REGRET TO ANNOUNCE THAT FROM THIS EVENING THE MANCHESTER OPERA HOUSE HAS CLOSED IN LIGHT OF OFFICIAL GOVERNMENT ADVICE. BACK TO THE FUTURE THE MUSICAL PERFORMANCES ARE THEREFORE SUSPENDED UNTIL FURTHER NOTICE.

YOUR BOX OFFICE/RETAILER FROM WHOM YOU BOUGHT YOUR TICKETS WILL BE IN CONTACT WITH REGARDS TO REFUNDS AND EXCHANGES.

PLEASE BEAR WITH US IN THESE UNPRECEDENTED TIMES.

INTERMISSION

LIFE IN THE TIME OF COVID

THE PREVIOUS COMPREHENSIVE CLOSING-DOWN OF LONDON THEATER was in 1665, due to the bubonic plague. Since that time, not even two world wars or the Spanish flu epidemic of 1918 had been able to completely keep the theaters dark.

In the West End, as well as the rest of the world, there was great uncertainty as to when, how, or if they would be able to move forward again.

Not long after he had announced the shutdown of the musical, Colin received an inquiry from the theater owner asking if he would consider reopening the show that August (2020) in Manchester, once things began to ease up. Even though the sets were still standing on the Opera House stage, the producer demurred. "I knew the pandemic wasn't going to be over by then, and everyone's contracts would end in June, and they were unlikely to be available. For the three months following the shutdown in March, the show remained in a tomb-like state in an apocalyptic film—personal possessions were abandoned, as the cast had left on the Sunday and we shut down on Monday before they could return to the theater. They didn't come back to pick up their belongings until June."

In July, Ingram had the sets broken down and trucked out of Manchester.

Having lived with the characters for more than two years, the cast members had their own ways of keeping them "nearby" as they waited out the government-mandated closure.

"It was a real wrench to have to put those characters down so quickly," reflects Rosie Hyland, "but Lorraine really did stick with me. I thought about her a lot. Every now and then I kept the dust brushed off her songs, made sure I could still sing them!"

Olly Dobson did what he could to "stay within the vibe of the show," but "it was really hard for me to do anything at all, given the circumstances. I kicked up a [skate]board every now and then, played the guitar, and listened to loads of music, because Marty is inspired by rock music. Other than that, my Marty life was on hold."

"I don't remember many of the specifics of that time, but the feeling was still there," says Roger Bart of pandemic-era Doc Brown. "Actually, there were many nights I lay awake in bed and would run what I remembered of the scenes in my head, see if I could remember the words, and try to put myself back to sleep that way. It was a wacky, wacky year!"

Even with only twenty-four performances, many of the creatives came away from Manchester with ideas they felt would benefit the show when it opened in London. To that end, semiregular international Zoom meetings were conducted, with Rando, Ingram, Hatley, and many others participating in the process.

Together Again (Kinda)

In the early months of the pandemic, there was an explosion of internet activity designed to entertain and to raise monies for many worthy causes. One of the most notable (and popular) efforts came from film, television, and stage actor/singer Josh Gad, who gathered the casts and filmmakers of some of the most iconic films of the eighties for a Zoom reunion for the fans, with a web series called *Reunited Apart*.

On March 11, 2020, episode two of the series premiered, with Michael J. Fox, Christopher Lloyd, Robert Zemeckis, Bob Gale, Lea Thompson, Mary Steenburgen, Elisabeth Shue, Alan Silvestri, and Huey Lewis appearing for the most epic reunion of *Back to the Future*. Acknowledging Zemeckis's and Gale's declaration that there would never be a *Back to the Future Part IV*, Gad came up with the next best thing—Olly Dobson, Cedric Neal, Courtney-Mae Briggs, and the entire ensemble and musicians performed "The Power of Love" to a global audience for the first time. To date, the episode has garnered more than three million views.

More "Relief"

In March 2021, the cast was asked to be a part of Comic Relief's Red Nose Day, a yearly tradition in the UK. There had been solid progress in the war against COVID, and it was deemed to be safe enough to allow the cast to perform, as long as safety measures were followed to the letter.

Bob Gale lent his talents to write the special segment for the show. Roger Bart had been unable to travel back to the UK due to COVID restrictions, but he did his part for charity, appearing as Doc via the magic of Zoom. Gale's scenario involved Marty, Jennifer, George, Goldie, the DeLorean, and performances of "Put Your Mind to It" and "The Power of Love." Although precious little physical contact was allowed, everyone was thrilled to don their costumes and perform in front of a live, appreciative audience after a full year of seclusion.

Are We Back?

In May 2021, the UK government announced its intention to begin a slow easing of restrictions on June 21, which included the theater industry. There were conditions, which included selling a reduced number of each theater's capacity in tickets, as well as everyone being mandated to wear masks indoors at all times.

Despite the limitations, more than twenty-five productions immediately began planning their returning shows, or the premieres of others.

ABOVE The power of social distancing: The cast, ensemble, and orchestra all reunited for a performance on Josh Gad's web series.

replace Ormson. He sang for the company one morning, danced that afternoon, and was asked to return the next day to read as the understudy for Biff. Unfortunately, that evening, he tested positive for COVID, so the company rescheduled his final audition three weeks later. Two days afterward, he was offered the position. Other ensemble/swing actors who joined the company for the London engagement included Matt Barrow, Josh Clemetson, Morgan Gregory, Ryan Heenan, Tavio Wright, and Melissa Rose.* More swings were added as insurance against a new wave of COVID. In July, a few days before rehearsals officially began, the new members of the ensemble were called in to go through the music and get as comfortable with it as they could, given the incredibly short three weeks of total rehearsal time before the Adelphi Theatre would open its doors to the public.

* West End debut for Clemenston, Gregory, Heenan, Wright and Rose.

The owners of the Adelphi Theatre approached Ingram about opening the show in July. "I felt late August was safer, and the press night, as always, would be two to three weeks later." His intuition proved to be remarkably prescient, as a new, faster-spreading variant of the coronavirus caused a surge in infections resulting in another—though much shorter—delay.

Ingram ultimately made the decision that rehearsals would begin in London on July 19, 2020, with the first preview performance on August 20.

West End Story

While still in a holding pattern, some productions had to replace cast members who, for various reasons, would not be returning. Ensemble members Jemma Revell (Babs) and Oliver Ormson (3-D) moved to Disney's *Frozen*. Revell was replaced by Nicola "Nic" Myers, making her professional and West End debut. Shane O'Riordan, who had appeared in the West End's *Les Misérables*, was invited to

Matthew Barrow
Swing

Josh Clemetson
Swing

Morgan Gregory
Ensemble

Ryan Heenan
Ensemble

Nic Myers
Ensemble

Shane O'Riordan
Ensemble

Melissa Rose
Swing

Tavio Wright
Swing

ACT THREE

A TRIUMPHAL RETURN

"There will always be people who haven't seen the movie, so our show had to work completely on its own. And it does."

—Robert Zemeckis

ON JULY 19, 2021, THE FIRST FULL REHEARSAL OF *BACK TO THE FUTURE THE Musical*'s London engagement took place at the National Youth Theatre, a charitable institution offering both on- and offstage opportunities to UK adolescents and young people since its inception in 1956. A small sampling of the world-class talent who have benefited from the organization includes Helen Mirren, Derek Jacobi, Idris Elba, Colin Firth, Ben Kingsley, Daniels Craig and Day-Lewis, Rosamund Pike, Chiwetel Ejiofor, and Kate Winslet.

The rules imposed by the government and the theater were stringent for cast and crew alike. No one minded the inconveniences for the opportunity to get back to work. "COVID restrictions had definitely changed the culture of the building," reflects Rosie Hyland. "There was less socialization and lots of mask wearing, but it hadn't dampened the atmosphere." Adds Hugh Coles, "It was nice to be back in a room working after so long. I was pretty happy to mask up for as much as possible. We were all keen to protect the show from COVID closure, so we really banded around the new protocols and made them part of the rehearsal experience. Weird? Yes. Distracting? No."

BELOW LEFT The National Youth Theatre was the site of the first rehearsals of the show as theater prepared to open again.

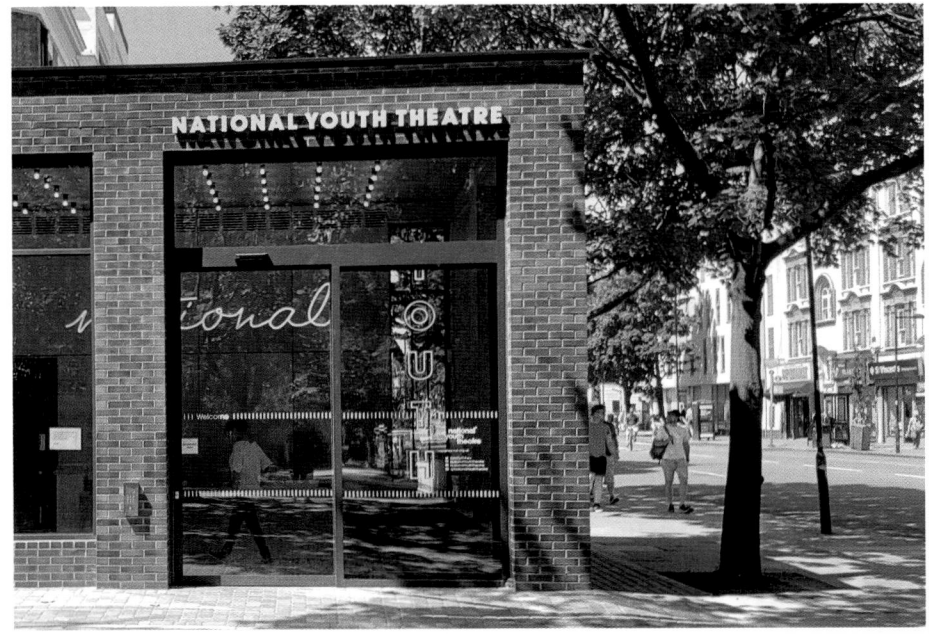

Change Is Inevitable

They had received rave reviews for the show in Manchester, and most producers and directors would have taken those kudos and waited until the health crisis had lifted to resume the show exactly as they had left it. This was never an option for the creatives of *Back to the Future*.

"Theater is never finished," states Ingram. "The view will always change, you always look to improve it, and no doubt, when we go to Broadway, we're going to make some improvements to what we've got in London." "Even with success, there could still be more to do," agrees Rando. "Maybe a cut here, a trim there, a new bit of music."

For Tim Hatley, the first priority was the theater itself. With a seating capacity of fifteen hundred, the Adelphi was four hundred twenty seats short of the Manchester venue. "In Manchester we had a lot of space by the side of the stage, and not very much depth. We were right up against that back wall, whereas in the West End, we had no wing space at all. The show itself, to the audience, would be the same, but there's a whole other show going on backstage. That's what we had to calculate, and make the cast comfortable with the revised dimensions." "We had to make Doc's lab smaller," adds Ingram, "and we had to remake the diner set because it just wouldn't fit in. These were costs we incurred

right off the bat simply because we never knew which theater we were going into in London when we built Manchester."

Back at the National Youth Theatre, as they had at both the Jerwood and Lanterns facilities, the floor of the studio was marked with tape, representing the dimensions of the Adelphi stage. Makeshift representations of the sets were moved on- and off-"stage" to simulate the flow and timing of the show, accompanied by furniture and props that would be returned to the theater when the company moved in for the final week of rehearsals leading to the opening of the show. Also on hand was the wood and metal framed DeLorean pushed back and forth by the crew, in and out of the scenes in which it appeared (and disappeared).

Any number of separate meetings were held at the same time. While Rando worked with the main cast, Chris Bailey and Darren Carnall rehearsed dancers in one studio; Maurice Chan and his assistants did fight training or stunts. Mornings were usually reserved for work on individual numbers, and afternoons found the company doing the entire show. Masks were required, except for those who were actually performing.

Great Expectations

In the time between Manchester and London, the Baines family were surprised with the wonderful news of an impending blessed event. Lorraine's mother, Stella, was going to have another baby! For the sake of brevity, Bob Gale cut the 1955 dinner scene where Marty met his four other aunts and uncles. Emma Lloyd, who portrays the Baines matriarch,

---

ABOVE Left: With the stage version of the DeLorean still being set up at the theater, Roger Bart turns to one equipped with "manual" transmission. Right: Gale and Zemeckis relaxed their "No *BTTF IV*" rule for this one exception: the book jacket of George McFly's new novel, designed by Tim Hatley.

mentioned to Gale that in the movie, Stella is pregnant with her fifth child. "We spoke of how it would be funny to have Stella heavily pregnant," she chuckles, "to touch on the fifties and the time period of the baby boomer, and also to see Marty's reaction of seeing his grandma pregnant. The scene of the Baines family gathered round the TV is such a lovely one, and I wanted that sense of Lorraine being from a big family, hence the added bump!" Bob readily agreed, admitting, "I was embarrassed to have not thought of it!"

"They said it would <u>never</u> happen!"

Since 1990, there have been many calls by the fans for yet another sequel. Both of the Bobs have steadfastly refused, insisting the trilogy would remain as such. When it came to the scene at the end of the musical when George unveils the cover of his upcoming novel, Gale decided to give a nod and a wink to the fans by having George announce the title of his new tome, *Back to the Future 4: The Further Adventures of Kelvin Klien*! "In Manchester," says Gale, "it had been *Back to the Future 2*, but one day in rehearsal, Al Silvestri suggested *4* would be funnier. He was right!"

A Trip Through Time and Space

It was mere days prior to the opening of the show in Manchester when Tim Hatley and Finn Ross were called upon to come up with a visual that would accompany the newly added overture. "We really had about a minute's notice to put it together, and so much of our energy was still very much being consumed by the car and a visual journey within the show," says Ross, laughing.

Starting with the original projection that audiences saw as they entered the theater, when the first musical notes sounded, the information on-screen indicated the location (Manchester, England), the date (keyed to each day of the show one was attending), and the time. During the overture, the date and time went backward to October 25, 1985, Hill Valley, California. The screen became translucent, revealing Doc's lab, and then Marty made his entrance.

"We left Manchester knowing we needed to do better," continues Ross. During lockdown, Ross and Hatley had the time to do that. "We were still going back in time, but we made it a journey from the present-day Adelphi Theatre to Doc's lab in 1985 Hill Valley and added a few fun details

---

RIGHT Tim Hatley and Finn Ross collaborated on a video time-travel journey from the Adelphi Theatre to 1985 to accompany Alan Silvestri's overture.

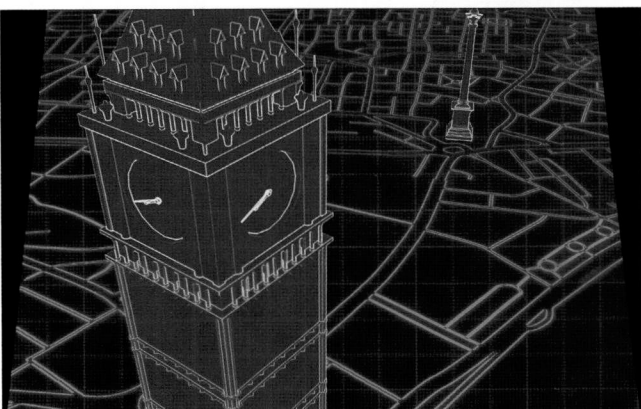

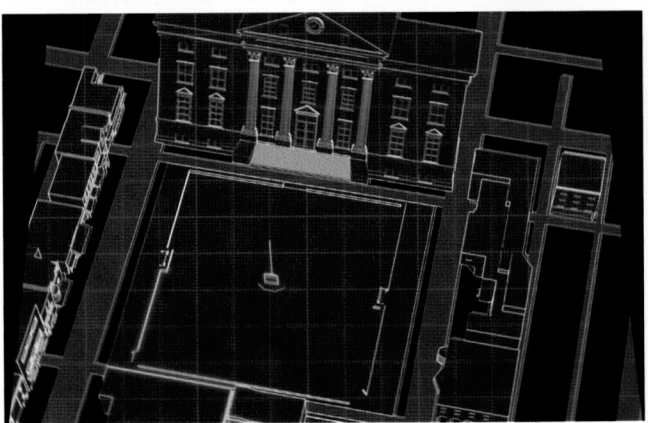

along the way. As we zoom past Big Ben, the hands are going backward. When it got to Hill Valley 1985, a signal was triggered indicating the presence of plutonium, which had the tracking mechanism take an immediate detour to the source—the home and laboratory of one Doctor Emmett L. Brown!"

We Can't Wait to Be

Hatley and Ross now turned their attentions to the opening of the second act, introducing Doc Brown's musical fantasy dream number, "21st Century."

In Manchester, it started with members of the ensemble inputting information into the circuit boards around them, with Doc appearing seemingly out of nowhere in his "command chair" as the circuit board gave way to a background of an expansive space station–like viewing port on which Ross could project imaginative objects, settings, and a few Easter eggs during the number.

Hatley felt they needed to do away with background distractions and have the first face the audience sees be that of Doc himself (especially since the chair illusion never worked!). In this revised variation, Doc would be doing the programming, but on a much grander scale.

After the lights dimmed, the circuit board surrounding the stage came to life, and projected on the front gauze was a Pac-Man screen, with ghosts chasing an 8-bit avatar of Doc Brown. "This was another of Tim's ideas," credits Ross, "but it was also kind of a tribute to the 1980s."

A giant control panel that suddenly manifests around Doc allows him to solve a projected Rubik's Cube, and then "pull the chain" on an oversize light bulb, which opens up the stage into the spaceship setting that had been part of the original show in Manchester.

Simultaneously, Chris Bailey and Darren Carnall took advantage of the forced "vacation" to rework the entire number. "When Tim and Finn changed the opening of the number to have Doc as the first person we see, that changed everything for me," says Bailey. "I put in a lot more dancing and action. I felt confident it was a better version for us, for the show, and for Roger Bart."

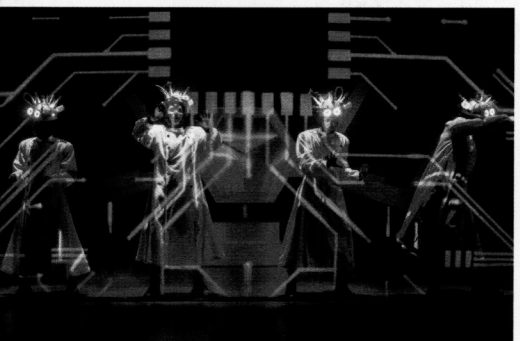
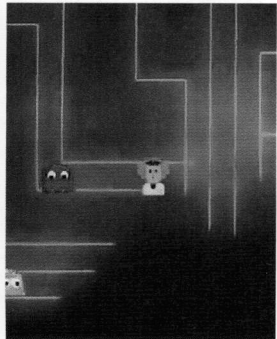

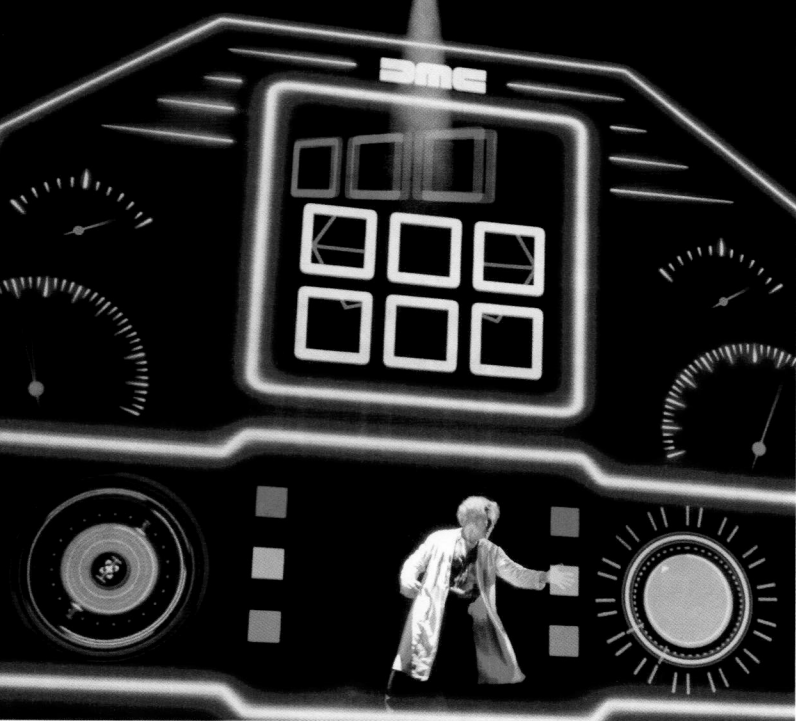

TOP As the overture ends and the curtain rises, the video journey deposits the audience in Doc's lab.

CENTER Left: The opening of the Manchester version of "21st Century." Right: In London, the second-act curtain opens to reveal a video avatar of Doc, being chased by ghosts.

BOTTOM Another video challenge faces Doc before the number gets underway.

126

A Banner Day

Another upgrade was the opening for George McFly Day. In Manchester, two members of the ensemble simply unfolded a banner proclaiming the day and hung it over the courthouse steps. For London, Hatley designed an elaborate hanging sign that dropped down, complete with George's image and a red, white, and blue tinsel curtain. Alan Silvestri rescored the opening to provide musical stings for the entrances of each of the "new, improved" McFly family members.

Back to the Theater

Rehearsals at the National Youth Theatre ended on August 6, 2020. When the cast gathered the following Monday, August 9, 2020, it was at the Adelphi Theatre, their final move for hopefully years to come.

There they were met by Colin Ingram and company manager David Massey, who escorted them all to the upper circle level in the theater, high above the stage. Once there, Ingram outlined the continuing health restrictions. He stressed that until the situation improved, this was the one and only time the performers would all be allowed in the general-public area. A strict edict had been issued that split the actors and the creative team: The cast would, of course, be given access to the stage, backstage areas where they would change costumes, and their dressing rooms. The entire body of creatives, including director Rando, Gale, Silvestri, and Ballard, were relegated to the orchestra (stalls) section in the theater. Masks were still de rigueur indoors, and social distancing was strongly encouraged.

ABOVE, LEFT George McFly Day gets an upgrade from Manchester to London.

TOP The company bids farewell to the National Youth Theatre on their way to the Adelphi Theatre in the West End.

MIDDLE If you're going to wear a mask to protect you from COVID, you might as well do it with style!

BOTTOM Producer Ingram instructs the cast about the company COVID protocols.

"Having a great show
 is useless if you
 don't have the right
 theater for it."
—John Rando

THIS SPREAD The company moves
into the Adelphi and prepares for
the beginning of previews.

While the rehearsals proceeded onstage, the rest of the Adelphi was getting its own face-lift. Taking inspiration from the tremendously popular Secret Cinema *Back to the Future* event, and Gale's descriptions of the elaborate work put into the public area of the *Back to the Future* theme park attractions, Ingram asked Hatley to undertake the project. The main-floor lobby was transformed into downtown Hill Valley, offering refreshments, merchandise, and eighties tunes with which to bop along. "My aim was to transform the front of the house into a welcoming *Back to the Future* environment from the moment the audience enters the theater," says the designer. "The entrance took its lead from the shop and business signs famously located in the town square, with the Town movie theater marquee being the entrance door to the stalls seating."

On the second floor, Hatley created the Plutonium Bar, where the walls are covered with chalkboards incorporating mathematical equations and working drawings. Even the name of the place is spelled out in letters representing the elements of the periodic table. And of course, it serves refreshments. "And because everybody loves a photo opportunity, I created a life-sized color-changing replica of the clock, along with an electrical cable and connector. It's been a huge hit with audiences and has appeared in countless internet selfies!"

Interspersed within the theme materials on all levels are reproductions of rare posters, photos, and props from the *Back to the Future* films. "We were going to do

Lorraine's Vodka Bar at the upper circle, but we ran out of budget and spent it on the stalls and mezzanine level," notes Ingram.

In the last days prior to the first public preview, the media had begun its descent on the production, with interviews being held on a daily basis with Gale, Silvestri, Ballard, Bart, Dobson, Hyland, Coles, et al. in various nooks and crannies in the theater, in the midst of the intensive final rehearsal schedule.

The Night Before

From the moment they moved to the Adelphi, the torrid pace of rehearsals and adjustments continued as the calendar pages seemed to fly off the wall until they froze on August 19, 2020. The opening of the show was not until the next evening, but the final dress rehearsal, as it had been in Manchester, would have the very first audience in attendance at the venue, comprised of the majority of the ushers and staff members of the Adelphi. Ingram couldn't help but recall the dismal reaction in Manchester under the same circumstances, and, even though he had sworn to keep from witnessing history repeat itself, he bravely

strode into the theater, secretly hoping he wasn't tempting fate with his presence at the event.

At the end of the night, his worries had been for naught. The show had been deemed "technically clean" by stage manager Graham Hookham, meaning that all of the elements, including the special effects and the DeLorean, performed to perfection. More importantly, the "audience" was explosive in its excitement and love for the show. "There were about eighty people," recounts Gale, "but if you closed your eyes, it sounded more like fifteen hundred! They were so taken by the production they gave it a standing ovation at the end of the first act, as well as at the end. We were all euphoric!"

Of course, the smoothness and success of the show on that night was a cause for concern in those who subscribed to theatrical superstition. "There are those who believe," continues Gale, "if there is an issue in the final dress rehearsal, your opening will be hugely successful." Now that they had successfully gotten through the London night-before performance in spectacular fashion, would troubles befall the production on their gala opening in front of thousands of first-nighters?

We Know Every Part by Heart!

Could one honestly say that not a single thing went wrong during the performance? One could not. For a show with so many technical elements, thousands of individual actions controlled and triggered by computers combined with human interaction, there is the occasional behind-the-scenes glitch that occurs, but such is the audience's engagement with the show that any are rarely noticed.

Such was the case on this Friday evening in August 2021. The energy, the excitement, the adrenaline were evident, coming both from onstage and from the sold-out audience in return. The minor issue of a TV monitor in Doc's lab not working at the top of the first act couldn't distract the audience from their exuberance of just having experienced the exhilarating overture and the first entrance of Olly Dobson as Marty McFly. Nobody lost focus on young Lorraine and her trio of selves as they serenaded the newly arrived and very alarmed time-traveler, when there was a minor set glitch in the bedroom.

During the tabletop model scene when the toy car caught on fire precisely on cue, did the audience realize that Roger Bart and Olly Dobson actually couldn't find the fire extinguisher normally on hand for Doc to douse the flames?

That one they noticed!

Roger Bart was also surprised as he quickly scanned the surrounding area, hoping the device had perhaps just shifted in its usual home space. Picking up on his partner's concern, Olly quickly joined the search.

ABOVE August 20, 2021: the first London preview performance.

For a time, the audience couldn't be sure whether there was a real issue occurring or whether it was simply part of the scene, such was the comedic mastery of the ad-libbing and the way Bart and Dobson responded to the situation. Neither of them ever broke character, and they kept the crowd in hysterics.

"Obviously, I hoped that we weren't going to have to bring down that lead safety curtain to protect the audience from the fire," Bart reveals. "Onstage, fire is as bad as fire on a boat, and so it did definitely cause panic. I hoped that the model was fireproof and that it wouldn't spread. (It was, and it didn't.) After that, it just became sort of absurdist. We just couldn't believe it. I was also hoping that the audience wouldn't get nervous, so we kept it very silly and jovial, but underneath I was thinking, *Please send someone! If it doesn't burn itself out, how are we going to put it out?*"

For Dobson, once he sensed the situation was safe, it was one of his favorite experiences to date. "That's live theater, and we live for it!" he enthuses. "These are the moments I treasure so much when anything goes wrong. As it was happening, I thought it was brilliant, and *Will we do it?*"

After enough time went by, a stagehand walked out, handed the extinguisher to Roger, and walked off.

As they resumed the scene, the actor's remarkable skills were clearly in evidence yet again, as moments later he commanded the audience's rapt attention for his heartfelt and touching ballad, "For the Dreamers."

Third Time's a Charmer

The rest of the show went stunningly, and the cast took their curtain calls to a full and prolonged standing ovation. This was, in fact, the musical's third opening night of

record, all of them special events, and each of which carried its own significance. The first two in Manchester established the show as a viable and powerful entry into the annals of theatrical history. London reinforced those perceptions and went even further as a promising response to the world's health conditions. Following scrupulous and meticulous procedures, actors were once again allowed to tread the boards, and audiences allowed themselves to be entertained.

"It was remarkable, because it was the light at the end of the tunnel like nothing else had ever been for me during the pandemic," comments Bart. "We had questioned whether or not there would ever be theater again for the next five years, and whether I would just age out of doing the part, or if this whole project would just fizzle and go away, because it's hard to get investors to keep their money in something like this for that long. To arrive at that evening after I had waited so long in my apartment for eighteen months after being sent home was just fantastic."

Although the actor had once previously performed in the West End, he considered that night at the Adelphi as his true debut. "I had been onstage there in 1996, but it wasn't really my part," he explains. "I was just minding it for somebody until they recovered. To be performing in *Back to the Future* in the West End was a dream come true."

"It felt like *We've been here before. Is it going to stick this time?*" adds Dobson. "There was a sense of joy being onstage after such a long time, and listening to the crowd, but I didn't let the occasion get to me. I've got to do my job. We all had to think about that audience—the people paying to be there—and we had to give them the show of a lifetime.

LEFT After a frantic search for a missing fire extinguisher, Roger Bart is able to dowse the flames caused by the toy car on the tabletop model of Hill Valley on the first night of previews in London.

Something they'll never forget. That's the feeling we went in with on that night, and it's the feeling we've taken with us into every show since."

"There was a palpable sense of gratitude," recalls Rosie Hyland. "The first night of previews is always exciting, but it was made all the more special being our first show back after all the heartache of lockdown. The audience seemed to feel the same. No matter what side of the proscenium you were on, it was a special night."

"To be honest, it was very much business as usual until I was backstage watching the car on the monitor work its magic," offers Hugh Coles. "After everything we had been through as a company, I'm not ashamed to say I cried watching that. It all meant so much—the pain of cancellation. The agony of waiting for news of our return. The faith of the audience to come and sit in a room with us. All because we believed theater was important and necessary, and life without it proved to be drab and colorless for so many months.

"All of those feelings all at once, alongside making my West End debut with people who meant so much to me. Truly special."

It Was the Best of Times, It Was the Worst of Times...

With the triumph of the show opening in London behind them, the team moved resolutely toward the night for which West End had been waiting for well over a decade: the official world premiere of *Back to the Future The Musical*. From August 20 through September 12, the company played to twenty-two sold-out previews. On the Saturday before press night, there had been both a matinee and evening performance, and another on Sunday. During that time, minor changes and adjustments were still being made by various departments, but the show was playing to standing ovations at each one of them.

The word of mouth was that the show was a sensation, and despite the still looming presence of COVID, guests were traveling from all parts of the globe to attend opening night. Those guests included Robert and Leslie Zemeckis, Christopher Lloyd and wife Lisa, an assortment of celebrities, including Andy Serkis, Tracey Ullman, Brian May, Caroline Quentin, show investors, and, of course, a large contingent of *BTTF* fans.

On the Day...

"Everything was going too well," remarks Ingram. "We hadn't missed one day of rehearsals or tech, which would have been a real disaster financially." A combination of attending to the pending event details and ensuring the show performed at its best throughout the preview period distracted Ingram from the preshow jitters he had experienced in Manchester.

On the day of the opening, the producer was indulging in his customary pre–press night massage. Upon its completion, he turned his phone back on to receive a call from his colleague Phoebe Fairbrother, who relayed, "Roger Bart has tested positive for COVID." Ingram's response? "Well, of course he has . . ."

"I didn't feel well the night before," admits the actor. "The process to get to opening

LEFT Celebrating the official West End opening of the musical. Top row, left to right: Alan Silvestri, Robert Zemeckis, Glen Ballard. Bottom row: John Rando, Bob Gale, Colin Ingram.

night is so arduous, and can run you down so much due to the pressure, the lack of sleep, the constant work, lack of sunlight . . . It's no wonder that my body would give out at a certain point, but the timing was horrendous."

Ingram immediately reached out to a number of the creative heads and then called Rando to break the news. "I told him that the team thought Mark Oxtoby could go on. It was going to be a bit touch and go, but he had to—the ship had sailed. We had people flying in from all over the world at great expense, and they'd all had their COVID tests to get here." As far as the theater critics who would be reviewing the show, Ingram had that covered. Earlier in the week, he had invited many of them to preview performances. "That's a pretty normal practice these

days," he offers. "It used to be they all came on one day, but if you have one bad show on press night, a technical mishap or some sort of glitch, it means all your reviews are affected. Almost all of the critics had seen the show with Roger, and they were all invited back for press night as well. To be honest, there was never any moment where I didn't think we weren't going to do it."

On Your Mark...

"It was around 12:15 in the afternoon, and I was just leaving for an appointment when my phone rang," recollects Mark Oxtoby. "It was David Massey, the company manager, so I answered and heard those immortal words: 'Are you sitting down?' Never in a million years did I think I would be going on to play Doc Brown at the West End press night in front of Robert Zemeckis and Christopher Lloyd!"

While Mark had *some* rehearsal in Manchester, it hadn't been nearly enough to comfort the actor as he rushed to

ABOVE Marty and Mark: Mark Oxtoby gives a stellar performance covering the COVID-stricken Roger Bart on press night.

the theater. "I'd hardly had any rehearsals. I'd never set foot in Doc's lab. I'd never had a show watch.* I didn't know the staging. A hundred other thoughts ran through my head at a billion miles per hour!"

When he arrived at the theater, there was no time to do a rehearsal of the entire show, so they concentrated on Doc's musical numbers, as well as the show's most important technical aspects to ensure the actor's safety. "There were so many! 'Make sure you turn this before you do that! This blows up! Don't get set on fire by this! The list seemed endless. Thankfully, I had thirty years of experience to draw from and was able to focus and take it all in."

As they had when Will Haswell had to step into the role of Marty when Olly Dobson got ill, the cast stepped up to help Mark in every way they could. "They were the best castmates that anyone could ever wish for! Cedric Neal went out and got me food. Will Haswell was constantly asking me if I was okay. Knowing the enormity of what I was about to do, everyone was so supportive and encouraging. During the performance, Olly was just wonderful and was by my side the entire show. Knowing I had no idea how props worked or where anything on the set was, from a light switch to the fire extinguisher, he held my hand through the entire show!"

"It was a pleasure," reflects Dobson. "We had to recognize it was Mark's moment. I thank him for clearly having read up on his script. He knew all of his lines and every lyric, and his version of Doc on that night was just wonderful. Still," he admits, "it was devastating to know that my partner in crime wasn't going to be there with me onstage."

While everyone was getting ready for this special performance, just minutes away from the Adelphi Theatre, a half-dozen DeLoreans lined the street outside of London's Corinthia Hotel. Inside, invited guests gathered for a pre-show cocktail party organized by Ingram as part of the day's festivities.

Outside the Adelphi, hundreds of fans amassed to get a glimpse of the celebrities, some of them ferried over by the DeLoreans, walking the blue carpet.

At 7:32 P.M. GMT on September 13, 2020, the curtain went up on the premiere performance of *Back to the Future The Musical*. The familiar overture thundered through

the theater, and the audience erupted in the first of many ovations as Olly Dobson took the stage.

For Bob Gale, it was a great start, but he wasn't ready to totally relax and enjoy the evening just yet.

"Press night, like a movie premiere, is stressful enough when everything is going right," he explains, "and now we had a scenario like something out of a movie, where the understudy has to go on at the last minute. Mark Oxtoby had never played Doc in front of an audience, so we were concerned. Intellectually, we shouldn't have been. Mark is a seasoned professional and, just as Will Haswell had been fantastic as Marty when Olly got sick in Manchester, and Katherine Pearson did an incredible Lorraine eight days prior, we had no real reason to think that Mark wouldn't be great. But this was a bigger deal than just a preview, so it puts you on edge, and you overthink everything. That all went away when Mark did 'It Works,' which played beautifully. Mark gave a fabulous performance, and it was an outstanding show."

* Show watch: when an actor sits in the audience and watches a performance of the show in its entirety.

RIGHT After the press night performance, Mark Oxtoby is embraced by an audience member of some notoriety.

"What was going through my head?" asks Silvestri. "This is no reflection on Mark in any way, but it was agonizing to know, sitting there watching the show, that Roger was a block away. But the old adage was never truer than it was on that night: 'The show must go on!' And it did. And it was amazing!"

"After three years on the job, the evening felt like a huge milestone," says Rosie Hyland. "I was so proud to have come this far. It was heartbreaking not to have Roger there, but seeing Mark Oxtoby rise to the occasion was really something to celebrate."

"It was truly special," agrees Hugh Coles. "The pain of cancellation by COVID. The agony of waiting for news of our return. The work we did to get back onto that stage. The faith of the audience to come and sit in a room with us. All because we believed theater was important and necessary, and life without it proved to be drab and colorless for so many months. All of those feelings, all at once, alongside making my West End debut with people who meant so much to me.

The show was described in the performance report as "technically clean." The same report notated, "Amazing, amazing, amazing . . . Well done to all on a spectacular opening night!"

Act Two, Scene Twelve

INT. ADELPHI THEATRE, LONDON - NIGHT
SEPTEMBER 13, 2021

The first official performance of "Back to the Future The Musical" has just ended. The full cast is taking their bows before the 1,500 members of the audience, each and every one on their feet applauding fervently. The cast parts, and seven men make their way onto the stage. BOB GALE, ROBERT ZEMECKIS, ALAN SILVESTRI, and GLEN BALLARD move to center stage. JOHN RANDO, COLIN INGRAM, and CHRISTOPHER LLOYD stand off to one side. After several moments taking bows and raising each other's hands in triumph, a microphone is handed to GALE, who moves front and center to address the still-cheering crowd.

                    GALE
Welcome back to live theater! We are all
honored to be part of the rebirth of
London's West End.

Some fifteen years ago, Bob Zemeckis, Alan Silvestri, Glen Ballard, and I had a dream. A dream of translating "Back to the Future" to musical theater. This was going to be a labor of love. And we all swore to each other that, if at any point, we felt we couldn't meet the high standards set by the movie, we wouldn't do it, we'd shut it all down. "Good enough" was never an option.

Tonight, you've seen the result: a show that's exceeded all of our dreams on every level. Because those high "Back to the Future" standards inspired everyone involved to do even better than their best.

Gale turns and gestures, indicating various factions as he addresses them.

                    GALE (cont'd)
From our incredible cast to our extraordinary production crew, to our

magnificent musicians and music team,
to the mind-blowing direction of the
absolutely brilliant John Rando, all
bolstered by the unwavering support
of our tireless producer Colin Ingram
and his partners, who never stopped
believing.

So, yes, this one's for the dreamers.
Dreamers like us. Dreamers like you.
Dream big, everybody! We need that now,
more than ever.

Thank you and good night.

More cheers as the music comes up and the
orchestra plays another chorus of "Back in
Time." Everyone onstage continues to dance,
hug, smile, and laugh as the curtain falls.

At the end of the evening, alone in his dressing room, Oxtoby reflected on what had just happened. "It was the first time that entire day I was on my own, so I just enjoyed the moment. I felt incredibly proud of what I'd just accomplished (with everyone's help). I'm a big believer in 'everything for a reason.' I nearly didn't take this job, but there was the reason I was meant to. And the fact that it will forever be part of the West End's theatrical and *Back to the Future*'s history is just crazy! Brilliant, but crazy!"

For Roger Bart, "It was devastating; I really just wanted to celebrate and perform. It was very hard for me not to be able to share that evening with everybody," he says frankly. But he did understand that there could be no postponement at what was essentially the last minute. "Colin made the right decision that worked best for the show. Fortunately, I recovered, got back to work in a week, and it was fine."

As for Mark filling the lab coat of Doc Brown on that night, Bart had nothing but praise and excitement for the journey his friend had taken. "Mark had to just jump in and trust his instincts. To add to that, it was opening night, with all of those people in suits out there. It must have been a mind-blowing experience, and I'm sure he felt the love, and deserved it. I was really happy for him, and happy for the show that he was able to step in and do such a great job in so little time with so little rehearsal."

On September 15, two days after press night, Mark Oxtoby tested positive for COVID-19, proof again of the unpredictability of the space-time continuum. For the rest of that week, the show would not go on.

The Reviews Are In! Again!

The day after press night, the media was awash with stories of the previous evening's unexpected cast substitution. Roger Bart understood that for the most part, they weren't about him specifically. "It's a story that would get picked up a lot," he reflects. "When I got COVID and was out for that week, it was also happening in the Broadway community, the rock-and-roll community, and with late-night TV show hosts. Everybody was getting it. People were watching very carefully, because they wanted to see whether theater was going to be able to come back in a way that was healthy."

But no matter the accompanying stories, the day after press night was still review day, a tradition that wasn't going to be pushed aside because of a "distraction." As the company had experienced in Manchester, the show itself touched, moved, amused, and excited the audience and the critics alike.

"Where to begin with a production that packs more energy than a nuclear reactor? ★ ★ ★ ★ ★" —*Daily Mail*

"Director John Rando, choreographer Chris Bailey and designer Tim Hatley have together crafted a near-seamless slice of escapist entertainment." —*Evening Standard*

"Great Scott! This musical based on the eighties classic shouldn't work—but it's magnificent. ★ ★ ★ ★ ★" —*Telegraph*

"A show that is, indisputably, a fantastic night out. ★ ★ ★ ★" —LondonTheatre.co.uk

"*Back to the Future The Musical* is a sensory delight from start to finish. ★ ★ ★ ★ ★" —LondonTheatre1.com

Two BIG Thumbs Up!

While the reviews were of interest to many involved in the production, there were two opinions of the show about which everyone was curious: What did Michael J. Fox and Christopher Lloyd think?

"At one of the *Back to the Future* anniversary events, Bob Gale mentioned it to me for the first time, and I thought it was an interesting idea," recalls Fox. "I remember Alan

Fox recalls Gale giving any number of interviews over the years where he'd be asked to describe what kind of a movie he considered *Back to the Future* to be. "He gave them the usual answers . . . 'It's a comedy, a time-travel movie,' and then one time, at the end, he added, 'It's a musical comedy!' And now it is, and it's a really good one!"

Christopher Lloyd had already been exposed to the musical when he traveled to Manchester in October 2019 to bestow the keys to the DeLorean time machine to Roger Bart at the media launch. Getting a small sample of the musical numbers performed by Olly Dobson and the cast whetted his appetite for what was to come. A filming commitment made him unavailable to attend the Manchester run, which was followed by that inconvenient pandemic, so a determined Lloyd made sure that Bob Gale would notify him and save him two seats in the Adelphi stalls [orchestra section] when the premiere finally came around.

In the thirty-five years since Lloyd first created the role, no other actor had ever played Doc (Dan Castellaneta had voiced the character in the animated *BTTF* series, but Lloyd also appeared in live-action wraparounds of each episode), so it would be a unique experience for him to watch someone else bring the character to life. "I'd been waiting to see this show ever since Bob mentioned it to me years ago," says Lloyd. "There was never any doubt in my mind that it was going to be amazing, because of everyone involved. With Bob, Robert Zemeckis, Alan Silvestri, and Glen Ballard behind it, this show wouldn't exist if they didn't believe it was worthy of the name *Back to the Future*. The movies have endured longer than anyone could have ever imagined, and are still going strong. This musical is the perfect companion piece. I don't see how they could have done it better, and I think it will deservedly have its own very long life."

And what did Christopher Lloyd think about the onstage antics of Doctor Emmett Brown on opening night in the West End? "As Marty McFly observed in 1885, I can finally confirm it—Doc can dance! And he can sing, too!"

Silvestri was there as well, but I didn't remember them saying it was going to be in London."

Due to the global pandemic, Fox was unable to travel to the UK for the premiere, and a video of a dress rehearsal was sent to him. One of the first things that came to his mind was that he was watching *Back to the Future*, and not some show that took the name and tried to be something else . . . either overblown and overreaching or, at the other end of the spectrum, cartoonish. He lauded every member of the cast for treading a fine line with seemingly no effort. "I was concerned before I saw it, that they [the actors] would be handcuffed by the way we had done certain things, and that they would have to physically resemble what we did, because those character behaviors have become iconic, and are as fundamental as the dialogue in some cases. When they did have choices to make, they were doing their own take on it; adding their own seasoning to the sauce. It really came through."

After viewing the show, Michael immediately sent off an email to Bob Gale, who shared it with the company:

"I'm buzzing from what is a truly great show. It captures the entire *BTTF* experience through sensational casting, effective story edits, great Techwork & Special FX. The actors were impeccable, with an energy and passion commensurate with us originals. And the music is freaking great, from the Huey Lewis songs to the Silvestri score and all the new songs and set pieces. It really is a small miracle. Congratulations to all of the amazing people involved. It looks like a hit to me!"

"Who's Playing Who?"

Roger Bart was far from the only cast member to be felled temporarily by COVID. While every stage production has the backup of understudies for its lead actors, none are ever guaranteed to make it in front of the footlights to perform for a crowded theater.

When performances of *Back to the Future* began again, having been temporarily closed for one week, COVID swept through the cast. It touched almost every actor, ensemble and swing member, some more than once, requiring other actors to take over different roles. Fortunately, in the parlance of baseball, John Rando had assembled a "deep bench" of talent who were always ready to step up to the plate, and who were able to keep the doors of the Adelphi open. And no matter which actor stepped into another role, no matter how little preparation they had, they never failed to entertain and delight the audiences.

Original Cast Recording

The morning after the gala press night premiere, Alan Silvestri, Glen Ballard, and Nick Finlow made their way to an old church in northern London that had been converted into a state-of-the-art recording facility, AIR Studios, in 1992 by legendary Beatles producer George Martin. Over the next weeks, the trio produced the original cast album of the musical.

Their work began recording the orchestral tracks and, for this venture, the show's orchestra was enhanced with some additional live strings. "When you're in the theater, there are sound effects and thunder and lightning as part of the experience," states Silvestri. "When we put something on a record, none of that is there, and we want to shine the light a little more brightly on everything that's being done to make sure it sounds just the way we want it." In the following weeks, the vocals of cast and ensemble were all added to the mix. The end result was a recording that the team was proud to present to the fans. "On any given day, only about 1,500 people can experience the show. The cast album is a way for us to reach out and give the entire world a closer, more tangible connection to the show with the hope that when it comes to a theater near them, they'll come and experience it live."

THE MUSIC OF THE NIGHT

ACT I

Overture . . . . Orchestra

SCENE 1: Doc Brown's Lab — October 25, 1985

SCENE 2: Hill Valley Town Square

"It's Only a Matter of Time" . . . . Marty, Goldie, Ensemble

SCENE 3: Band Audition

"The Power of Love" (abbreviated) . . . . Marty and the Pinheads

SCENE 4: Hill Valley Town Square

"Wherever We're Going" . . . . Marty, Jennifer, Clock Tower Woman

SCENE 5: McFly House

"Hello, Is Anybody Home?" . . . . . . Marty, George, Lorraine, Dave, Linda

SCENE 6: Twin Pines Mall Parking Lot

"It Works!" . . . . Doc, Marty, and the DeLorean Girls

SCENE 7: Barn — November 5, 1955

SCENE 8: Hill Valley Town Square

"Cake" . . . . Clock Tower Lady, Mayor Red Thomas, Ensemble

SCENE 9: Lou's Café

"Got No Future" — Reprise . . . . Marty

"Gotta Start Somewhere" . . . . Goldie and Ensemble

SCENE 10: Baines House

"My Myopia" . . . . George

SCENE 11: Lorraine's Bedroom

"Pretty Baby" . . . . Lorraine and the Lorraine Baines Trio

SCENE 12: Doc Brown's Lab (1955) / Barn

"Future Boy" . . . . Marty, Doc, and Ensemble

SCENE 13: Ext. Hill Valley High School

SCENE 14: High School Lunchroom

"Something About That Boy" . . . . Lorraine, Biff, and Ensemble

(As performed on September 12, 2021.)

Overture

Typically, the overture of a musical features snippets of the songs and themes that will be heard throughout the show. Glen Ballard and Alan Silvestri had created close to twenty original crowd-pleasing songs for the show, any number of which could have contributed to a bouncy and engaging orchestral arrangement, played as the curtain rose to begin Act One.

But, as the production went through the rigors of development and refinement, precious little thought was given by Rando, Ballard, Silvestri, Gale, or Ingram as to what the first strains of musical exposure to the audience would be. As the production began rehearsals and previews in the Manchester Opera House, the "creatives" were surprised to find that a great deal of work had already been done in that regard.

In addition to their regular orchestration chores, Bryan Crook and Ethan Popp also took on the challenge of proving the efficacy of Popp's aforementioned concept for the system that would combine live musicians with a computer server "housing" a virtual orchestra's worth of instruments. To do so, they needed a piece of music to serve as a proof of concept.

In 2014, with the blessings of Robert Zemeckis and Bob Gale, Alan Silvestri had embarked on an "In Concert" offering in which the film would be projected in concert halls, with a symphony orchestra performing the score in sync with the film before a live audience. Because the film didn't feature any original score during the first twenty minutes, Silvestri created additional music to fill that gap, including an overture. It was that specific piece that Crook and Popp chose as the "guinea pig" for their euphonious undertaking.

"Bryan and I wanted to dive into the largest, most 'bombastic' piece of music we could to show this was possible," says Popp of this untried, revolutionary new approach. "We decided upon Alan's overture from the *Live in Concert* series as it ticked that proverbial box, and at the time, the show didn't use the main fanfare and theme in its entirety."

When that revised composition debuted in front of cast and crew at the *sitzprobe* event, its place in the show was undisputable.

What better welcome could there be for *Back to the Future* fans and musical theater aficionados than to be greeted by the majestic strains of Alan Silvestri's quintessential score?

NICK FINLOW

Alan didn't know Bryan and Ethan had done this. When he opened the score and saw the arrangement, he asked, "Are we playing this?" When he heard it in the first orchestra call, he was bowled over. We hadn't necessarily done it to be in the show, and maybe would have put it at the end when the audience was walking out, but Al quite rightly said, "I think it needs to be at the beginning of the show."

It's Only a Matter of Time (My Future)

Although it had been identified fairly early in the process, the change in Marty's musical outlook on life from negative to positive took several months to accomplish. When the first efforts to change the tone were undertaken, everything that could be deemed questionable about the number became immediately apparent: the Hill Valley citizenry singing about the deterioration of their town and their lives and Marty as a sullen, angry, beaten-down teen. The only note of positivity was provided by mayoral candidate Goldie Wilson, who promised a brighter future for Hill Valley if he was elected.

As had been espoused by everyone with musical theater experience (Rando, Ingram, Ballard, Bailey), the first number is arguably *the* most important in establishing a tone for the show. Morose Marty McFly was clearly the wrong way to go. But by the time the curtain went up in Manchester, the audience was greeted by an energetic, upbeat company, led by an optimistic, buoyant, positive, and magnetic Marty McFly.

It was the skill and talent of Ballard and Silvestri that made it possible to keep the winning music and rhythms of the song intact and make the necessary changes without having to take apart the entire number and start from scratch.

BOB GALE
I chalk up our collective myopia about the tone of "Only a Matter of Time" to being too immersed in the movie. In the downbeat version, we were doing in song what we saw in the visuals when Marty is in the 1985 town square. But the story is about Marty, so once we changed the song to be about him instead of the town, we put the focus where it belonged.

GLEN BALLARD
Originally we wanted to introduce the ensemble cast in a traditional Broadway musical style. To reveal the 1985 town square and introduce most of the cast—they may be in different roles, but we know we have got a lot of people here, and the dance sequence would firmly remind the audience that we're in 1985.

SCENE II: EXT. HILL VALLEY
TOWN SQUARE - DAY, 1985

Town Square features the Hill Valley Courthouse (now the Department of Social Services)
with a clock on its pediment stuck at 10:04,
charred black, with a twisted lightning rod
above. Townspeople in the square go about
their lives and join MARTY as he sings.

MARTY
I'M LOOKING AROUND
THERE'S NOTHING HERE CAN SLOW ME DOWN
IT'S FEELING LIKE MY LUCKY DAY
GONNA MAKE IT AND THEN SKATE AWAY

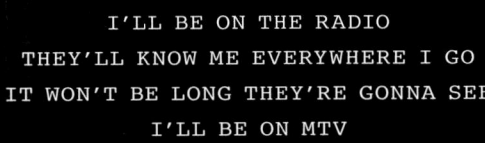

I'LL BE ON THE RADIO
THEY'LL KNOW ME EVERYWHERE I GO
IT WON'T BE LONG THEY'RE GONNA SEE
I'LL BE ON MTV

MARTY

I'LL ROCK MY FUTURE
(I'M) A WINNER NOT A LOSER
NOTHING ANYONE CAN SAY
CAN MAKE IT ANY OTHER WAY
I'VE GOT MY FUTURE
A PLAYER NOT A CRUISER
I'LL BE JUST WHAT I WANNA BE
ROCKIN' ALL THE WAY THRU HISTORY

IT'S FEELING LIKE A NEW DAY
NOT ANOTHER INSTANT REPLAY
GONNA FIN'LLY DO IT MY WAY

YEAH!

A PERFECT FUTURE
FOR A SHAKER AND A MOVER
EV'RY NOTE IS IN ITS PLACE
LOTS OF TREBLE, LOTS OF BASS

I'LL ROCK MY FUTURE
COULD IT BE ANY COOLER?
ALL I GOTTA DO IS PLAY
MY TROUBLES DISAPPEAR AND GO AWAY

TOWNSPEOPLE

NOTHING ANYONE CAN SAY
CAN MAKE IT ANY OTHER WAY

BE JUST WHAT I WANNA BE
ROCKIN' ALL THE WAY

OOOOOOOH
OOOOOOOH
OOOOOOOH
OUTLOOK LOOKING GOOD
YEAH!

EV'RY NOTE IS IN ITS PLACE
LOTS OF TREBLE, LOTS OF BASS

ALL I GOTTA DO IS PLAY
MY TROUBLES DISAPPEAR

Goldie Wilson, 50, enters, with a few campaigners carrying big "Goldie for Mayor" signs that have a headshot showing off his gold front tooth. He hops up on a soapbox.

GOLDIE WILSON

Elect me! Goldie Wilson for mayor! My new progress platform means more jobs, lower taxes, and bigger civic improvements!

VOTE FOR ME
IF YOU WANT TO ADVANCE
I'LL SERVE YOU FAITHFULLY
IF YOU'LL GIVE ME A CHANCE
I BELIEVE THE FUTURE CAN BE BRIGHTER THAN BEFORE
HEY, WHEN I GOT STARTED
I WAS SWEEPING UP THE FLOOR

CHRIS BAILEY

The opening number is always tricky, because you're setting the tone for the whole show. I did one version of the dancing in New York. Spent three days with eighteen dancers. This had Marty in his negative head-space where he's angry at life. I didn't think the first number that our star does should be negative. So I did a version of it where I changed some of the words around and made it, "I'll rock my future." It was just for a workshop—so I had it that he was really up, and then at the end he does the audition and then he crashes back down to earth. And John [Rando] came to see it and he hated it. So I worked out the negative version. But later, when we went back to London and did that version, John came back to me and said, "You know what? You might have been right. Can we work on it?"

ALAN SILVESTRI

Even though we moved away from the idea of introducing most of the other characters in the beginning, we always felt right about bringing Goldie Wilson to the forefront. Even though he only had just a few lines in the original film, the Bobs always knew that Goldie was a central character in the story, because he represents change, and it was Glen's idea to have him in that number singing about running for mayor.

HONESTY
DECENCY
INTEGRITY

GLEN BALLARD

When you make a movie, you've got about ninety minutes to make your point. In a musical, you can take a little longer. We have this arc of who Goldie Wilson is. We start with him in 1985: "Vote for me." He's running for mayor in 1985. Trying to change things. In 1955, we see where the possibilities began for this busboy. When we get back to 1985, he's actually mayor. And any time you have a chance to put Cedric Neal in a number, you take it!

NICK FINLOW

From a musical point of view, Glen, Alan, and I were desperate to get that voice into the show as early as possible!

CEDRIC NEAL

I couldn't be happier with my numbers in the show beginning with this one. There were several versions of Goldie's verse in the workshops. I think the initial one was "Vote for me if you want to advance, just give me the chance. I'll serve you faithfully. I believe that the future is bright, and not only white . . ." [laughs]

GOLDIE

'CAUSE IT'S ONLY A MATTER OF TIME
TILL THE BELLS OF PROSPERITY CHIME
WE'LL BE PART OF A NEW DAY
A LONG OVERDUE DAY
I'LL LEAD US AS WE MAKE THE CLIMB

MARTY

I'M BREAKING THROUGH THE
FOURTH WALL

I'M FLYING AND I CAN'T FALL

OUTLOOK OH SO GOOD
YEAH!

COME ON NOW FUTURE
LET'S HIT THE TURBO BOOSTER
BUCKLED UP WITHOUT A CARE
NOW YOU CAN TAKE ME ANYWHERE

WRITE MY FUTURE
FOR SIMON AND FOR SCHUSTER
THE TALE OF HOW I CAME TO BE
A ROCK-AND-ROLL BIOGRAPHY

ONLY A MATTER...

YEAH, I KNOW I'M GETTING
OUTTA HERE
THE GREATEST FUTURE OF ALL!

IT'S ONLY A MATTER OF TIME!

TOWNSPEOPLE

OOOOOOOOH
OOOOOOOOH
OOOOOOOOH
OOOOOOOOH
WOOOAAAAH

IT'S ONLY A MATTER OF TIME

A NEW PARADIGM SO SUBLIME

ONLY A MATTER OF
IT'S JUST A MATTER OF
OUTLOOK OH SO GOOD
YEAH!

COME ON NOW FUTURE
LET'S HIT THE TURBO BOOSTER
BUCKLED UP WITHOUT A CARE
NOW YOU CAN TAKE ME ANYWHERE

WRITE MY FUTURE

TALE OF HOW I CAME TO BE
AAAAHHHHH!

BUT IT'S ONLY A MATTER OF TIME
ONLY A MATTER OF
ONLY A MATTER OF TIME.

WHAT A FUTURE!
HERE'S HIS FUTURE!
IT'S ONLY A MATTER OF TIME!

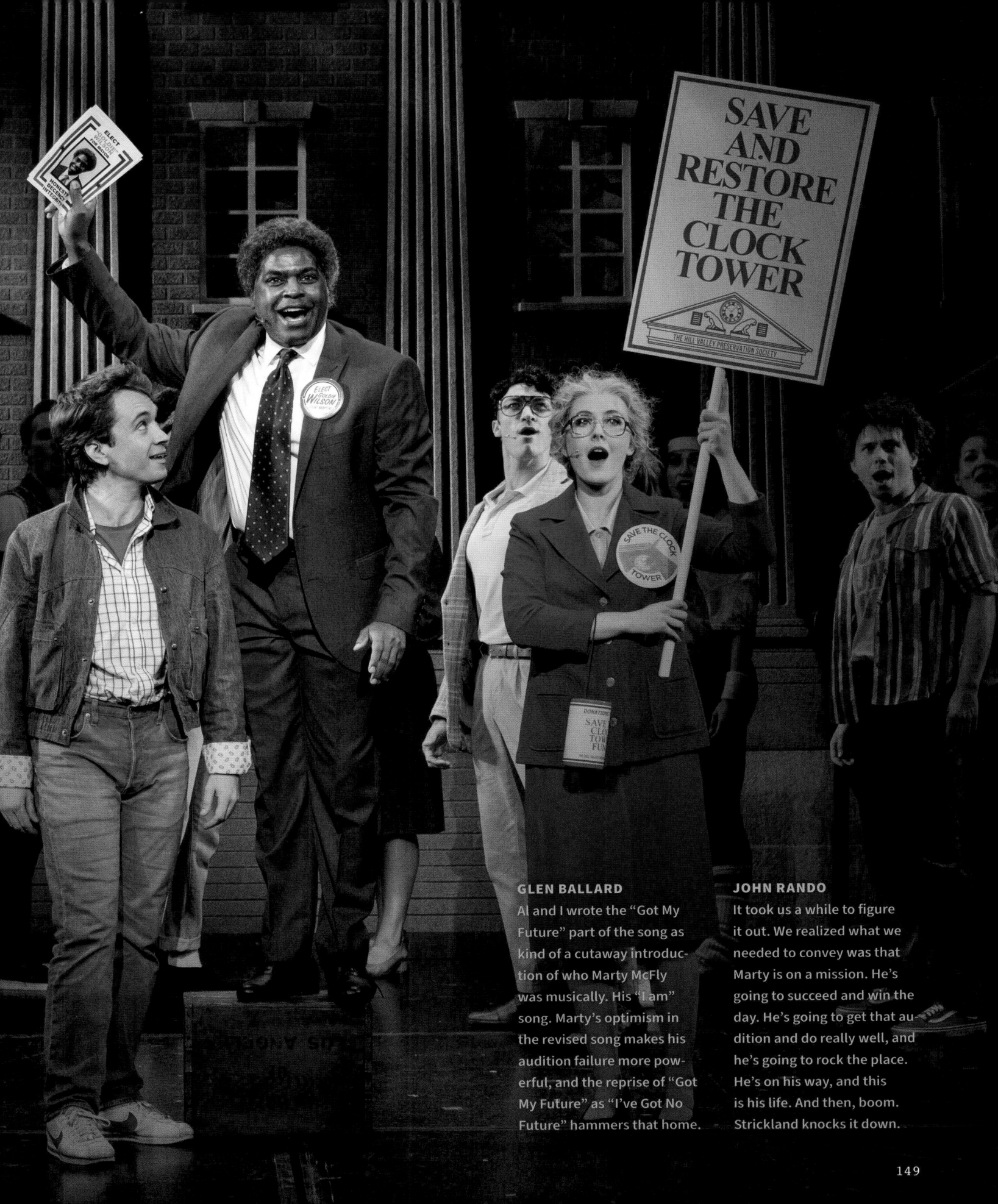

GLEN BALLARD

Al and I wrote the "Got My Future" part of the song as kind of a cutaway introduction of who Marty McFly was musically. His "I am" song. Marty's optimism in the revised song makes his audition failure more powerful, and the reprise of "Got My Future" as "I've Got No Future" hammers that home.

JOHN RANDO

It took us a while to figure it out. We realized what we needed to convey was that Marty is on a mission. He's going to succeed and win the day. He's going to get that audition and do really well, and he's going to rock the place. He's on his way, and this is his life. And then, boom. Strickland knocks it down.

149

Wherever We're Going

The 2017 song showcase first debuted a hybrid version of "Wherever We're Going" with "A Matter of Time," and it remained as such through the first reading at the Dominion. It became one of the first numbers to get a revision for the very next version of the book, dated some sixty days later. There had been numerous discussions to have a more balanced version of "A Matter of Time" and "My Future" in the opening number, and that "A Matter of Time" would be removed from "Wherever We're Going," which would be expanded to give the song its own identity.

Its appearance in the book closely echoed its placement in the film, both scenes appearing immediately after Marty is rejected in his band audition and in great need of positive reinforcement. In theater, a film "close-up" translates into a song for the stage performers. Establishing Jennifer and Marty's strong love and mutual support for each other was an obvious choice for a "vocal close-up."

GLEN BALLARD
One of the first things we did was to go through the movie script and say, "Who deserves a song?" In the movie, we sort of breeze through their scene about having the car to go to the lake. We wanted to give them a more emotional moment, so we created a song for them; the second song we wrote based on the script. It cements the relationship between Marty and Jennifer.

BOB GALE
It was an obvious place for a song between the two of them, because after the crushing disappointment of the audition, Marty needs to have his spirits lifted, to have hope, and Jennifer gives it to him.

JENNIFER
Marty! I just heard about your audition. I'm so sorry. Strickland's such a jerk. But listen, do you remember--

MARTY
(interrupting)
What if he's right, Jennifer? What if I'm just not cut out for music? What if I never get a chance to play for an audience?

JENNIFER
Oh, come on. One rejection isn't the end of the world. And you're good! You're really, really good! Now, do you remember the time--

MARTY
Jennifer, what if today was a sign? I just don't think I can take any more rejection. (sighs) Jeez, I'm starting to sound like my old man.

JENNIFER
(sits next to him on the bench)
WHY DO YOU LET PEOPLE PUT YOU DOWN?
IT'S NOT FOR THEM TO SAY
JUST KEEP YOUR FEET PLANTED ON THE GROUND
AND LOOK THE OTHER WAY

THEY'LL DEFINE YOU
UNLESS YOU HAVE A DREAM
YOU GOTTA TAKE TIME TO
BE WHAT YOU CAN BE
AND LET ME REMIND YOU
YOU'RE EVERYTHING TO ME
SOMETHING GOOD IS FLOWING

WHEREVER WE'RE GOING
IS ALRIGHT WITH ME
THERE'S NO WAY OF KNOWING
WE'LL JUST WAIT AND SEE
WE'LL GET WHERE WE'RE GOING EVENTUALLY
WHEREVER WE'RE GOING
IS ALRIGHT
ALRIGHT, ALRIGHT
ALRIGHT WITH ME

So listen--

Suddenly, CLOCK TOWER LADY inserts
herself between them, shaking her donation
can and alternately pointing to the clock.

CLOCK TOWER LADY
Save and restore the clock tower! You
want to know when our town died? Almost
thirty years ago, on Saturday night,
the twelfth of November, 1955! At ten-o-
four, a lightning bolt struck the tower
and fried the clock! It's all explained
right here!

She folds a "Save the Clock Tower" flyer
and shoves it in his pocket.

CLOCK TOWER LADY (cont'd)
Get Hill Valley unstuck in time!

BOB GALE (cont'd)
I added a fun little bit
in creating the character of
Jennifer's uncle Huey, a record
company executive who's
coming to visit Hill Valley to
hear Marty play. John Rando
also made the suggestion that
we remove the Clock Tower
Lady's singing the story of the
lightning hitting the clock tower from the opening "A Matter
of Time" number and moving
it here, as dialogue.

JOHN RANDO
The Clock Tower Lady was
originally singing the exposition in the opening song at
the town square. It felt a little
unspecific. "Wherever We're
Going" seemed like the perfect
spot to get both the exposition
of the clock tower and the plot
point of putting the flyer in
Marty's hand. It also matched
the film structure, interrupting
the young romance of Marty
and Jennifer.

COURTNEY-MAE BRIGGS
My introduction as Jennifer is
minutes after we've just finished that huge opening number in which I'm part of the ensemble. Then, all of a sudden,
third number in, the spotlight
is on us two. I found it tricky
as an actor because I feel our
relationship is established in
that scene, and we're going
into "slow ballad" territory. I
tried to keep it a little upbeat,
and a little fun and playful,
because we're singing about
how much we love each other,
and that I believe in him.

OLLY DOBSON

It ticks off another box on the list of giving the audience *Back to the Future*. Right after the classic Strickland put-down, we get the classic girlfriend trying to get her boyfriend out of his rut. She's going to accomplish that, and the audience is going to see that they're in love. We get this lovely, bouncy song, because that's what they do when they walk home. They enjoy themselves.

COURTNEY-MAE BRIGGS

I also have to do a really quick costume change. In the opening-number outfit, I've got fishnets on my arms, a leotard, and really tight boots. I've got to change my wig and get on these high-waisted jeans and the rest of Jennifer's familiar outfit in a very short period of time. I kind of fly into the scene, but that works since Jennifer is running in anyway, so it's quite good energy. I love the adrenaline of a quick change.

MARTY
(drops a coin in the can)
OK, lady, here's a quarter.

CLOCK TOWER LADY
Thank you!
(chases two joggers
running by...)
Save the clock tower!
Save the clock tower!

JENNIFER
So listen this time:
remember I told you about
my uncle Huey?

MARTY
From LA? He works at the
record company?

JENNIFER
(nods)
Well, he's coming to town
tonight. And he wants to
hear you and the guys play.

MARTY
Really?

JENNIFER
Noon tomorrow!

MARTY
No way! Seriously?

JENNIFER
And I told him how great you
are. So don't make me a liar.

152

MARTY
You're the best, Jennifer!
(They kiss.)

JENNIFER
I KNOW YOU BETTER THAN ANYONE
AND YOU BELONG TO ME
AND WE WILL FINISH WHAT WE'VE BEGUN
YOU'LL WRITE A SONG FOR ME

Marty grabs her camera and takes
a "selfie" of the two of them. She
takes the photo, and they move
dance-like around the bench.

JENNIFER
I CAN HEAR IT
WHEN YOU SING TO ME
I WANT TO BE NEAR IT
IT'S YOU I WANT TO SEE
AND LET ME BE CLEAR THAT
YOU'RE EVERYTHING TO ME
SOMETHING GOOD IS FLOWING

JENNIFER
WHEREVER WE'RE GOING
IS ALRIGHT WITH ME
I'M LOVING JUST KNOWING
YOU'RE GOING WITH ME
A FUTURE TOGETHER
IS OUR DESTINY

IS ALRIGHT, ALRIGHT
IT'S ALRIGHT

WE'RE BOTH GONNA SEE
OUR STORY
A GREAT MYSTERY
I KNOW IN MY HEART THAT
WE'RE HOLDING THE KEY
WHEREVER WE'RE GOING
IS ALRIGHT, ALRIGHT
IT'S ALRIGHT, IT'S ALRIGHT
IT'S ALRIGHT
IT'S ALRIGHT WITH ME.

MARTY
WHEREVER WE'RE GOING
IS ALRIGHT WITH ME

YOU'RE GOING WITH ME
A FUTURE TOGETHER
IS OUR DESTINY
WHEREVER WE'RE GOING
IS ALRIGHT, ALRIGHT

WHEREVER WE'RE GOING
WE'RE BOTH GONNA SEE
OUR STORY UNFOLDING
A GREAT MYSTERY
I KNOW IN MY HEART THAT
WE'RE HOLDING THE KEY
WHEREVER
IT'S ALRIGHT, ALRIGHT,
ALRIGHT
IT'S ALRIGHT
IT'S ALRIGHT WITH ME.

Hello, Is Anybody Home?

Within the first few minutes of the show, the audience has witnessed Marty's drastic emotional swings—from his exuberant, full-of-hopes-and-dreams entrance to a soul-crushing low when Strickland throws him out of the band audition, and back to a good place with the loving encouragement of his girlfriend, Jennifer. Returning to the McFly family home, there's only one way to go. Escorting him back to the catacombs of despair are father George, mother Lorraine, brother Dave, and sister Linda.

BOB GALE

Bob [Zemeckis] and I loved it instantly, because it was so wacky. Glenn and Al captured the dysfunctionality of everybody so well, plus the idea that each character had their own theme. It kept changing with each character, which just seemed perfect to do with a musical. Everyone has their own separate song, and as we kept developing it, the song improved, and more people got involved with figuring out how it was all going to come together. The idea that it all intertwines is just marvelous.

GLEN BALLARD

The family sequence was a big number for Al and me. We knew that they would be sitting at a table onstage, and we have four characters who come in and inform the audience who they are; in effect, our "I Am" songs at once.

ALAN SILVESTRI

It would have been easier to assume that everyone in the audience knew the film and the backstory, but it was agreed upon very early that

---

GEORGE
I know what you're gonna
say, son. And you're right,
you're right. But Biff just
happens to be my supervisor,
and I'm just not very good at
confrontations.

Marty turns to the audience
while George pours himself a
bowl of peanut brittle.

MARTY
MY FATHER DOESN'T HAVE A SPINE
HE GROVELS, SCRAPES,
AND TOWS THE LINE
HELLO? IS ANYBODY HOME?

COMPLETELY LOST, A HOPELESS CASE
HE'D COME IN THIRD,
IN A TWO-MAN RACE
HELLO? IS ANYBODY HOME?

GEORGE
Marty, take my advice. Don't
waste your time auditioning
for that silly event. It'll
only bring you rejection and
headaches. Just look at me...

GEORGE
I DON'T HAVE AMBITIONS
BIG DREAMS OF MY OWN
HAPPY WITH THE WAY THINGS ARE
JUST LEAVE ME ALONE!

I DON'T NEED THE HEADACHES
THAT TOO MUCH MONEY BRINGS
FANCY CARS, TAILORED SHIRTS
SHINY DIAMOND RINGS

DON'T NEED THE COMPLICATIONS

SUCCESS IS OVERRATED,
OVERSTATED, OVERBLOWN
LISTEN TO MY MANTRA:
JUST LEAVE ME ALONE!

MARTY
IS ANYBODY HOME?

Brother Dave, 21, enters in his
fast-food uniform.

DAVE
He's right, Marty, the last
thing you need is headaches.

MARTY
Right, big brother, like standing behind a burger counter
makes you an expert on life?

DAVE
I'M THE MAN, OH YES, I AM
I GOT THIS THING WIRED
HAVE YOU HEARD
TEN BILLION SERVED
GETS ME SO INSPIRED
SALTY SATISFACTION,
SATURATED FAT

AND ALL I EVER HAVE TO SAY...
YOU WANT FRIES WITH THAT?

WHOA, WHOA
I'M A MAN IN UNIFORM
ARCHES ON MY HAT
AND ALL I EVER HAVE TO SAY...
YOU WANT FRIES WITH THAT?

Sister Linda, 19 and overweight,
enters, faces Dave.

LINDA
GIVE ME BACK MY PRINCE CD.

DAVE
YOU WANT FRIES WITH THAT?

LINDA
AND MY WALKMAN, IF YOU PLEASE.

DAVE
YOU WANT FRIES WITH THAT?
THE ANSWER IS A QUESTION
MUSIC TO THEIR EARS

THEY ALL COME BACK
IT'S JUST A FACT
YOU WANT FRIES WITH THAT.

Marty, Dave, Linda, and George
move to the dinner table, and
George begins writing his
report for Biff.

LINDA
Hey, Marty...?

MARTY
Yeah, sis?

LINDA
I am not your answering
service. Jennifer Parker
called you. Twice.

Lorraine enters with a platter
of meat loaf and a bottle of
cheap vodka. She looks older
than her 47 years, the toll of
an unhappy life.

ALAN SILVESTRI (cont'd)
we would walk a fine line,
making sure that anyone seeing it for the first time would
get this vital information, and
it would still be entertaining
for the fans of *Back to the
Future* in seeing how we presented the stage incarnations
of their favorite characters.

GLEN BALLARD
Bob Gale was very much into
deepening these moments
with these characters
because that's the family
against which Marty is rebel-
ling. He loves them, but he's
disappointed with them. We
had to show his disappointment and at the same time
reveal who they were in this
dystopian, original version of
suburban life in 1985.

OLLY DOBSON
Marty is spiraling out of
control. Isn't it enough that his
dreams have been crushed?
He's had a bummer of a day:
His audition got shut down,
he's not with Jennifer anymore, and he still needs that
comfort. But at home, as usual,
he's not getting heard, and he
is just at the end of his tether.

CHRIS BAILEY

There was some staging involved. Dave McFly does a little bit with the French fries, and we gave George some quirky body movements. Because we're meeting these people for the first time, we don't want the audience to hate or pity them. You want to show that there's something appealing about them, despite their dysfunction.

ROSIE HYLAND

It's just another night at the McFly house. George has his peanut brittle, Linda is whining about not being able to get a date, Dave thinks that working at the golden arches is the greatest job in the world, and Lorraine has her vodka. The whole number is about how disconnected we all are. Is anybody home? We're all here, but is anyone really here? We're all just kind of in our own little glazed-over worlds. And Marty is frustrated with that.

HUGH COLES

What's fun about this number is that everyone gets a couple of lines in a section of the song, and then continues with their daily life. Before I sing, I have a scene with Biff with the peanut brittle, and then I sing a little bit to Marty about not having any ambitions or big dreams of my own. This is who George is, but it's not a huge song or dance. Then you just get to exist in your own world when someone else is singing.

LORRAINE
Marty. I don't like her.
Any girl who calls up a boy
is asking for trouble.

LINDA
Oh, Mom, there's nothing
wrong with calling a boy.

LORRAINE
I think it's terrible, girls
chasing boys. Here, have
some meat loaf.

LINDA
Again?!

LORRAINE
When I was your age, I never
chased a boy or kissed a boy
or sat in a parked car with
a boy.

LINDA
Then how am I supposed to
meet anybody?

LORRAINE
When the time is right, it'll
just happen.

LINDA
(stands)
SHE TELLS ME IT'LL HAPPEN
THAT THE SUN WILL RISE
AND THE STARS WILL SHINE
ALL I EVER SEEM TO DO
IS SIT AROUND AND WAIT
I JUST WANT A DATE

SHE SAYS SHE NEVER CALLED A BOY
OR CHASED A BOY, EVEN KISSED A BOY
WHAT DOES SHE EXPECT FROM ME?
'CAUSE SHE CAN'T RELATE

I JUST WANT A
I JUST WANT A
I JUST WANT A DATE

LORRAINE
Patience, Linda, it'll just
happen, like the way I met
your father.

LINDA
That was so stupid! He fell
out of a tree in front of
your house!

LORRAINE
It was meant to be.

WHEN LIFE ROLLS BY SO
BEAUTIFULLY
WITH PERFECT FRIENDS AND FAMILY
WHEN LOVE FALLS ON YOU
FROM A TREE
WELL, THAT'S MEANT TO BE

DAVE, LINDA, GEORGE
KNOW IT'S MEANT TO BE

LORRAINE
YOU LOOK AROUND
AND YOU START TO SEE
THAT YOU'RE LIVING OUT
YOUR FANTASY
IT STARTS TO FEEL LIKE DESTINY
LIKE IT'S MEANT TO BE

LORRAINE, DAVE, LINDA, GEORGE
KNOW IT'S MEANT TO
YOU WERE SENT TO
MUST BE MEANT TO BE

LORRAINE
Anyway, if Grandpa hadn't
found him lying out in the
street, none of you would
have been born.

LINDA
Yeah, Mom, you've told us a
million times. Grandpa
brought him in the house and
you felt sorry for him, so
you decided to go with him

to the "Fish Under the Sea" dance.

LORRAINE
No, no, it was the "Enchantment Under the Sea" dance. Our first date. It was the night of that terrible thunderstorm. Remember, George?

GEORGE
(obliviously writing
his report)
No thanks, Lorraine, I'm stuffed.

LORRAINE
(to Linda)
Your father kissed me for the very first time on that dance floor. And it was then that I realized I was going to spend the rest of my life with him.

Dave gets George's attention and makes a goofy expression. George guffaws.

LORRAINE
THERE WAS SOMETHING ABOUT
THAT BOY

MARTY
HELLO? IS ANYBODY HOME

LORRAINE
THERE WAS SOMETHING ABOUT
THAT BOY

MARTY
(jumping up on the table)
HELLO HELLO HELLO
(jumps down from the table)
AND NOW THE WALLS JUST
KEEP CLOSING IN
AND I DON'T KNOW IF
I'LL EVER WIN
IT'S JUST THE SAME AS
IT'S ALWAYS BEEN
NO GO
HELLO
TOO SLOW
HELLO

The family encircles Marty as the scenery slides away, ultimately leaving everyone

on a surreal, dark stage, each in their own pool of light.

FAMILY
HELLO

        ENSEMBLE
GEORGE
DON'T NEED THE
COMPLICATIONS   HELLO

DAVE
DO YOU WANT
FRIES WITH THAT?   HELLO

LINDA
I JUST WANT   **MARTY**
A DATE   AAAAAAAAH!
        HELLO
LORRAINE
YOU KNOW IT'S
MEANT TO BE

MARTY
IS ANYBODY HOME?

MARTY & FAMILY
HELLO HELLO HELLO
HELLO HELLO

It Works!

After watching Marty tormented by the insanity of his home life, it was time for the audience to finally meet Doctor Emmett L. Brown live and in person!

His sudden and startling appearance in his miraculous invention in the parking lot of the Twin Pines Mall, as staged by John Rando and realized by Roger Bart, is one truly worthy of the genius inventor. In the words of Bob Gale, "I think Doc's entrance may be the greatest entrance of any actor in theater."

MARTY
It's a time machine? A TIME MACHINE? Doc, are you telling me you built a time machine out of a DeLorean?!

DOC
Well, if you're gonna build a time machine into a car, why not do it with some style?

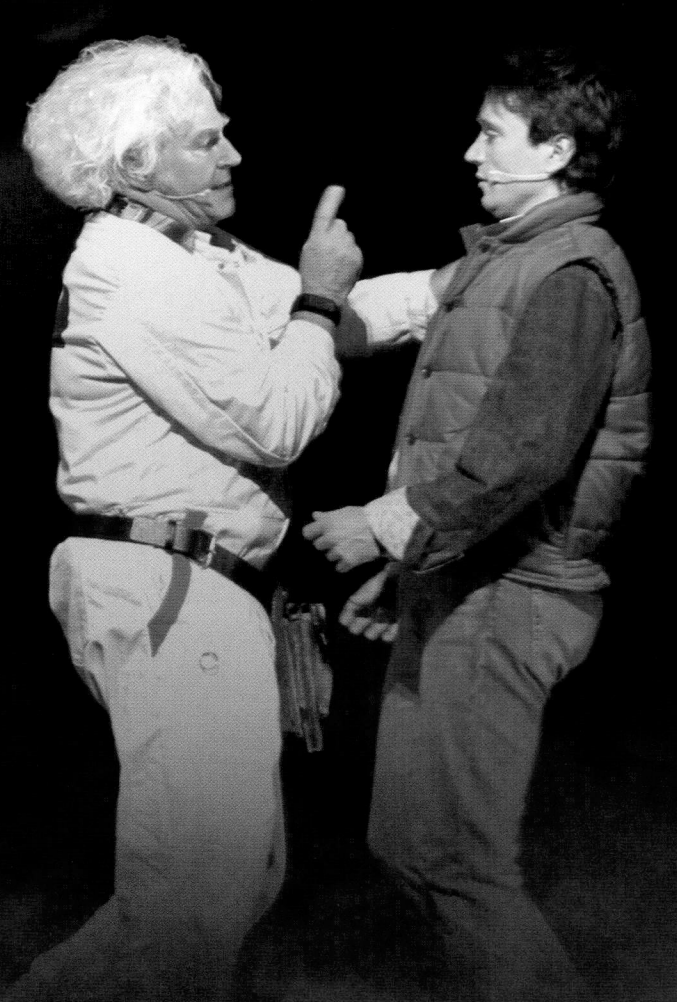

ROGER BART

It's a very funny number, but it's quite a few words. Glen [Ballard] sometimes writes where he forgets that I actually have to breathe in. I like it. I like the length of it. I like the way the girls appear and disappear. I like the fact that I managed to get in a Barry White impersonation, which I never thought I'd ever be able to do in a show.

GLEN BALLARD

This was an early song, part of our 2017 showcase. We originally approached it as a really traditional piece with a real fifties feeling to it. It had a kind of zaniness to it musically, and we knew this is the first time one of Doc's wild ideas actually works. For Doc, it is so unprecedented that we just wanted to make this as joyful and funny as possible. And then Roger made it better. Once you see Roger perform any of the songs that we do, we automatically know we've got to give him more "real estate," because he's so good with it. In having Roger in several workshops and labs, the song kept evolving. On every level, he elevates you.

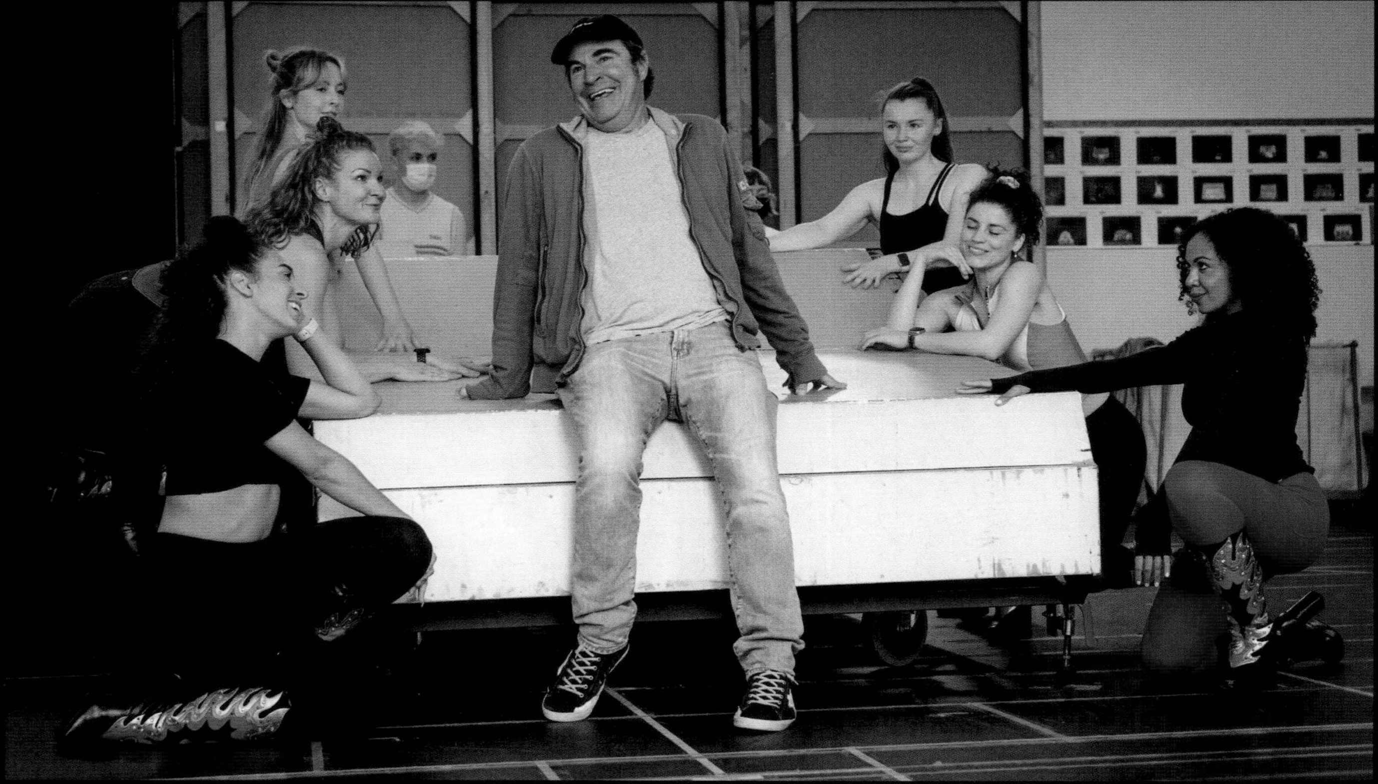

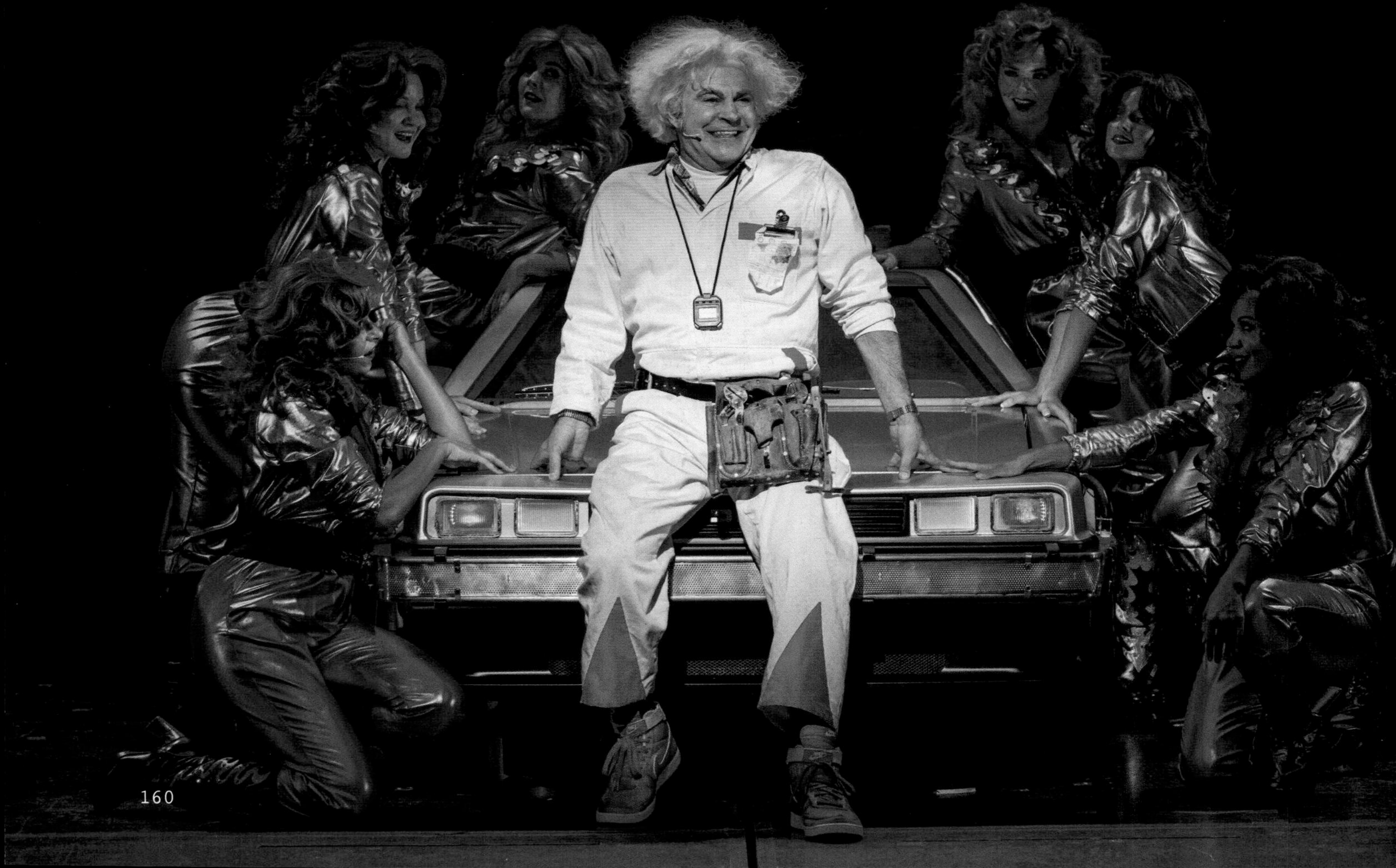

DOC

I'M THE ARCHITECT
OF TICK-TOCK TECH
A FREQUENT FLIER
ON A COSMIC TREK
I'VE SORTED THROUGH
THE QUARKS AND QUIRKS
AND FOR ONCE I KNOW I'VE MADE
A THING THAT REALLY WORKS

IT'S A TIME MACHINE
THAT GOES BOTH WAYS
TO NEW TOMORROWS
AND TO YESTERDAYS
IT'S A CAR FOR THE STARS
LIKE CAPTAIN KIRK'S
AND FOR ONCE I KNOW I'VE MADE
A THING THAT REALLY WORKS

Doc is joined by six girls in shiny silvery outfits as the mall set dressing vanishes. The background becomes a surreal video display celebrating the DeLorean.

DOC	GIRLS
IT WORKS	IT WORKS
IT WORKS	IT WORKS
IT WORKS	IT WORKS

IN TERMS OF THE
VERNACULAR IT'S
SPECTACULAR BECAUSE

IT WORKS	IT WORKS
IT WORKS	IT WORKS
IT WORKS	IT WORKS

DOC

AND NOW I FIND MY GLORY IN
A STAINLESS-STEEL DELOREAN
IT'S GRATIFYING KNOWING
I WAS FIRST
BECAUSE IT WORKS

MARTY

Hey, Doc, who are the girls?

DOC

I dunno. They show up every time I start singing.

BOB GALE

Putting chorus girls in this number was one of the very first ideas we had. It was insane. This was also, at the beginning, what Bob Zemeckis was talking about when he wanted a video screen with the gears going around showing how Doc's brain worked. What we ended up doing has that same flavor, but much cooler in how we are able to use the high-tech video wall. When I saw the number in rehearsal in Manchester, with the DeLorean with all the lighting and animations and girls and their costumes and Chris Bailey's choreography, I was laughing so hard I had tears in my eyes. It's one of my favorite memories of this whole process.

OLLY DOBSON

It's just this epic, awesome musical excuse to show everyone what comedy we can give you, and how we can tell this story. It's a car. It's showgirls. It's all a bit mad and crazy, and this is him. This is Doc. This guy is mad, but he's got the brains. He's totally wacko, and Marty loves to be able to run around and follow him because it's like, "Oh my God! Look at this wonderful, crazy world, and oh my God! There are girls here now. How did he do that?"

ROGER BART

It launches us. It sets the wonderful precedent of the ensemble and how they seem to be in a world where Doc is capable of magic. I think that for kids coming to the show, I like the idea that they are looking at Doc, thinking that when Doc is onstage, anything can happen. The rules are very different, so the idea that my car would spin with strobes and colored lighting and I'd have beautiful girls all around me is very exciting. Let's face it. When you're around somebody who is the chief designer at imagineering, you want to go in their house and have your mind blown. Ultimately, we ended up with a really fun tune.

DOC

BLUNT FORCE TRAUMA
UP AGAINST YOUR HEAD
CAN PUT YOU IN A COMA
YOU COULD END UP DEAD
OR CALLING FOR YOUR MAMA
BUT FOR ME INSTEAD
THAT BLUNT FORCE TRAUMA
WHEN I SLIPPED AND HIT MY HEAD

SHOOK SOMETHING LOOSE IN ME
SOME HIGH FRUIT IN THE TREE
AND THAT'S WHEN I COULD SEE
HOW FLUID TIME CAN BE
IT GAVE ME THE CONNECTION
AFTER DECADES OF REJECTION
I NEVER REALLY THOUGHT
I'D GET TO SEE HOW WELL

IT WORKS
IT WORKS
IT WORKS

AND WITH THIS NEW INVENTION
I'LL CUT THROUGH THE FOURTH
DIMENSION
'CAUSE IT WORKS
IT WORKS
IT WORKS

I FOUND WHAT I WAS
SEARCHING FOR
IT'S CALLED THE FLUX CAPACITOR
IT'S THIS YEAR'S BREAKTHROUGH
SCIENTIFIC FIRST
BECAUSE

GIRLS

IT WORKS
IT WORKS
YES, IT WORKS

DOC

THE SECRET WAS CONFINED
AND IT'S LIKE I WAS BLIND
THE SOLUTION WAS SUBLIME
AND I KNEW IT ALL THE TIME
I DIDN'T SEE HOW I COULD DO IT
UNTIL I PUT MY MIND TO IT

IT WORKS
IT WORKS
IT WORKS

A SPACE AND TIME FUNICULAR
BUT IT'S VEHICULAR BECAUSE

IT WORKS
IT WORKS
IT WORKS

THE WORLD WILL WRITE MY
STORY IN
THIS STAINLESS-STEEL DELOREAN
THE TIME CONTINUUM SHALL
BE TRAVERSED
BECAUSE (MARTY)
IT WORKS
IT WORKS
IT WORKS

DOC & THE GIRLS

IT WORKS
IT WORKS
IT WORKS

IT WORKS
IT WORKS
IT WORKS!

The girls disappear
and the mall set
dressing returns.

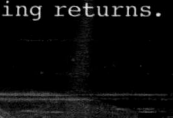

HONESTY
DECENCY
INTEGRITY

Cake

In the film, when Marty McFly sets foot in the 1955 Hill Valley town square, it was to the accompaniment of the Four Aces' classic "Mr. Sandman." The song immediately established the era as the viewer saw the "unblemished" version of Marty's hometown through the eyes of the youth as he tried to grasp his incredible circumstances.

The song was included in the book for the first workshop, and an a cappella version performed. After viewing a recording of the event, Robert Zemeckis was underwhelmed. "Having 'Mr. Sandman' open that scene didn't do anything for the show except to remind people of the movie," he explains. "I thought there was an opportunity to do something musically that would be equivalent to the movie's visuals."

Dire
did not
songs.
idea an
so muc

In *B*
look ba
of hind
well-me
things
ed. In t
identify
the Hill
to an ir

SCENE 8 - EXT.
1955 HILL VALLEY - DAY

Marty enters from stage right and does a double take at the billboard. He slowly turns around in disbelief.

CLOCK TOWER LADY, 30, enters from stage left. In 1955, she's a member of the Chamber of Commerce.

CLOCK TOWER LADY
A visitor! The Chamber of Commerce welcomes you to Hill Valley -- it's a nice place to live! Here's why!

CLOCK TOWER LADY
YOU FOUND THE FUTURE
AND IT'S HERE
JUST LOOK AROUND
YOU'LL SEE IT CRYSTAL CLEAR
BUSINESS IS BOOMING
FLOWERS ARE BLOOMING
AND 1955 HAS BEEN A BANNER YEAR

Four uniformed Texaco attendants enter from stage right.

TEXACO GUYS
OUR SUPER LEADED GASOLINE
(spoken) Only nineteen cents a gallon!
WILL KEEP OUR ATMOSPHERE
SO FRESH AND CLEAN
PRECISION TOOLING
AND FOSSIL FUELING
WILL KEEP YOU CRUISING IN YOUR
SUPER-SLEEK MACHINE

Three stylish ladies in sunglasses and bright dresses enter from stage left, all smoking cigarettes.

CIGARETTE LADIES
THESE FILTERED CIGARETTES
ARE NEW (SO NEW)
AND EVEN DOCTORS SAY
THEY'RE GOOD FOR YOU
AND THERE'S NO QUESTION
THEY'LL AID DIGESTION
AND PICK YOU UP
WHEN YOU FEEL BLUE

Clock Tower Lady offers Marty a cigarette. As he refuses, the gauze lifts to reveal the 1955 town square, a lively, picture-perfect place dominated by the pristine courthouse under a bright blue sky. The clock shows 8:25. There are period streetlights and park benches. Townspeople are dressed nicely in 1955 attire (men in ties, women in dresses and heels, some with strollers).

ENSEMBLE
IT'S A GOOD OLD-FASHIONED
MODERN WAY OF LIVING
AND NO ONE DOES IT BETTER
THAN WE DO
FINALLY, IT'S TIME WHEN
ALL OF THESE FINE MEN
GET TO HAVE THEIR CAKE AND
EAT IT, TOO!!

A guy in a white coat with a can of asbestos paint approaches Marty.

GUY IN WHITE COAT
FOR HOME INSULATION,
ASBESTOS IS BEST
IT KEEPS YOU COZY AND WARM

A guy in overalls with a large pesticide sprayer labeled DDT moves center stage.

GLEN BALLARD
It was important for us that we didn't celebrate 1955 blindly. It was a great time for white guys, but for some people, like Goldie Wilson, it wasn't. At the same time, it has so many nostalgic high points that we all kind of relate to the period. So when Marty arrives in 1955, there's something wrong about it, but at the same time, there's something familiar about it. We use the song to transform it from the movie into a stage musical. The fifties were the fifties. And we weren't going to gloss over them.

BOB GALE
When we made the film, we wanted to have more of those period references, but weren't able to include them due to time constraints. We shot a cigarette commercial in which a surgeon walks out of an ER, looks at the camera and says, "After doing two lung operations in a row, I like to light up a Sir Randolph." We ultimately didn't use it because it interrupted the movie's pace. When we decided to replace "Mr. Sandman" with an original song, a cigarette gag was a must. I gave Glen a great reference book, *All-American Ads of the 50s*, from which we could draw further inspiration.

JOHN RANDO

I wanted the audience to experience Marty's arrival in fifties Hill Valley as if he had been trapped inside a 1950s musical. Glen and Al really made us see the 1950s through 2020 values. We tested it out in our November 2018 lab at the American International Church in London. Although not fully realized, it was very evident we were going to move the story forward through song with "Cake." I also suggested to Bob and Glen that we needed a guide for Marty to be welcomed to 1950s Hill Valley, and that we could use a young version of the Clock Tower Lady, thinking it would be nice to see her roots in the 1950s as well [Katharine Pearson would ultimately play the Clock Tower Lady in both time periods].

OLLY DOBSON

It's a great comedic number: "Look how outrageous we were back in the day. Look at the times!" It's about comparing the life they led to the one the audience is leading now. "Mr. Sandman" sets the tone perfectly in the film. Lyrically, it didn't make sense for the introduction of the 1950s for the stage, but if you listen carefully to the score preceding "Cake," you'll hear a few bars of "Sandman." Just enough to remind people that the show is in safe hands.

CHRIS BAILEY

"Cake" is a full-on number, with basically everybody in the ensemble involved. When Marty arrives in Hill Valley, he's having this sort of out-of-body experience, but it's real. When we started

GUY IN OVERALLS
WE SPRAY DDT ON THOSE WORRYSOME PESTS
AND WE'VE REENGINEERED THE FOOD FROM THE FARM

A woman proudly shows Marty a big can of SPAM.
He takes it.

CLOCK TOWER LADY
What'd I tell you? It's like utopia!

MARTY
It's a nightmare!

He gives her the SPAM can. A campaign worker
for mayor Red Thomas sets a soapbox down and
the mayor steps up.

RED THOMAS
Reelect me, Mayor Red Thomas! My new
progress platform means more jobs, lower
taxes, and bigger civic improvements!

ENSEMBLE
Yay!

RED THOMAS   WOMEN
THIS IS OUR   OOOOAAAAAH

DREAMLAND U-S-A

THE PERFECT COMBINATION   AAAAAAAAAH

OF WORK AND PLAY

IT'S NO MALARKEY

OUR PATRIARCHY

WILL SHOW THE WHOLE   AAAAAAAAAH

WIDE WORLD

THE WAY TO LIVE THIS WAY

MEN   WOMEN

IT'S A GOOD   IT'S A GOOD

OLD-FASHIONED   OLD-FASHIONED

MODERN WAY OF LIVING   MODERN WAY OF LIVING

AND NO ONE DOES   THEY MAY THINK THEY

IT BETTER   DO IT BETTER

THE FACT IS   THE FACT IS

NO ONE DOES IT BETTER NO ONE DOES IT BETTER

THAN WE DO   THAN WE DO

CHRIS BAILEY (cont'd) to work on it, we watched lots of commercials, and they're reflected right at the start of the number. We have the Texaco boys, the cigarette-smoking housewives, and continue with different vignettes of people telling Marty how amazing it is in the fifties because they have all these great products like DDT and asbestos. We tried different versions of that. I'm always a fan of going more and more theatrical. The musical inspiration came from "Put On Your Sunday Clothes" [from *Hello, Dolly!*]. This is what we were sold in the fifties. The American dream [Zemeckis had also featured the four Texaco attendants in the feature].

BRYAN CROOK (CO-ORCHESTRATOR) This song is definitely the "Broadway show tune" of the musical. Given that and its setting in the fifties, the lush orchestration emulating a full thirty- to thirty-five-piece orchestra was assumed. We're using the full resources of woodwind doubling, different brass mutes, keyboard sounds (pizzicato and arco strings, percussion, woodwinds), and our brilliant percussionist, who is running back and forth between timpani, glockenspiel, xylophone, orchestra chimes, vibraphone, and toys.

A lot of the varied styles contained in the number come from Nick Finlow's arrangement, which carves out moments specific to the Texaco boys, smoking women, Mayor Red Thomas, etc. These special moments onstage were ripe for some musical variety.

167

JOHN RANDO

When it came to designing and staging it, we worked hard to give Marty a sense of entrapment, including a massive painted drop that descends behind him and traps him on the edge of the stage. We also worked hard to show a kind of 1950s town square opening number reflective of the same town square revealed in our 1980s opening number.

ALAN SILVESTRI

We had a lot of fun with the lyric content. Clearly, no one would have dreamed back then, when their kids playing in the basement came out looking like snowmen because they were covered in asbestos, that it was a real nightmare, or that DDT would have poisoned entire communities. The great irony of it is that we haven't changed. There's a timeless aspect to that metaphor, because we aren't doing anything different. People may have something in their homes, or a material on their couch, and fifty years from now, we're going to say, "How could they have used *that* for upholstery back then?" So while we're laughing at these people singing the false praises of the 1950s, we're also laughing at ourselves.

MEN (cont'd)	WOMEN (cont'd)
USE SUPER LEADED	
GASOLINE	WE LOVE OUR
	CIGARETTES, IT'S
TRUE... 'CAUSE	TRUE, 'CAUSE
IT JUST FEELS	IT JUST FEELS
RIGHT WHEN	RIGHT WHEN
ALL OF THESE	ALL OF THESE
WHITE MEN	WHITE MEN
GET TO HAVE	GET TO HAVE
THEIR CAKE	THEIR CAKE
SO LET THE	SO LET THE
WOMEN BAKE	WOMEN BAKE
WE GET TO HAVE	WE GET TO HAVE
OUR CAKE	OUR CAKE
AND EAT IT TOO	AND EAT IT TOO

The clock BONGS--it's 8:30, and the townspeople disperse. Marty is amazed that the clock tower clock is NOW WORKING!

MARTY
It works. The clock works.

Gotta Start Somewhere

Another song that had its roots in the 2017 song showcase was "Gotta Start Somewhere," in which the 1955 Goldie Wilson imparted words of advice to young George after his routine session of bullying from Biff. Cedric Neal performed the song at his audition, and that was more than enough to clinch the role for him. "He knocked the hell out of it," remarks Bob Gale, "and even though he was a little bit older than the part was written, there was no way we weren't going to have Cedric in the show."

Goldie sidles up to George, takes the bowl off his head.

GOLDIE
Say: Why do you let that boy push you around like that?

GEORGE
Well, he's bigger than me.

GOLDIE
Stand tall, boy, have some respect for yourself. If you let people walk all over you

GOLDIE (cont'd)
now, they'll be walking all over you for the rest of your life. Look at me. You think I'm gonna spend the rest of my life in this slop house?

LOU
Watch it, Goldie.

MARTY
(realizes who this is)
Goldie? Goldie Wilson?

CEDRIC NEAL
I call it the Big Black Woman Gospel Number of the show. I think in the first workshop it felt like a forty-five-minute song, and Glen Ballard and Nick Finlow said, "Cedric, there's something in this." So we reworked it, we brought the cast in, and I don't think I've ever felt as much joy as I do when I'm doing that number.

GLEN BALLARD

It's a huge number, and Cedric is maybe the best singer in all of England. What's important is the message he's imparting to George, and the audience, and he leads by example. Goldie is using the system—it's not the other way around. He's got a plan, and he doesn't care if he has to start from the bottom and sweep up, but whatever he does, he's going to make something of himself. It's a statement of confidence I think resonates in today's times.

CHRIS BAILEY

When we're planning out the dance and choreography, we try to make sure that everything is thought through in the same way that Bob would write the script. It had to make absolute sense why this person is in that situation and how they're affected by everything around them, rather than just singing a song and dancing. That's always going to be on a very basic level. It seemed like a really good opportunity to go into Goldie's world of the people he would probably hang out with in his social circle and economic status. So all of the ensemble here are working class: workmen, waitresses, gas station attendants. It reminds me of the lower decks for the third-class passengers on the *Titanic*. The passengers on the upper decks were limited by the social structure as to how they could behave. Belowdecks, it was a party—a celebration.

GOLDIE
No, sir, I'm gonna make something of myself. I'm going to night school and someday, I'm gonna be somebody!

MARTY
That's right, he's gonna run for mayor!

GOLDIE
Yeah, I'm--mayor! Now that's a good idea... I could run for mayor...!

LOU
A colored mayor. That'll be the day.

GOLDIE
You wait and see, Mr. Carruthers! I will be mayor! I'll be the most powerful man in Hill Valley, and I'm gonna clean up this town!

LOU
(hands him a broom)
Good! You can start by sweeping the floor.

GOLDIE
Mayor Goldie Wilson. I like the sound of that!

During the number, George tries to get away from Goldie, but Goldie keeps pulling him back to give him his advice.

GOLDIE
WHAT ARE YOU WAITING FOR?
PICK YOURSELF UP OFF THE FLOOR
IF YOU DON'T RESPECT YOURSELF
WON'T GET IT FROM NO ONE ELSE

NO SHAME IN WORKING HARD
LET THEM KNOW THAT'S WHO YOU ARE
THOUGH I'M LOW MAN IN THE ROOM
I'M STILL THE BEST ONE WITH
THIS BROOM

THIS AIN'T NO STEP AND FETCH IT
IT'S ALL PART OF THE CLIMB
THERE'S A TRAIN,
I'M GONNA CATCH IT
IT'S A MATTER OF TIME

BUT YOU GOTTA START SOMEWHERE
YOU GOTTA START SOMEWHERE
YOU GOTTA GET GOING
OR YOU'RE NEVER GONNA GET THERE
AND ONCE YOU GET MOVING
YOU'LL FIND SOME WAY, SOMEHOW
AND IT MIGHT AS WELL BE RIGHT
HERE, RIGHT NOW

GOLDIE & KITCHEN HELP
COME ON, BOY.

GOLDIE
YOU GOTTA START SOMEWHERE

The set flies out, putting us back in the town square, where working-class townspeople join the number.

GOLDIE

Listen up. Sometimes you just gotta sweep
that negativity away.

SOME PEOPLE'S ROAD TO FAME
BEGINS ON STREETS THAT HAVE NO NAME
DOESN'T HAVE TO HOLD YOU BACK
ONCE YOU'RE MOVIN' ON THAT TRACK

DON'T BE CONFINED TO IT
IF YOU PUT YOUR MIND TO IT
YOU CAN ALWAYS GET YOUR WAY
IF YOU'RE WILLING JUST TO SWEAT YOUR WAY

DON'T DEMEAN THE MENIAL
DO THE BEST YOU CAN
REMAIN CONGENIAL
AND SOMEDAY YOU'LL BE THE MAN

ENSEMBLE

HOO HOO HOO
HOO HOO HOO
HOO HOO HOO
YEAH!

AAAAAAAAH
YOU'LL BE THE MAN

Ensemble claps and dances as Goldie continues.

GOLDIE

BUT YOU GOTTA START SOMEWHERE
YOU GOTTA START SOMEWHERE
AND MAKE YOURSELF USEFUL
OR YOU'RE NEVER GONNA GET THERE
AND ONCE YOU GET MOVING
YOU'LL FIND SOME WAY
SOMEHOW
SO IT MIGHT AS WELL BE
RIGHT HERE, RIGHT NOW
COME ON, BOY

YOU GOTTA START SOMEWHERE
YOU GOTTA START SOMEWHERE
YOU GOTTA GET GOIN'
OR YOU'RE NEVER GONNA GET THERE

AND ONCE YOU GET MOVING
YOU'LL FIND SOME WAY SOMEHOW
SO IT MIGHT AS WELL BE
RIGHT HERE, RIGHT NOW
COME ON, BOY

ENSEMBLE

GOTTA START SOMEWHERE
GOTTA START SOMEWHERE

NEVER GONNA GET THERE
HOOOOOO

MIGHT AS WELL BE
RIGHT HERE
COME ON, BOY

GOTTA START SOMEWHERE
GOTTA START SOMEWHERE

NEVER GONNA GET THERE
HOOOOOO

MIGHT AS WELL BE RIGHT HERE

COME ON, BOY

[INSTRUMENTAL/DANCE BREAK]

George has exited amid all of the dancing, and Marty can't find him.

171

CEDRIC NEAL

When I started the show, I'll be the first to admit, I wasn't a triple threat. I will sing you under the table, act you under the table, but I wasn't a dancer. So I wanted to step out of my box and make Goldie a full-fledged triple threat. It was daunting, but Chris Bailey and Darren Carnall and the whole team were very patient and rallied around me, and in the end, I think we got to something we were all satisfied with. I like swinging that broom around!

GOLDIE	ENSEMBLE
KEEP MOVIN' AND A-GROOVIN' IT'S ALL A STATE OF MIND AS LONG AS YOU'RE IMPROVING YOU WON'T GET LEFT BEHIND	YEAH-EE-YEAH!
BUT YOU GOTTA START SOMEWHERE YOU GOTTA START SOMEWHERE MOVING OR YOU'LL NEVER GET THERE AND ONCE YOU GET MOVING YOU'LL FIND SOME WAY SOMEHOW IT MIGHT AS WELL BE RIGHT HERE, RIGHT NOW COME ON, BOY MIGHT AS WELL BE RIGHT HERE	GOTTA START SOMEWHERE GOTTA START SOMEWHERE NEVUH NEVUH NEVUH GUNNA YEAH! MOVIN' YOU'LL FIND SOME WAY SOMEHOW MIGHT AS WELL BE RIGHT HERE COME ON, COME ON, BOY! MIGHT AS WELL BE RIGHT HERE

GOLDIE	MEN	LADIES
GOTTA START SOMEWHERE YOU GOTTA START SOMEWHERE	GOTTA START SOMEWHERE RIGHT NOW! GOTTA START SOMEWHERE RIGHT NOW!	GOTTA START RIGHT HERE RIGHT NOW! GOTTA START RIGHT HERE RIGHT NOW! AND YOU'LL BE THE MAN!
YOU'LL BE HEY! HEY! YOU'LL BE!	AND YOU'LL BE THE MAN!	YOU'LL BE THE MAN!

YOU'LL BE THE MAN!

The ensemble moves downstage as the Hill Valley billboard gauze drops down.

GOLDIE
YOU GOTTA START SOMEWHERE

ENSEMBLE
GOTTA START SOMEWHERE
GOTTA START SOMEWHERE
GOTTA START SOMEWHERE
GOTTA START SOMEWHERE
WHERE YOU'RE GOIN'S UP TO YOU
YOU KNOW WHO HE'S TALKIN' TO

GOLDIE
YOU AND YOU AND YOU AND YOU

George, on his bicycle, pedals across the stage, with Marty in pursuit.

MARTY
Dad! George! Hey, you on the bike!

ENSEMBLE
TAKE THE FIRST STEP,
THEN TAKE TWO
DOIN' NOTHIN' JUST WON'T DO
YOU GOTTA START SOMEWHERE
SOMEWHERE
SOMEWHERE
SOMEWHERE
SOMEWHERE

Ensemble dances off stage right, leaving Goldie alone onstage.

GOLDIE
HEY!
HEY!
HEY-AY-AY-YAY!

NICK FINLOW
It's a great, uplifting moment in the show, and we need a song like this at this point. We are so lucky to have Cedric Neal. He's got the most phenomenal voice, and it's lovely in my role as the music supervisor to be able to sit back and think when Cedric's onstage, I have nothing to worry about. I was, however, asked to write a reprise of the number for the scene change—first to get the cast off the stage, and second to get the scene change done to bring in Lorraine's house. We discovered before we went into rehearsals for Manchester that it was actually going to take quite a long time to get off, so this reprise I'd written suddenly had to be pretty much doubled. We managed to fix some of the issues when we moved to London, but in Manchester, the reprise was not far off the length of the original song itself. We had two amazing moments of Cedric, which I was thrilled about!

OLLY DOBSON
It's a powerhouse. If you don't have any sort of a positive outlook on life, then you're screwed. Generally speaking, it's just a bit of good advice, and it's nice that he's telling George to do that now. As for Marty,

I don't even get to savor the number. That's another comedic value thing—the protagonist who is not enjoying this. "Can everyone stop singing and dancing, please, because I'm trying to find Doc Brown?"

HUGH COLES
For George, this number is like being in a blender. I think that's my favorite thing, viewing all of these songs and numbers through the perspective of George, which is usually people singing at him, dancing around him, pushing him around. Each time it's strengthening the perception that George just gets acted upon by the world.

CEDRIC NEAL
This song is my testimony about anything in life. I'm the person who delivers the message eight times a week, just say to the people in the audience, this is what this show is about—this is what life is about. Times are hard. Put your mind to it and you can do anything. Start somewhere. And that resonates in my life. And I get to minister that message. To encourage somebody else, to encourage a little brown boy sitting in the audience who's always wanted to sing, always wanted to dance, to act . . . you've just got to start somewhere.

My Myopia

With the Baines house firmly in place onstage, Cedric and the ensemble have a brief but well-deserved respite. Marty has trailed George to a well-appointed home on a tree-lined street.

GLEN BALLARD

It's pretty much assumed that in a musical version of *Back to the Future*, the audience is going to expect a certain level of technology on display, but if that's all you've got, you'll never win at theater. You still have to have the heart and soul of a story. One of the things we discovered in writing the songs was that there was a huge opportunity to have the characters sing about their lives and motivation, and reveal who they really are to an audience that is predisposed to love them.

BOB GALE

"Myopia" rhymes with "utopia"—one of the greatest rhymes in the history of music, a brilliant play on words. But more importantly, it totally captures George's characterization. It's actually a reprise and permutation of what 1985 George sings in "Hello, Is Anybody Home?" but to a different tune. It's taking the same idea and seeing it through different time periods.

GLEN BALLARD

In the movie, audiences see a guy in a tree, staring through binoculars, then he falls, almost gets hit by a car, and

George's bicycle leans up against the mailbox of a house. A tree trunk is nearby. GEORGE sings.

> **GEORGE**
> I DON'T NEED TO LOOK AROUND
> I KEEP MY FOCUS ON THE GROUND
> HOPING NO ONE CATCHES ME
> WITH SKETCHES NO ONE ELSE
> CAN SEE
>
> I DON'T NEED TO HAVE A LOOK
> BEYOND THE PAGES OF THIS BOOK
> I WANT TO BE LEFT ALONE
> WITH THE THOUGHTS THAT ARE
> MY OWN

As George pulls the binoculars from his bag, we reveal a clapboard house behind him. As he sings, a teenage girl appears in a second-story window wearing a slip. She primps, brushes her hair, stuffs tissues in the bra portion, then checks her face for zits, totally oblivious to George outside, who throws glances toward her with the binoculars.

> MY MYOPIA
> IS MY UTOPIA
> AND I'M HOPIN' YA
> FEEL IT TOO
> WHEN YOU NARROW YOUR
> POINT OF VIEW
> YOU SEE ONLY WHAT YOU WANT TO

> MY MYOPIA
> IS MY UTOPIA
> AND I'M HOPIN' YA
> UNDERSTAND
> THAT I'M DOING THE BEST I CAN
> TO SEE ONLY WHAT I WANT TO
>
> BUT DEEP INSIDE
> ALL I EVER WANTED TO DO
> WAS RUN AND HIDE
> AND YES, I KNOW I CAN DO BETTER
> THAT'S THE ONLY WAY
> I'LL EVER GET HER
> AND CONSIDERING
> I HAVEN'T MET HER YET

George disappears to climb the tree. Marty enters and watches.

> **MARTY**
> He's a Peeping Tom!

Our scenery adjusts to "move us upward" so we lose Marty to see George on the tree bough, climbing along to get a better look at the girl in the second-story window.

> **GEORGE**
> I HEARD ABOUT THIS
> BIRD DOWN UNDER
> HE'S TERRIFIED BY THE
> SOUND OF THUNDER
> HE DOES SOMETHING THAT
> I UNDERSTAND
> HE TAKES HIS HEAD AND (SORT OF)
> BURIES IT IN THE SAND

GLEN BALLARD (cont'd)
runs away. Marty calls him a Peeping Tom. That's all we know. We thought this was a moment to reveal young George to the audience in a more sympathetic way. "My myopia is my utopia." That's who George is, a very insecure teenage boy. Biff beats him up every day, so George escapes by cutting everything out of his life to focus on his own fantasies, one of which is Lorraine. He sees just what he wants to see. He draws his sketches and writes stories that he keeps to himself. He's very protective about his artistic nature, and he's got a crush on a beautiful girl. The song is a fun way to reveal that he's not a pervert, but rather a lonely seventeen-year-old kid who's struggling with who he is and how to cope with life. It also gives Hugh Coles a chance to take the character to the next level as he reveals his heart to the audience.

HUGH COLES
There's one bit in the song that reveals something important about George that you don't get to see in the film. "Deep inside, all I want to do is hide. Yes, I know I can be better . . ." It's not like he's just this kid that everybody else sees. He knows he's like this, and he doesn't want to be. He doesn't want the life we see when the curtain comes up at the beginning, doing Biff's work. Nobody wants that. That's why the song is such a gift, to be able to act that

LORRAINE'S BEDROOM.

GEORGE IS A PEEPING TOM ..

FLY UP TREES WHEN GEORGE FALLS TO GROUND.

ABOVE Tim Hatley design sketch of George up a tree.

HUGH COLES (cont'd)

song and then get that moment with the audience. Such is the beauty of musical theater, where you can turn to the audience and go, "Yeah, I know. I know. But I can't . . . I can't change." George gets pushed around and pushed around, and finally he gets in his tree and it's just George and the audience. "This is how I feel all the time. And I don't want to feel like this, but I can't change it anyway, and there's Lorraine . . ." and I fall out of the tree. That tiny bit where you get to sit with George. I love it. It's one of my favorite bits in the show.

ROSIE HYLAND

While George is peeping at Lorraine, she comes and goes throughout the number. The audience sees her through the window and she's doing various things, checking her reflection, popping pimples, primping. Each time I come on and do a little bit of reflection acting in the window, then I pull the shade down so Hugh can keep singing and the audience is not distracted by the bedroom. Then raise the shade, do some more acting, and pull the shade down. Could I get the shade to stay on the roller? NO! It just insisted on falling off every time. Sometimes the whole deal collapsed, and one day I pulled it and I fell through the window! So that was hideously embarrassing because I'm only dressed in a slip. I felt for poor Hugh. During previews, over the course of weeks, it happened too many times. Eventually, they changed the mechanism so it worked every time.

GEORGE

TRYING TO AVOID A
CONFRONTATION
I WOULD RATHER BE IN
HIBERNATION
I RETREAT INTO IMAGINATION
AND MY RELIANCE ON
SCIENCE FICTION

TO LAND A PRETTY GIRL,
OH WELL, I WISH
BUT I FLOAT JUST LIKE
A JELLYFISH
HUMBLE PIE IS MY FAVORITE DISH
I LIVE IN FEAR OF
CONTRADICTIONS

MY MYOPIA
IS MY UTOPIA
AND I'M HOPING YOU'RE
FEELING IT
SEE HOW I'M DEALING WITH IT
AND... I'M... HOPING YOU'RE
FEELING IT TOO

The tree cracks. George loses, then regains his balance. A bigger crack causes George to fall. Marty, unseen, calls out from below.

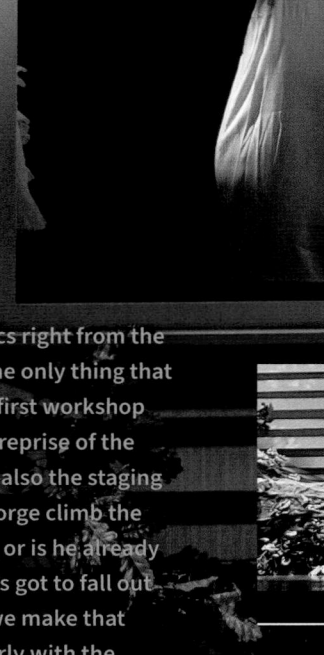

BOB GALE

Glen got these lyrics right from the very beginning—the only thing that changed from the first workshop was dropping one reprise of the chorus. There was also the staging question: Does George climb the tree while singing, or is he already up there? Then he's got to fall out of it, and how do we make that action meld properly with the song? John was really great about knowing what to do there.

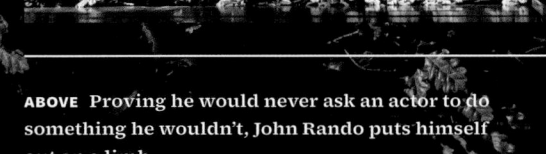

ABOVE Proving he would never ask an actor to do something he wouldn't, John Rando puts himself out on a limb . . .

MARTY (offstage)
Dad--George! Don't worry,
I'll catch you!

George falls out of view,
and we hear a body thud and
some grunts. The tree bough
rises, revealing that George
has fallen on top of Marty.
George gets up and sees who he
landed on.

GEORGE
You again? Just leave me
alone!

George hops on his bike and
pedals off, leaving Marty out
cold. SAM BAINES, 45, runs
in from stage right with a
briefcase.

SAM
What was that? What's
going on?
(calls at the departing George)
Hey, you! Did you do this?!
(calls to the house)
Hey! Stella! Another one
of these damn kids fell
out of the tree! Help me
get him in the house!

JOHN RANDO
There is a natural inclination for
the audience to want to applaud
at the end of every song, but
there are times when dramatically, you don't want them
to applaud, and break up the
moment. In Manchester he ended
up on Lorraine's roof right next to
her window and then "fell" from
the roof to land on Marty. We felt
it was a little too close to the window for comfort. When we moved
to London, I decided to keep him
in the tree, allow him to finish the
song and give the audience their
chance to applaud, and then he
falls off the branch. Other than
that, it's pretty much the same as
what we started with back at the
first reading. Hugh delivers it with
such quirky genius, we didn't
want to change much.

Pretty Baby

Having been knocked unconscious by the combination of a falling tree limb and his teenage father, we next find Marty in bed in a darkened room. When the audience hears him stirring, they know exactly where he is, with whom, and when, as he mutters one of *Back to the Future*'s most iconic lines: "Mom, is that you?" And as he did on celluloid in 1985, he wakes to find himself face-to-the-fresh-faced 1955 teenage version of his mother, Lorraine Baines. While tending to the youth's cranial injury, Lorraine has become totally smitten with this young stranger, and she makes her intentions abundantly clear to the flabbergasted Marty upon his return to consciousness. Only, in the musical, she gets to make those intentions clear with a song!

"Pretty Baby" made its first appearance in Bob Gale's October 17 draft of 2011. The core of Ballard and Silvestri's song remains in the show to this very day, with some embellishments and additional lyrics added over the years.

GLEN BALLARD

When Alan Silvestri and I addressed the scene, we thought it needed a fifties motif, so we listened to a lot of music from the fifties and early sixties. While that was important to the development of the song, we always had to remember the intent of the scene: Lorraine is coming on to her son, unaware of his identity. Marty's trying to avoid her. We spent a lot of time trying to figure out how to soften what was really happening, which they did very successfully in the movie. We created the song, which was essentially a Shirelles-inspired number, and that's where the concept of the "Lorraine Chorus" was born.

ALAN SILVESTRI

This could very well be my favorite number in the show. It was a very controversial scene back when the movie was made because it was implying something that was not just outside of the culture of the

SCENE 11: INT. LORRAINE'S BEDROOM - NIGHT, 1955

A dimly lit girl's bedroom. A bed is center stage under a curtained window. There is also a makeup table with a mirror, and a chest. A woman tends to an unconscious Marty in the bed with a wet cloth. Marty stirs.

                    MARTY
        Mom? Is that you?

                    WOMAN
        There, there, just relax.
        You've been asleep for
        almost nine hours.

                    MARTY
        I had a horrible nightmare. I
        dreamt I went back in time.

                    WOMAN
        Well, you're safe and sound
        now, in good old 1955.

She flips the light switch. Lights come up and we (and Marty) see that this is his mother, Lorraine, a beautiful 17-year-old.

                    MARTY
        1955? 1955?! You're my--you're
        my--you're...

                    LORRAINE
        My name's Lorraine. Lorraine
        Baines.

                    MARTY
        Yeah... but you're so--so--thin!

                    LORRAINE
        Just relax, Calvin. You got
        quite a bruise on your head.

Marty pulls off the covers only to find he's in his underwear. He quickly pulls them back.

MARTY
Where are my pants?

LORRAINE
Over there. On my hope
chest. I've never seen
purple underwear before,
Calvin.

MARTY
Calvin? Why do you keep
calling me Calvin?

LORRAINE
Well, that is your name,
isn't it? Calvin Klein?
It's written all over your
underwear. Oh--I guess
people call you Cal.

MARTY
Uh, no. Actually, they call
me Marty.

LORRAINE
(moving closer to him)
Pleased to meet you.
Calvin. Marty. Klein.

As she sings, she advances on
a very uncomfortable Marty,
and he backs away. She relent-
lessly moves forward, and he
moves backward, creating a
reverse courtship dance, which
can involve him climbing onto
and off furniture to avoid her
advances.

LORRAINE
PRETTY BABY
GOT THIS FUNNY FEELIN'
PRETTY BABY
I MIGHT NEED SOME HEALIN'

IT'S GETTING HOTTER
AND IT'S GIVING ME THE CHILLS
I THINK I'D BETTER REST HERE
FOR A WHILE

TRIO
AHH, AHH, AHH

The window curtains part,
revealing a female trio in
fifties wardrobe who all
resemble Lorraine. As the
number proceeds, they enter
the room as accompaniment.

ALAN SILVESTRI (cont'd)
time, but it was a real taboo that
Bob and Bob were flirting with . . .
literally! I think the reason the
number works as well as it does is
that we took it very seriously, as
the guys did in the movie. And what
we realized, and how we treated it,
was that it was all innocent. Just as
she was in the movie, Lorraine was
innocent and irresistibly charming,
because *she didn't know!* How
could she? Marty can't tell her. It
was one of those things, just as we
talked about having fun with what
goes on fantasy-wise in Doc's mind,
we get to do it here with Lorraine,
in a crazy, coy-ish fifties-style flirty
song, singing it to her son. And it's
all completely innocent!

JOHN RANDO
Glen and Al had written this very
1950s period-feel girl song for
Lorraine, complete with female
backup singers. When we first
went to work on it for the Dominion workshop, Nick Finlow was
eager to make those backup voices sound really good. He worked
on early vocal arrangements for
six ensemble women. Even as far
back as that reading, I was thinking the backup singers had to be
multiple Lorraines. It would be
almost as if Marty was trapped in
multiple universes with his teenage mom. When I went to work
with Tim Hatley on the design
idea for the set and costumes,
the big inspiration for us was
"Beauty School Dropout" from
Grease. As Chris Bailey went to
choreograph the song, he wanted
to cut the number down to only
three Lorraines, keeping with the
period style of the Ronettes or the
Shangri-Las.

179

CHRIS BAILEY

The first priority was to give Rosie Hyland some vocal backup so the song became a "number" and we could theatricalize it, rather than having a single actor singing to another, which might make it too real. I wanted three ladies so the number would stand out from the others where we had massive ensemble numbers, and vocally, ladies work better in trios because there are three vocal parts, à la the Andrews Sisters. At first, I was asked if they could come out from under the bed, through the bedroom door (which didn't exist), and other suggestions, all of which needed very specific set designs to keep things safe for the actors. It was my idea to have them come through the window. I wanted their entrance to appear initially as uncomfortably close to Olly so we could see him squirm. For me, this is all through Marty's eyes: "My mom is coming on to me and has octopus hands! They are every-where!" I wanted their entrance to be immediate, no walking on or elaborate entrance.

LORRAINE	TRIO
PRETTY BABY	
GOT A LITTLE SECRET	
	SHH...
OH, PRETTY BABY	
I HOPE THAT YOU CAN KEEP IT	
GOOD GIRLS NEVER DO IT	
	NO!
THEY WON'T DO IT	
	NO!
'TIL THEY DO	
YOU KNOW THAT I'D BE	
OH SO GOOD FOR YOU.	
WHEN I SIT BY YOUR SIDE	
	BY YOUR SIDE
I JUST CAN'T DESCRIBE	
	CAN'T DESCRIBE
FEELING THESE FEELINGS	FEELING THESE FEELINGS
I FEEL...	
	AHH, AHH, AHH
IT'S SOMETHING DEEP INSIDE	
	DEEP INSIDE
THAT CANNOT BE DENIED	
I CAN'T CONCEAL IT	
THIS CAN'T BE REAL	THIS CAN'T BE REAL
TELL ME IT'S REAL	TELL ME IT'S REAL
	AHHOOH
PRETTY BABY	PRETTY BABY
DID YOU COME TO SAVE ME?	SAVE ME
MY PRETTY BABY	
OH, HOW YOU DRIVE ME CRAZY	CRAZY
I'M IN A HURRY	SHA LA LA
GOT TO HURRY	SHA LA LA
CAN'T YOU SEE	AHH...
IT'S UP TO ME AND YOU	BA DA
AND WE BOTH KNOW WHAT TO DO	BOTH KNOW BA DA DA DOO DAH
PRETTY BABY	BABY
WON'T YOU FEEL IT TOO?	WON'T YOU FEEL IT TOO?
FEEL IT TOO?	
	FEEL IT TOO?
PRETTY BABY I WANT YOU TO	
FEEL IT, TOO	

ROSANNA HYLAND

This is chemistry like Lorraine has never felt before. There's this kind of space-time continuum-y connection to this guy, but she doesn't know what it is. I see it as sort of the hypnosis of Lorraine. She's kind of under a spell with him, and I think this is the moment where you see her just go all doe-eyed and she can't control herself. In the number, all of her inner world is coming out. She's explaining what's happening on the inside, which is just that she's obsessed, and she's so sure that this is meant to be to the point where she is convinced that he feels the same. She keeps interpreting him backing away from her as playing hard to get!

OLLY DOBSON

It's one of my favorite parts of the show. Rosie is impeccable in her attention to detail in flirting, and she is really funny. All these things are going through everyone's minds. She's flirting, but naturally relaxed, yet a little tense. She's Marty's mom, but she's far from motherly. For me, it's just the fact that my mother is hot and I need to get the hell out of there! There's no other option.

I must leave, but I can't, I haven't got any trousers on! And then the music starts. It's a brilliant song. I think it's really a wonderful way for an audience to be exposed to what musical theater can be. It's heightened and it's straight out of a cartoon, and it's playful, it's funny, and ridiculous, just as the situation is. And the audience loves the appearance of the multiple Lorraines!

The trio exits through the window. Lorraine reaches over to touch Marty. He backs away, slips, loses his balance, and falls. THUMP! A female voice calls out.

STELLA (offstage)
Lorraine!

LORRAINE (to Marty)
It's my mother! Quick, put your pants back on!

She throws him his pants, then straightens up the bed.

Future Boy

Having located the 1955 version of Doc Brown on Riverside Drive, Marty has convinced the scientist to follow him to the barn where he's hidden the DeLorean to enlist Doc's help in returning him to 1985. Glen Ballard wrote the original version of the song as a bluesy Pink Floyd–type rock ballad. "It was like 'Wish You Were Here,' and Doc would pull out a sax and start wailing," says the songwriter. Comments John Rando, "I loved Glen's instincts that there should be a lot of heart between Doc and Marty, but it was coming out at the wrong time, because this Doc has just met Marty. Roger was concerned as well, knowing that a rock ballad with long notes was going to be hard to sustain."

BOB GALE

The song began as a Doc/Marty duet, with only the "Future Boy" portion, which went on for several verses. But John thought a song at this part of the story should focus on the plan to get Marty home. So as we prepped the Jerwood Lab, "Future Boy" was jettisoned and Glen wrote a new, peppier song called "One-Way Street." This included the syncopated section of Doc getting the idea. After living with that for a day or two, lightning struck, and we realized that we could do a shorter version of "Future Boy" with the syncopated section as a bridge.

```
                MARTY
        Right. And you've always
        said that you can accom-
        plish anything if you
        just put your mind to it.

                 DOC
        I said that? That's good
        advice. But I just don't
        know how we can gener-
        ate that kind of power,
        Future Boy.
```

NICK FINLOW

In the original opening, it was both Marty and Doc singing. We took Doc out of it, giving the opening to Marty.

```
                MARTY
            FUTURE BOY
         I'M NO FUTURE BOY
       'CAUSE I THINK I'M HERE
              TO STAY
        WHAT'S THE FUTURE FOR
         IF I DON'T GET MORE
             THAN TODAY
         I'M NO FUTURE BOY

          I'LL NEVER FIND
        WHAT I LEFT BEHIND
     THERE'S NOTHING FOR ME HERE
         THERE'S ONLY MORE
        OF WHAT CAME BEFORE
      MY FUTURE'S DISAPPEARED

    NOW EVERYTHING'S UNCERTAIN
    CAN'T SEE BEHIND THE CURTAIN
            I CAN'T GO
           I DON'T KNOW
      WHERE THIS ALL WILL LEAD
```

NICK FINLOW

Then we asked Glen and Alan for something that was more appropriate, not just musically but also in terms of the character of Doc.

JOHN RANDO

I realized I could put dialogue in the middle of it. We needed to reshape the number in order to push the story forward.

Doc, who has been examining the car, hits his head on the gull-wing door, and his face lights with an idea.

DOC
Marty, there <u>is</u> one energy source capable of generating 1.21 gigawatts of electricity: a bolt of lightning!

MARTY
What did you say?

DOC
A bolt of lightning. Unfortunately, you never know when or where it's ever going to strike...

MARTY
We do <u>now</u>.

Marty produces the clock tower flyer, hands it to Doc. Doc reads it, then his eyes light up.

DOC
This is it! It says here that a bolt of lightning is going to strike the clock tower at precisely 10:04 p.m. next Saturday night!!

ROGER BART
I got out of that song line by line, and then the guys wrote a patter section, which we were all happy with:

DOC
THE PHYSICS OF THIS PROBLEM
ARE PERPLEXING
THE MUSCLES IN MY BRAIN
ARE BUSY FLEXING

AS THE GEOMETRIC FORM
OF A PENDING THUNDERSTORM
IS HARD TO CALCULATE
BUT NOW WE HAVE A DATE
AND ALL MY COMPUTATIONS
MUST CONFORM

MARTY
Come on, Doc. Put your mind to it...

DOC
Put my mind to it. Put my mind to it. If we could somehow harness this lightning, and channel it into the flux capacitor...

THE WAY TO GET YOU BACK
TAKES AN EQUATION
AND A ME-TE-OR-O-LO-GI-CAL
OCCASION
AND THEN A LIGHTNING CRACK
BECOMES A POWER PACK

DOC (cont'd)
THAT'S WHAT IT'S GONNA TAKE
NO ROOM FOR MISTAKE
IT'S THE ONLY WAY WE KNOW
TO GET YOU BACK...

In the moment where Doc has the epiphany of how to return Marty to 1985, the musical had reached the same point in the film where Christopher Lloyd looks straight in the camera and utters the line "Next Saturday night, we're sending you back to the future!"

In the musical, Doc's 'Eureka!' moment deserved a full-on celebration. It was Robert Zemeckis who took the number to the next level.

When he had uttered the words "I see tap dancing" to choreographer Chris Bailey, he didn't mean for it to be taken literally. "I do like tap dancing," allows Zemeckis, "but I was trying to convey that I thought the number should have the potential of a big, crowd-pleasing, Busby Berkeley–inspired piece of entertainment." Both Bailey and Rando seized upon that thought. With the earlier number "It Works," they had established that when Doc started singing, the girls show up! They could use that same motif, and this time, the girls would bring along their male counterparts.

Bailey collaborated with David Chase, his dance arranger, to work it out. Despite the word "dance" in his title, Chase explains that he has nothing to do with the movements of anyone performing in any given number. "Chris Bailey has the essential job of the choreographer," he says, "which is to figure out the way that human bodies move through space to help tell the story. My job is to write music for the choreography that supports the movement, that honors what the composer's intention is melodically and even stylistically."

CHRIS BAILEY
David and I played with what it could be and tried to figure out the genre of it. We went the Vegas route with a piece of music which was really cool and totally ridiculous. After that, we just went for it, the whole ensemble dressed in top hats and tails.

A large ensemble in top hats and tails enters from both sides and fills in around Doc and Marty. The barn set disappears, and the video background becomes a moving Busby Berkeley-esque design in celebration of the plan.

ENSEMBLE
THE ONLY WAY TO EVER GET
YOU BACK!

DOC & ENSEMBLE
BACK TO THE FUTURE BOY
YOU'RE THE FUTURE BOY
'CAUSE YOU KNOW WE FOUND
A WAY
YOU'RE THE FUTURE BOY
AND IT'S GONNA BE OKAY
AAH-AAH-AAH
AAH-AAH-AAHAAH-AAH-AAH

DOC
(speaking during the singing)
Alright, Marty, we'll get my car and a winch to tow the time vehicle back to the lab.

MARTY
Y'know, Doc, I can stay a week in 1955. It won't be so bad; it could be cool! You can show me around, we could go to the movies, meet some people. Hey! I could buy some souvenirs and comic books that might actually be worth something when I get back!

MARTY	ENSEMBLE
TO THE	HE'LL STAY!
FUTURE BOY	HE'LL STAY!
	HE'LL STAY!
I'M THE	HE'LL STAY!
FUTURE BOY!	HE'LL STAY!
	HE'LL STAY!
I'M THE	HE'LL STAY!
FUTURE BOY!	HE'LL STAY!
	HE'LL STAY!
	HE'LL STAY!
I'LL STAY!	HE'LL STAY!
	HE'LL STAY!
	HE'LL STAY!
	HE'LL STAY!

Doc had been nodding along, but now it's a terrible idea. He shakes his head and waves his hands, trying to put an end to it.

DOC
Whoa. Whoa! Whoa!!!

Doc's "whoas" put an abrupt end to the song. Most of the ensemble exit as the set transforms back into Doc's lab. But a few remain, with one oblivious chorus girl still singing and dancing "He'll stay! He'll stay!" Doc gets right in her face.

                    DOC
        WHOA!!!!

She stops and holds her hat in embarrassment.

        Marty, that is absolutely
        out of the ques--

Doc notices the remaining ensemble members, gives them a "what are you doing here"

look, opens the door, and shoos them out.

OLLY DOBSON
Oh, it's just so good. Top-notch silliness!

BOB GALE
Giga-kudos to John and Roger for coming up with this gag. It's basically Olsen and Johnson–style vaudeville mayhem, and right out of the classic Daffy Duck cartoon *Duck Amuck*. What makes it so wonderful is that the audience first thinks it's a mistake—which they enjoy, because they want to see how the performers recover. But then they realize that it was all precisely planned and choreographed, so they

love both the joke itself and the fact that the joke is on them too. I think that's why it always gets applause.

ROGER BART
One of the wonderful things about theater, and about the nature of collaboration between the actors and the director, is that we are all in the room, all willing to take chances and try new things, even if they fail miserably. On that specific rehearsal day, John and I were playing with the idea of: What happens when dancers come onstage and things go horribly wrong? It's a unique gag, and one that's not done often. In this number, it became an applause moment, exceeding our expectations.

Something About That Boy

With each new workshop and iteration, everyone's enthusiasm for this number grew. The Dominion version had Lorraine and her girlfriends singing a few stanzas in the lunchroom, followed by a quick chase of Marty and George by Biff and his goons. For the Sadler's Wells showcase, Biff had found his voice to counter Lorraine's doe-eyed verse of infatuation.

"After the Sadler's workshop, Chris Bailey and I began to brainstorm about how to convert 'Something About That Boy' into a full-on Broadway-style production number with the potential to end Act One," says Rando.

In lieu of the film's skateboard chase, Gale simply wrote in the book, "Choreographed Lunchroom and School chase." "The rest was up to John and Chris Bailey," he says with a laugh.

"When we started, it was just a short song, followed by a chase," says the choreographer. "It ended up as the biggest production number in the show." Even before numerous rehearsal sessions at both the Jerwood and Lanterns facilities, Chris Bailey and Darren Carnall did workshops in New York, aided and abetted by Nick Finlow and David Chase.

Rather than navigate a skateboard chase around Hill Valley's town square, as they had in the movie, the "Scooby-Doo chase" (as it was dubbed by Olly Dobson) takes the company through a complete tour of Hill Valley High. Tim Hatley's turntable magic, combined with Finn Ross's video wall and Tim Lutkin's sophisticated lighting, allowed the action to start in the lunchroom and progress through corridors, classrooms, and the gymnasium locker room without ever leaving the confines of the stage.

The priority was to provide an exciting and engaging spectacle, with the safety of the cast being an uppermost priority. "We had talked about George going through the scene with food all over him, either milk or mashed potatoes, courtesy of Biff," recounts Rando, "but our prop guy pointed out that it could get in his wig, or microphone, or on the stage where someone could slip, fall, and injure themselves—far too risky. Then he suggested spaghetti, which was perfect! I remember spaghetti day at school growing up, and it was always wild, with spaghetti everywhere!" One serving of prop, non-skid pasta over George's head later, Coles was properly "dressed" for the event. Earlier in the scene, when summoning the courage to talk to Lorraine, Coles requested that a food cart have a supply of chocolate milk for him to swig before he approaches her and declares himself her "density."

In addition to Chris Fisher and Ben Stevens providing their magic throughout the chase, the physicality of the action would also require the supervision of accomplished stunt performer and fight director Maurice Chan.

"When I first met with John, he explained what he wanted," says Chan. "A spectacular fight with a lot of fun!" Chan and his team, CASCADE, put together several proposals, which they forwarded to the director. "They created this whole stunt sequence with the lockers that was really funny and exciting," says Rando. Once everyone was in sync with the proposed action, Chan and his associate Alexandre Vu traveled from Paris to Manchester, where they conducted intensive workshops with Dobson, Cutler, Coles, Will Haswell (Slick), and Oliver Ormson (3-D). "The actors adapted very quickly to what they were asked to do: body work, fights, reactions, and falls. Their desire to learn made our work a pleasure."

BIFF
(shoving Marty)
Well, well, well. If it ain't the new
butthead in town. You're history now, punk!

MARTY
Hey, whoa--Biff! Your shoe's untied!

Biff falls for it, and Marty decks him. Time
freezes for everyone but Lorraine, who is
delighted by her defender.

JOHN RANDO
It's the perfect opening for the beginning of the song, and it's
very period—where the girl talks before the song kicks into
gear, à la "Leader of the Pack." The "freeze" is a technique
used a lot in theater, and I love it because it's very focused.
"Everyone pay attention *here* for this one moment to get

inside what she's feeling," and then everything happens from
there. I always thought that was such a cute image of her
head framed by the power of the masculine arms, and her
being so teenagey about it, fawning over him.

LORRAINE
A MAN SHOULD BE STRONG
A MAN SHOULD BE TRUE
A MAN CAN BE HANDSOME
BUT HE'S GOTTA COME THROUGH

HE'S GOT TO HAVE MANNERS
BUT NOT TOO POLITE
THERE'S NOTHING MORE BORING
THAN SOMEONE TOO TIGHT

Time moves in slow motion...

RANDO
The women are the first to slowly unfreeze and back up
Lorraine in song.

LORRAINE	GIRLS
	AAAAAAAH
HE'S GOT EVERYTHING	
I'M LOOKING FOR	
HE'S GOT SOMETHING DIFFERENT	AAAAAAAH
HE'S GOT MORE	AAAAOOOH

LEFT Maurice Chan and his stunt team with the cast and
director Rando.

Time now resumes its normal flow.

AIDAN CUTLER

In rehearsals, after the punch we had Biff fall back onto the stage in loads of different ways. One day John asked me to fall straight back on the floor so that I was profiled to the audience. In the last couple of weeks of rehearsal, I got hit, landed with a big thud on the ground, and as the musical cue came for the song to begin, I thought it'd be a great idea to stick my leg straight up in the air at a ninety-degree angle for, like, a forty-five-second freeze-frame. I thought I was either going to get told off or be asked not to do it again. Bob and Glen and Alan were in the room chuckling away, and John Rando was howling. He said that *has* to go in. To this day, it's one of my favorite things to do and at the same time one of the things I regret the most, because every single night, I have a cramp in my thigh and have to get through a five-minute number with the top of my leg completely seized up. But totally worth it for the forty-five seconds of pure laughter it evokes!

BIFF
(to his stooges)
Get him!

OLLY DOBSON

I will never be able to contribute to a number as much as John encouraged us to. He came into a workshop one day with a set of lockers and went, "Let's go!"

Biff and his guys chase Marty and George around the lunchroom while Lorraine and her girls sing. At some point, a janitor moves through with a rolling bin, dumping half-eaten food into it. Biff grabs some knives from the cart.

LORRAINE
THERE'S SOMETHING ABOUT THAT BOY
THERE'S SOMETHING ABOUT THAT BOY
HE'S BRINGING ME SO MUCH JOY
I DON'T KNOW WHAT IT IS
BUT THOSE EYES OF HIS LOOK THROUGH ME

LORRAINE	GIRLS
HE'S GOT EVERYTHING	
THAT A GIRL	THAT A GIRL
COULD NEED	COULD NEED
HE'S NOT LIKE	
THE OTHERS	
HE'S SO SWEET	HE'S SO SWEET
AND THERE'S ALMOST	
NOTHING I WOULDN'T DO	WOULDN'T DO
TO MAKE SURE THAT	
HIS DREAMS COME TRUE	WOOAAAH

Biff throws cutlery knives, which Marty blocks with a lunch tray.

LORRAINE	GIRLS
HOW SPECIAL WE COULD BE	OOOOOH
HE'S SUCH A MYSTERY	WOOAAH
WE COULD MAKE HISTORY	OOOOOH
'CAUSE THERE'S	
SOMETHING ABOUT	SOMETHING ABOUT
SOMETHING ABOUT	SOMETHING ABOUT
SOMETHING ABOUT	SOMETHING ABOUT
THAT BOY	THAT BOY

Our turntable has rotated into a locker area. Marty and George have donned football helmets and jerseys and do calisthenics with three real football players. Biff and his goons look at these guys suspiciously, removing their helmets to see who they are.

BIFF	3-D & SLICK
THERE'S SOMETHING	
ABOUT THAT BOY	ABOUT THAT BOY
THAT I DON'T LIKE	
IT'S JUST NOT RIGHT	HE'S JUST NOT RIGHT
THERE'S SOMETHING	
THAT I'LL DESTROY	I'LL DESTROY
HE'S GONNA PAY	HE'S GONNA PAY
IT STARTS TODAY	
THERE'S SOMETHING	THERE'S SOMETHING
ABOUT THAT PUNK	ABOUT THAT PUNK

3-D

A NO-GOOD CRUMB

SLICK

A FIRST-CLASS BUM

BIFF, 3-D & SLICK

THERE'S SOMETHING THAT JUST AIN'T RIGHT

OLLY DOBSON

Hugh and I suggested that Biff should throw something at us, to get everyone's eyes drawn our way. The illusionist team came in and worked with us on the knife-throwing bit. They also helped us with the gag where we step into two lockers. When Biff opens them, they're empty, and as he turns away, we step out of them again and the chase continues.

ENSEMBLE

THERE'S SOMETHING ABOUT THAT BOY

LORRAINE

I KNOW I JUST MET HIM

ENSEMBLE

THERE'S SOMETHING ABOUT THAT BOY

LORRAINE

BUT I HAVE TO GET HIM

ENSEMBLE

HE'S BRINGING YOU SO MUCH JOY

LORRAINE

AND I JUST CAN'T FORGET HIM
I'M READY TO LET HIM KNOW NOW

3-D
HE'S ON SOME LIST

SLICK
LIKE HE'S A COMMUNIST

Marty and George hide in lockers. Biff and
his guys check the various lockers in search
of them.

BIFF	**3-D & SLICK**
I'M GONNA FIND HIM	
AND WHEN I DO	AND WHEN YOU DO
I'M GONNA UNWIND HIM	GONNA UNWIND HIM
AND BREAK HIM RIGHT	BREAK HIM RIGHT IN
IN THREE	
	(Spoken) Two, Biff.

Biff opens a locker and finds Mr. Strickland
inside, smoking.

BIFF
Oh. Hey, Mr. Strickland.

Biff closes the locker, then Marty and George
exit other lockers. Biff spots them.

BIFF
Get 'em!

STRICKLAND
(also giving chase)
Tannen! You wait till I get hold of you,
young man! You're heading the wrong way
down a one-way street, my friend!

Marty and George run past a cleaning woman
mopping the floor from a bucket on a wheeled
plank. Marty removes the bucket, creating a
makeshift skateboard.

CLEANING WOMAN
Hey! Don't run there! It's wet!

The goons, then Biff, chase after them, each
sliding across the wet floor and offstage.

Our turntable has rotated into a French class,
where Lorraine and her girls are at desks. Other
students have books in front of their faces.

ENSEMBLE	**LORRAINE**
THERE'S SOMETHING	
ABOUT THAT BOY	I CAN'T PUT MY
	FINGER ON IT
THERE'S SOMETHING	
ABOUT THAT BOY	I JUST WANNA
	LINGER ON IT
HE'S BRINGING ME	
SO MUCH JOY	AND THERE'S

LORRAINE & ENSEMBLE
SOMETHING ABOUT THAT

LORRAINE
SOMETHING ABOUT THAT BOY

Marty and George run into the classroom and
sit at empty desks, putting workbooks in front
of their faces. Biff and his guys thunder in
and look for them.

Eagle-eyed viewers might get a glimpse of a French phrase
on the chalkboard behind the lockers, which reads "*La route.
Là où on va. On n'a pas besoin de route.*"* With a special assist
from John Rando's sister Joyce, who provided an appropriate
"lesson plan" for that day's class!

*   Try Google Translate!

LORRAINE	ENSEMBLE	BIFF	STOOGES
		I'M GONNA FIND HIM	
SO I'LL LET THIS FEELING GUIDE ME	OOH WAH OOH	AND WHEN I DO	
	WAH OOH		AND WHEN YOU DO
HE'S TURNED UP THE HEAT INSIDE ME		I'M GONNA UNWIND HIM	
			AND BREAK HIM
AND I JUST CAN'T FORGET HIM		AND I JUST CAN'T FORGET HIM	AAH
I'M READY TO LET HIM KNOW NOW	THERE'S SOMETHING ABOUT THAT BOY	I'M READY TO LET HIM KNOW NOW	
I KNOW I JUST MET HIM	THERE'S SOMETHING ABOUT THAT BOY	HE'LL BE DESTROYED	HE'LL BE DESTROYED
BUT I HAVE TO GET HIM	HE'S BRINGING ME SO MUCH JOY	HE'LL BE DESTROYED	HE'LL BE DESTROYED
SOMETHING ABOUT THAT	SOMETHING ABOUT THAT	SOMETHING ABOUT THAT	SOMETHING ABOUT THAT

[UNDERSCORE]

Using his makeshift skateboard, Marty glides across the stage and right into the arms of Biff! Before the bully can strike, Strickland separates them and Marty escapes. Another piece of the chase ensues, but this time accompanied by an underscore.

When everyone was satisfied with the blocking up to this moment, Alan Silvestri planned to score this specific piece of the action but found that two other crucial scenes had to take priority. As he had on many other numbers, David Chase was more than happy to contribute his considerable talents to the piece.

DAVID CHASE

I consider what I do as the theatrical/dance equivalent of underscoring a movie. I often say that my job is to be invisible. No one should be able to identify the seams between my work and the composer's. I'm most successful if you can't figure out what I did.

ALAN SILVESTRI

It was great that David and Nick had worked on this for Manchester, because we were out of time. When we got back to London after the break, that was one of the things on my list to revisit. I did a full-on mock-up that was all written and designed around that piece of the chase, using motifs and elements from the original score, which we did constantly. We never wanted to reinvent any wheel that was already so beautifully invented.

"There were two things I had immediately excised from the story in very early drafts," states Bob Gale. "One of them was the skateboard chase. It was never going to look very good on the stage, and someone could have gotten hurt." He did, however, pen a brief homage to the boards: "One of the few things I wrote for this number was including the description of a cleaning woman mopping the floor from a bucket on a wheeled plank."

The second omission from the book was the scene where Marty visits George in the middle of the night as "Darth Vader from the planet Vulcan." "With Darth Vader, you wouldn't see your actor's face, and it's pretty difficult to do a song that way." John Rando came up with the idea to resurrect the rogue villain, but not in the same context as Gale and Zemeckis had done in the film. "Again from my grade school memories is the janitor with the toolbelt, and he's got that really big, long box of fluorescent bulbs. I was really keen on the idea that Marty could invent a light saber with a flashlight

and a fluorescent tube. I didn't tell anyone, including Bob." When it occurred during the rehearsal, Gale's distinctive burst of laughter echoed through the room. "When you get that laugh," says Rando, smiling, "you know you got it right!"

From the classroom, the chase proceeds into a locker area. Marty and George climb on top of a bank of lockers and hold off Biff's goons. When George jumps down, Biff climbs up and faces Marty. George grabs a fluorescent tube from a custodian and hands it up to Marty, who wields it like a light saber.

                    MARTY
            BIFF, I AM YOUR FATHER!

                    BIFF
                    WHAT?

Biff disarms Marty, then Marty kicks Biff in the butt and Biff falls down behind the lockers. Marty jumps off and runs stage left. Turntable rotates again, as Lorraine, Betty, Babs, George, Strickland, more students, cheerleaders, and football players fill the space for the number's finale.

LORRAINE   ENSEMBLE
SOMETHING ABOUT
    THAT BOY...   THERE'S SOMETHING
                        ABOUT THAT BOY
                        THERE'S SOMETHING
ABOUT THAT BOY...   ABOUT THAT BOY

                        THERE'S SOMETHING
                        ABOUT THAT BOY

Marty skateboards across the stage past Lorraine, Betty, and Babs, while George is completely ignored.

                    BETTY
            You weren't kidding, Lorraine!

                    BABS
            Where did he come from?

                    BETTY
            Where does he live?

                    LORRAINE
        I don't know, but I'm gonna find out.
        Calvin Klein, I'm gonna make you mine.

Biff has fallen into the janitor's garbage bin we saw earlier and emerges covered in half-eaten spaghetti and other food, humiliated.

In Manchester, the number ended with Biff falling from the top of the lockers into a laundry bin and emerging with a piece of "athletic equipment" draped over his face. For London, it was decided Biff would get a taste of what he gave to George. After landing in a garbage bin, the lunchroom lady loses her grip on a big pot of spaghetti, which Biff now wears as a wig, while Lorraine and company sing the final notes of the glorious number.

                ENTIRE SCHOOL
            SOMETHING ABOUT THAT

                    BIFF
            SOMETHING ABOUT THAT

                ENTIRE SCHOOL
            SOMETHING ABOUT THAT BOY!

Biff stumbles back into the garbage bin.

CURTAIN: Front gauze drops. "To Be Continued" is projected on it.

                END ACT ONE

193

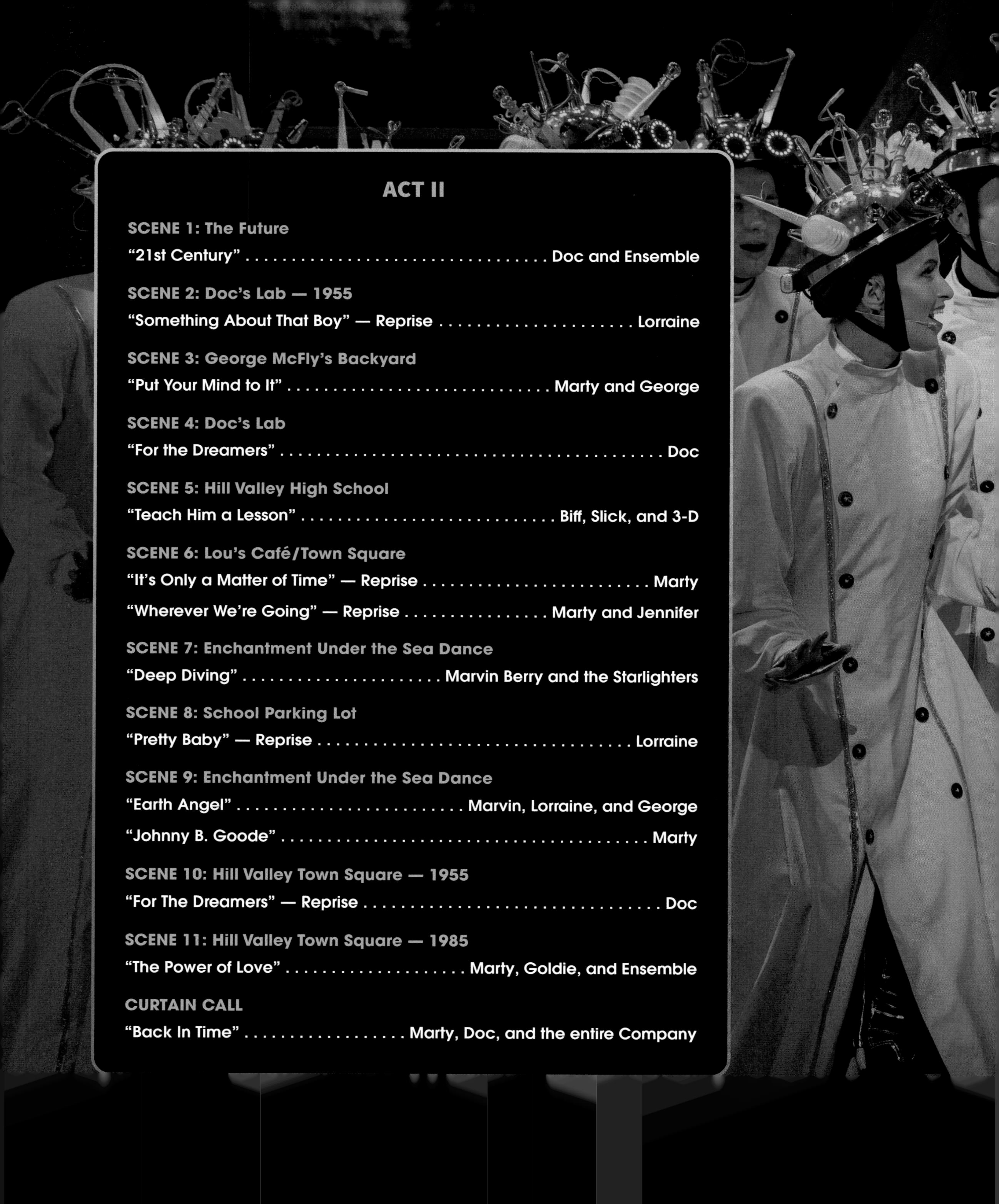

ACT II

SCENE 1: The Future

"21st Century" . . . . Doc and Ensemble

SCENE 2: Doc's Lab — 1955

"Something About That Boy" — Reprise . . . . Lorraine

SCENE 3: George McFly's Backyard

"Put Your Mind to It" . . . . Marty and George

SCENE 4: Doc's Lab

"For the Dreamers" . . . . Doc

SCENE 5: Hill Valley High School

"Teach Him a Lesson" . . . . Biff, Slick, and 3-D

SCENE 6: Lou's Café/Town Square

"It's Only a Matter of Time" — Reprise . . . . Marty

"Wherever We're Going" — Reprise . . . . Marty and Jennifer

SCENE 7: Enchantment Under the Sea Dance

"Deep Diving" . . . . Marvin Berry and the Starlighters

SCENE 8: School Parking Lot

"Pretty Baby" — Reprise . . . . Lorraine

SCENE 9: Enchantment Under the Sea Dance

"Earth Angel" . . . . Marvin, Lorraine, and George

"Johnny B. Goode" . . . . Marty

SCENE 10: Hill Valley Town Square — 1955

"For The Dreamers" — Reprise . . . . Doc

SCENE 11: Hill Valley Town Square — 1985

"The Power of Love" . . . . Marty, Goldie, and Ensemble

CURTAIN CALL

"Back In Time" . . . . Marty, Doc, and the entire Company

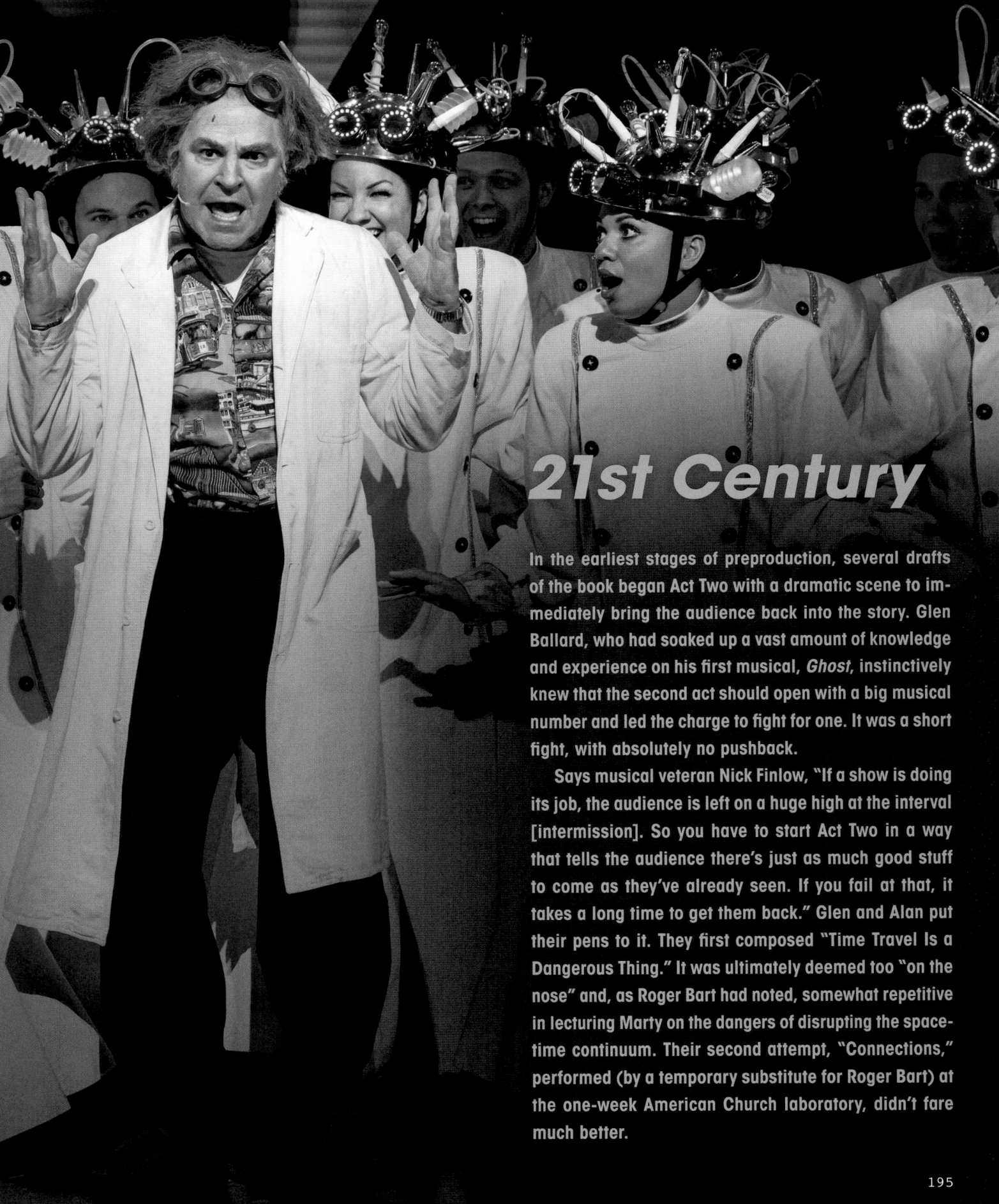

21st Century

In the earliest stages of preproduction, several drafts of the book began Act Two with a dramatic scene to immediately bring the audience back into the story. Glen Ballard, who had soaked up a vast amount of knowledge and experience on his first musical, *Ghost*, instinctively knew that the second act should open with a big musical number and led the charge to fight for one. It was a short fight, with absolutely no pushback.

Says musical veteran Nick Finlow, "If a show is doing its job, the audience is left on a huge high at the interval [intermission]. So you have to start Act Two in a way that tells the audience there's just as much good stuff to come as they've already seen. If you fail at that, it takes a long time to get them back." Glen and Alan put their pens to it. They first composed "Time Travel Is a Dangerous Thing." It was ultimately deemed too "on the nose" and, as Roger Bart had noted, somewhat repetitive in lecturing Marty on the dangers of disrupting the space-time continuum. Their second attempt, "Connections," performed (by a temporary substitute for Roger Bart) at the one-week American Church laboratory, didn't fare much better.

Although the number wasn't seen as a vast improvement on the previous version, the songwriting team had introduced two new concepts to the framework that would carry over to their next attempt to musically welcome the audience back to their seats. Per John Rando's written assessment: "The idea of the Act Two opener being in Doc's mind [a dream] is super fun. The idea that we are in a fifties vision of a futuristic lab is also a real winner!"

In thinking further about what the number needed to accomplish, they examined the basics. It needed to be fun, exciting, a spectacle, clever, tuneful, and engaging. "And then Glen had an epiphany," reveals Bob Gale, "that we could do something that was a complete, absolute non sequitur with everybody going crazy and doing it in a different style. We wanted the audience to think that maybe they walked into the wrong theater!" It

could be anything they could imagine. The possibilities became endless.

In addition to the vast talents of everyone behind the scenes, the show also had musical theater superstar Roger Bart, who would be front and center. Says Alan Silvestri, "The amazing thing about Roger is that we know if all of the electricity went out in a packed theater, Roger could walk out with a lighter in his hand and entertain that room for the next hour and a half until the lighter ran out of gas. He can have that audience in the palm of his hand ad-libbing all by himself. He's that talented."

Roger wouldn't need Glen and Al to provide him with a lighter, but they did give him the brilliant number the show needed. As the curtain rose to begin Act Two, the 1955 Doc Brown appeared out of the ether to introduce the audience to the year 2020.

ACT TWO - OPEN
SCENE I - FUTURISTIC TABLEAU

DOC
NO MORE HUNGER
NO MORE PAIN
THEY'RE THINGS OF THE PAST
PEACE AND LOVE IS
ALL WE'LL EVER KNOW
WITH NO MORE WORK OR MONEY
WE'LL BE HAPPY AT LAST
THE SUN WILL FOLLOW
EVERYWHERE WE GO

ENSEMBLE
THERE'S NO MORE CRIME
IN THE FUTURE
JUST SUMMERTIME
IN THE FUTURE
WE'RE OUTTA TIME
'CAUSE THE FUTURE'S
NOW

DOC
I'VE GOT MYSELF A TIME MACHINE

ENSEMBLE
IMAGINE WHAT WE'LL SEE
IN THE TWENTY-FIRST CENTURY

Images through the porthole
illustrate some of the lyrics.

DOC
FLYING CARS AND STRANGE
MACHINES
WILL FILL UP THE SKIES
TRIPS TO MARS WILL HAPPEN
EVERY DAY
EXERCISING WHILE YOU'RE
SLEEPING
GIVE IT A TRY
WATCH TV WHILE INCHES FALL AWAY

ENSEMBLE
THERE'S NO MORE GLARE
IN THE FUTURE
YOU'LL HAVE GREAT HAIR
IN THE FUTURE
TIME TO PREPARE
'CAUSE THE FUTURE'S NOW

DOC
(Runs his hands over the chair)
I DIG THE WAY THIS BABY FEELS

ALL
I CAN'T WAIT TO BE
IN THE TWENTY-FIRST CENTURY

BOB GALE
Amazingly, what Glen and Al came up with, without any prompting from anyone else, tied into a concept that Bob Z. and I had from the very first days of thinking about a movie called *Professor Brown Visits the Future*. Bob and I had discussed creating a future as seen at the 1939 World's Fair, where we would have flying cars, and all this crazy technology that we'd been promised but never came to pass. Glen created a great framework for this stuff. I sent out a bunch of materials from books that I had about silly predictions of the future, and he took what he could use and put them in there, and later I sent the same stuff to Tim Hatley. Along with Finn Ross, we were trying to figure out what we were going to have on the viewing screen, the imagery and the images. That allowed for a few Easter eggs flying through space.

GLEN BALLARD
It actually started as a bad dream induced by a pastrami sandwich Doc ate for break-fast! Alan and Bob and I were constantly talking about the idea that there's nothing so dated as yesterday's version of the future, and what the future is going to look like. Al and I had a complete vision in mind for our first iteration,

GLEN BALLARD (cont'd)

a vision of the future that's completely utopian and also science-fiction utopian. The whole song was supposed to be the 1950s Doc's view of the future. It's a dream sequence, and it gives us the opportunity for about four minutes to step out of the straight narrative.

ALAN SILVESTRI

The idea of Doc and fantasy was always part of *Back to the Future*. In the original score, the filmmakers are always talking about themes for the characters. The theme for Doc was a manic, up-tempo piece. What that represented was the neurons firing in Doc's mind. It still does, and with the addition of the video wall we can also see what those neurons are creating. So as Glen and I are looking at this completely free field, we're back in Doc's fantasy, as we were in "It Works!" It was always fun to have the freedom for Doc to let his mind run free. And that's what "21st Century" is, but it also had to set up the energy and enthusiasm for the continuation of the show. The number didn't have to be about anything. It just had to get everybody back in the theater, feeling great to enjoy a really fun Roger Bart performance. After that, it becomes "Meanwhile, back in *Back to the Future* . . ." and we start the "movie" again. We were trying to accomplish all of that in that one number spot. I think we got it working pretty well!

JOHN RANDO

I remember when Glen sent me the first draft, thinking it wasn't really a musical theater number, but more of a kind of eighties house music. But I also saw a real potential to it. By that time, Glen had Roger's "voice" fully inside his head. I loved the idea of it being a dream. I did it on another show in China. You can open the act in a dream, and the audience doesn't know it until the end of the song. When we put "21st Century" on its feet in the winter of 2019, I thought it was a super-cool song. Roger was going to be really good in it, and we could do some interesting things with the ensemble.

ROGER BART

It was established that in the number, it was going to be in the future. There was a lot of debate as to whether to set the song as a dream or a nightmare for Doc. I thought of it as potentially a much darker number, with Doc worrying about the potential ramifications of his brilliant invention.

But Glen is kind of an old hippie, a love child, and he and Al wrote Doc as being a true explorer and adventurer, and at his core, everything is about peace and love. He's really caught up in this idea that this is the greatest thing he's ever done, and everything is going to be beautiful and the world is going to be fantastic. That's what the song ended up being.

SO MANY THINGS
I NEED TO SHARE   NEED TO
I'LL GET TO PROVE
THEM EVERYWHERE   PROVE THEM
EXPERIMENTALLY   EXPERIMENTALLY

IN THE TWENTY-   IN THE TWENTY-
FIRST CENTURY   FIRST CENTURY

THE NEW WORLD WILL BE   AAAAAAH
SHINY AND BRIGHT
IT WILL BE A DELIGHT   WOOOAAH
EVERYTHING BA-KE-LITE

AND SINCE WE'VE GIVEN
UP CASH   AAAAAAH
NO MORE MARKETS WILL CRASH
AND WE'LL VAPORIZE TRASH   WOOOAAH

JUST IMAGINE PLAYING ALL DAY   AAAAAAH
AND FOR DOUBLE THE PAY
WOULDN'T THAT BE OKAY   WOOOAAH

IT'S LIKE THE   IT'S LIKE THE
NEW KINGDOM COME AND   NEW KINGDOM

IT'S NOTHING BUT FUN   NOTHING BUT FUN
THE NEW MILLENNIUM   NEW MILLENNIUM

                                   HE'S GOT
I'VE GOT MYSELF   STAR POWER
A TIME MACHINE

                                   A METEOR SHOWER
IMAGINE WHAT WE'LL SEE

                                   AND IT'S HIS HOUR
IN THE TWENTY-FIRST   TWENTY-FIRST
CENTURY   CENTURY

JUST THINK OF WHAT
WE'RE GONNA FIND   HE HAS FINE-TUNED
                                   IT
A WORLD THAT'S GONNA
BLOW YOUR MIND   PUT HIS MIND TO IT

IMAGINE WHAT WE'LL BE   THEN DESIGNED
                                   THROUGH IT
IN THE TWENTY-FIRST   TWENTY-FIRST
CENTURY   CENTURY

Doc joins the ensemble in a dance break. Toward
its conclusion, he gets on a wheeled hoverboard
and glides around as he sings the last verse.

NICK FINLOW

There was a very clear brief from Alan and Glen that it had to sound very EDM,* very eighties. It had to have a very specific sound that didn't exist anywhere else in the show, and necessarily so because it lives in a completely different world from the rest of the show. It doesn't exist in normality, and it doesn't exist in reality. When it came to me, the only thing I did was to write some ensemble parts for it. Glen and Alan not only wrote but "programmed" an incredible dance break in the middle, full of so many sounds, figures and riffs and sound effects. They also wrote to a video of Chris's choreography, which is Alan's usual modus operandi. The whole song is pumping right from the start. There's no way to ignore it, but as everyone

else has said, the clever thing about this number is that it's not really telling any story, and it gives the audience a chance to sit back down and relax without really having to take care of storytelling. It's a bit of an entr'acte.†

TIM LUTKIN

They've got all sorts of weird sounds, and pops and bars of music in, and the lighting mimics the craziness of the soundtrack. It flips and changes and strobes, and its color shifts and energy bleed out into the rest of the number, so it gives Doc and the ensemble a kind of crazy, saturated world like an add-on to the show. I chose to use red, green, and blue as the base palette, as they're the primary colors of light and video technology. It gave the number a real techno feel.

*   Electronic dance music.
†   A dance, piece of music, or interlude performed between two acts of a play.

DOC	ENSEMBLE
I'VE GOT MYSELF A TIME MACHINE	
	IT'S EMPIRICAL
I NEED TO KEEP IT REALLY CLEAN!	
	ASTRO-LYRICAL
BEYOND THIS GALAXY	
	IT'S A MIRACLE.
IN THE TWENTY-FIRST CENTURY	TWENTY-FIRST CENTURY
I REALLY DIG THE STAINLESS STEEL	
	HE'LL GO SO FAR AND WIDE
IT FEELS SO GOOD BEHIND THE WHEEL!	
	HE'LL BE STARRY EYED IN THE COOLEST RIDE.
I CAN'T WAIT TO BE IN THE TWENTY-FIRST- CENTURY	TWENTY-FIRST CENTURY
I CAN'T WAIT TO BE IN THE TWENTY-FIRST CENTURY	WAIT TO BE TWENTY-FIRST CENTURY

[21ST CENTURY PLAYOFF]

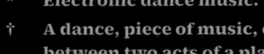

200

COURTNEY MAE BRIGGS

We had these huge, black rubber gardening gloves, which got thrown away because no one could keep them on. When you put your arm out, a glove flew off into someone else's face. They had to go!

JOHN RANDO

Bob Gale had specified they were all in lab coats. We did research and there were lots of images of 1950s versions of what they predicted the future would look like. We looked at fabulous stuff in certain outfits and shoulder pads, buttons in certain ways, and lots of other fun things. That all settled in Tim [Hatley]'s imagination and he drew these outfits. And they dance so well. The shape of the body is really what's important, and Chris Bailey made adjustments to make the costume do the dancing too.

BOB GALE

For Roger's entrance, in the first version I wrote that Doc appeared in what resembled a *Star Trek* teleportation tube. It's a tried-and-true stage effect, and there was no doubt it was going to work. We had another version where he appeared in the DeLorean, and the ensemble actually disassembled the vehicle and then put it back together at the end. That was not going to happen!

ROGER BART

Production had hired a company that was going to help us with the magic and a lot of the illusions. And the old "man in the chair disappearing" was in their bag of tricks. They built a chair in which I was going to be onstage, and it was clearly quite empty, and with a flash of smoke, I would be sitting in it and

create a kind of "How did he get there?" vibe. The mechanics of the chair were tricky.

BOB GALE

It never worked. Every time we tried it, it never worked.

ROGER BART

When the audience saw the chair, and me rotating around à la Captain Kirk, "What am I doing here?" vibe, it sufficed. It turned into one of those things where we had other problems, so we moved on. The hoverboard was an interesting journey . . .

COURTNEY-MAE BRIGGS

We were told there was going to be smoke going across the stage, and with the enhanced lighting, it would look like we were hovering, which was an incredible idea. But to get twenty ensemble members doing it safely was going to be very tricky, because your feet are solidly strapped in. At one point in rehearsal, I fell completely forward and just crawled off the stage because I couldn't get back

up, which was highly amusing to everyone! Strapping on the boards would be quite time-consuming with the large contingent of dancers involved, but because the scene started first thing after the intermission, the ensemble would have had ample time to get into the devices. Removing them to continue the number in an especially small backstage area had the potential to grind the number to a halt.

ROGER BART

They were so incredibly noisy. Every time they tried to do a leap or jump, it sounded like we were living

under a family of elephants. I think the boards were used for probably a single three-hour rehearsal and then they were piled in a box. When you come to the theater and you see your set piece in an alley in the garbage, you know your song's been cut!

[Despite the failure of the custom-made boards to be of use, Roger Bart had a thought about Doc taking a stab at this futuristic mode of transportation.]

ROGER BART

I said to Chris that Doc should be more technologically advanced than everybody

else. Why couldn't I just hoverboard around them? Chris said OK, so we bought a hoverboard.

(This so-called hoverboard was one of the self-balancing battery-operated scooters that hit the market in 2015, labeled as "hoverboards" by merchandisers trying to cash in on the *Back to the Future* connection.)

ROGER BART

I had to use one in a television show, and I had to learn it fast, but I told everyone I wasn't great, and I wasn't promising I could do any tricks. And on that first

Hoverboards Don't Work on Water...or Onstage

In 1989, while doing publicity for the release of *Back to the Future Part II*, Robert Zemeckis, tongue firmly in cheek, made the statement that hoverboards were real and had existed for a number of years, but the efforts of alarmed parents' groups had kept them from mass consumer consumption. Thousands of letters poured into the studio from kids who urged, pleaded, or demanded they be made available to the public. Despite a number of attempts over the ensuing decades, working hoverboards remain solely a conceit of the movie world. In 2019, Chris Bailey attempted to bring them back to life for the musical stage.

After Doc's remarkable arrival at the lab, Bailey and Darren Carnall had developed a routine which saw the ensemble performing the first part of the number with the boards strapped to their feet, performing a synchronized routine around Doc as he tunefully regales the audience with the wonders of the perfect society he's discovered.

The boards themselves were copied from Marty's hoverboard in *BTTF II*, with the addition of two rubber balls embedded in the body, under the foot straps. The inherent problems didn't take very long to surface.

ROGER BART (cont'd)
afternoon, I fell. I was not promoting a lot of confidence.

COURTNEY-MAE BRIGGS
Because we couldn't pull off the hoverboards safely, Roger got the hoverboard, and we'd just see him in the rehearsal room on breaks, just whizzing past, which was very surreal. He was always practicing.

ROGER BART
In over two hundred performances, I haven't, knock wood, fallen [onstage] yet. You know, it's kind of hard to sing while gliding, but it's silly, and people seem to like it. I think it's a great number.

COLIN INGRAM
The number always gets me excited. I just love the fact that we take the audience to a completely different place. The whole concept of what they thought the future would be in the 1950s is such a funny idea. The dance break is great fun and goes into this kind of a nightclub number. It's not what you expect *Back to the Future* to be. I love it when we can do stuff like that.

Put Your Mind to It

In the film, having been asked by Lorraine to take her to the Enchantment Under the Sea dance, Marty pays a visit to George to outline a plan that will help his teenage dad win over his mother and set the timeline back on course. For the stage, this was one of the opportunities identified by Glen Ballard and Alan Silvestri to give the characters a chance to connect in a way that wasn't possible on the big screen. As they had espoused on many occasions, "A song is the musical version of a film close-up," and they took advantage of an already popular segment of the film and gave it a fresh personality, offering a spirited song and dance, as well as a surprisingly emotional moment for George and Marty.

BOB GALE

The first version of this number that Glen and Al wrote for the scene was called "When You're Really Cool," and Marty is teaching George how to *be* cool. It was a good song, but Marty's real focus was to teach George his plan, and whether one was cool or not really had nothing to do with it. I said what we needed here was for Marty to convince George that he could accomplish anything

---

BELOW Left: "Hey you! Get your damn hands off of her!!!" Right: The first recorded instance of the "double wardrobe malfunction."

GEORGE
"Hey, you, get your damn hands off her!" You really think I should swear?

MARTY
Yes, George, dammit-- definitely swear! Then you hit me in the stomach, I go down for the count, and you and Lorraine live happily ever after.

GEORGE
You make it sound so easy. I just wish I wasn't so scared.

MARTY
There's nothing to be scared about. Remember...

MARTY
WHEN YOU WALK
TAKE IT SLOW
LIKE YOU'RE GOING SOMEPLACE
ONLY YOU CAN GO
AND WHEN YOU TALK
DON'T BE LOUD
(GEORGE: WHAT? WHAT?)
FRIENDS ARE FINE
BUT DON'T BE PART OF A CROWD

AND DON'T BE IN A HURRY
EVEN WHEN YOU'RE RUNNING LATE
YOU SHOULD NEVER WORRY
GEORGE, YOU'VE GOTTA CONCENTRATE

Marty indicates that George should mimic his movements, but George's attempt is awkward, to say the least.

```
    PUT YOUR MIND TO IT
    DON'T BE BLIND TO IT
    AND WE CAN FINE-TUNE IT
    JUST PUT YOUR MIND TO IT
            YOUR MIND
```

Marty gives George a disappointed look, shaking his head.

GEORGE
I thought I was doing
exactly what you were doing.

MARTY
Not even close. Let's try
again.

```
    WHEN YOU PLAY
    HAVE SOME FUN
    MAKE IT LOOK LIKE
    YOU HAVE ALREADY WON
```

Marty tosses away his jacket.
George struggles to remove his.

```
    AND WHEN YOU DANCE
        ON THE BONES
    TRY TO SWAGGER LIKE MICK
    JAGGER OF THE STONES
```

GEORGE
What stones? And who's Dick
Jagger?

Marty hops up on a picket fence.
George does the same.

MARTY
STOP APOLOGIZING
(GEORGE: SORRY)
BE ANYTHING YOU WANT TO BE
(GEORGE: NOW I WANNA BE
DICK JAGGER. WHAT DOES HE DO?)
NO OVERANALYZING
LET THE MAN INSIDE GO FREE

```
    PUT YOUR MIND TO IT
    DON'T BE BLIND TO IT
    AND WE CAN FINE-TUNE IT
    JUST PUT YOUR MIND TO IT
            YOUR MIND
```

BOB GALE (cont'd)
if he put his mind to it. With
that direction, they came back
with "Put Your Mind to It."

I intended "put your mind
to it" to be a theme echoing
through the entire show. We
hear Doc say those words
in the very first scene in the
show, and it recurs in several
places, where it's quoted by
Marty, Goldie, and George
as well. This song helped to
crystallize it. It's a testament
to great songwriting, great
performance, and great
choreography that the song
is as crowd-pleasing as it is,
because it's just two guys.

GLEN BALLARD
That was Bob Gale's mantra
from the very beginning, "Put
your mind to it," and for us,
the duet between father and
son was one of our proudest
moments of the whole show. It
couldn't be done in the movie
for obvious reasons, but given
the talents we had, it was a
natural for the scene. Olly's got
moves, and Hugh's physicality and the way he portrays
George are incredible.

JOHN RANDO
This number was solid gold
from the time we had the
first reading. We had these
two great actors with Olly
and Hugh, who was just the
goofiest, most wonderful guy
I'd ever worked with. They
sang it a couple of times, and
I said I think we're going to
really just rock this out. I kept
referring to Mick Jagger and
David Bowie in that video

205

JOHN RANDO (cont'd)

"Dancing in the Streets," and they were both like, "Huh?" I had forgotten that video was almost thirty years old at the time, so I showed it to them on the phone, they thought it was hilarious, and it took off right from there. It was a big, big moment in Act Two, and it's remained that way from the beginning with minimal changes.

CHRIS BAILEY

This was a wonderfully easy number for me, because it's really clear what's happening. They have this great relationship, and what Marty is basically saying is, "Dad—be cool and do this." And what we chose to do was tell him to try some dance moves, and let's get you to try and loosen up, and of course, Hugh, being such a wonderful physical actor, gets to just have some fun by obviously copying Marty badly, and we just theatricalize it through the lyrics of the song and the dance. "When you walk, take it slow . . . follow me." Then there's a Mick Jagger reference and trying to do some Jagger moves. It's a fun way of seeing this gangly guy "stepping" out of his comfort zone.

OLLY DOBSON

When we meet Marty at the beginning of the show, he doesn't have a great relationship with his father. You see that he has a wonderful relationship with Doc, who could be his father or grandfather, and he holds on to that with a great deal of loyalty and love, because he doesn't get that at home. When he sees his mom as a young woman, he wonders: What happened? Then he sees his father, and it all makes sense. Marty has to teach his father what his father should have taught him. It's a lovely moment for people who might not have that relationship with a parent—just to see how Marty loves him and wants to make him feel comfortable and let him know it doesn't really matter what you look like, as long as you're up there trying. Even though it's rock and roll, I've always looked at the song as quite a solemn moment, and a touching one.

Of course, Hugh adds the element of silliness to the song, with George cracking one-liners. As we're dancing, bobbing our heads in sync, I keep encouraging him, saying, "Oh my God, you're doing it! How are you feeling?" And one night, he randomly went, "In my neck."

Marty prompts George to copy his gestures: a pose, a flick of the hair, a little jerk of the head.

MARTY
IT'S A STATE OF MIND
IT'S A POINT OF VIEW
IF YOU WANT THAT GIRL
MAKE UP YOUR MIND TO

Finally, George "gets it."

MARTY
YOU FEELIN' IT, GEORGE?

GEORGE
YEAH! RIGHT IN MY NECK!

Now it becomes a real dancing duet.

MARTY & GEORGE
PUT YOUR MIND TO IT
DON'T BE BLIND TO IT
DRAW A LINE THROUGH IT
JUST PUT YOUR MIND TO IT
PUT YOUR MIND TO IT
AND YOUR BEHIND TO IT
DON'T BE CONFINED TO IT
JUST PUT YOUR MIND TO IT

GEORGE
(points to his head, proudly)
I GET IT! MY MIND!

Marty gives George a hug. Then Marty raises his hand to "high-five" George, but it's a gesture unknown in 1955, so George just waves.

OLLY DOBSON (cont'd)
Someone out there might be thinking, *Is that an appropriate moment?* Everyone else is thinking, *Yes, that is exactly what he would say.* It just adds to the joy of that moment. George is unlocked. For the first time, there's a togetherness, a partnership.

HUGH COLES
It's my favorite moment of the show, and I have so much fun doing that every single night. I love it because I don't have to do anything. It's all on Olly's shoulders. He's doing all the heavy lifting with the singing and dancing. I just get to be George and

listen to what he's saying. It's such a joyous number to go from George not getting it to *getting* it through dance, which was the key for that. I cannot dance, which is apparent, and then George slowly starts to get it and look like Mick Jagger. In that one moment where Olly and

I come to the front [of the stage] and do our headbanging bit, that's the moment where it's really just Olly and me and the audience, and we're all having a really good time.

For the Dreamers

Shortly after the Dominion workshop, Glen Ballard surprised the visiting John Rando and Bob Gale with a new song, "For the Dreamers." Gale had actually heard it a few days prior and couldn't wait to see Rando's reaction.
    "Rando was blown away when Glen sang it," said Gale. Both men knew immediately that it was going to be a moving, heartrending number that would show audiences a side of Doc Brown never before seen, and a telling moment in the relationship between the scientist and the youth.

GLEN BALLARD

Creating this song harkened back to the early steps of the process that Al and I established in determining which characters would get a song, what that song revealed about their characters, and/or what their motivations were in singing it. Here, Doc is very seriously concerned that he may not be able to return Marty back to 1985, but he can't admit that to Marty, so he tries to put a good face on it, not just for Marty, but for himself, too. There's also the subtext of the dawn of the Atomic Age, "What have we unleashed," and that's what Doc is thinking about his invention. *Have I done something terrible in creating this? Have I ruined the life of this innocent kid? Am I just a failed dreamer, destined to be forgotten by history?*

ROGER BART

I found it to be a very personal exploration of what it is to be human, to make mistakes, and to doubt. It was a unique opportunity to finally be asked, where does Doc see himself in

DOC
Ready, set, release!

Marty releases the car. Doc uses the cables to electrify the wire, but as the car passes the wire, a spark sets the model on fire! Doc gasps. He grabs a fire extinguisher and puts it out. Marty reacts in horror.

MARTY
You're instilling me with a lot of confidence, Doc. I can see the handwriting. I'm not gonna make it back, am I? I've got no future.

DOC
Nonsense! This is a small setback, meaningless in the cosmic scheme of things. Do you think I haven't had any setbacks or disappointments before?
(indicates portraits of Edison, Einstein, Franklin, and Newton)
Or these great geniuses? Do you know how many failures Edison had before he figured out the light bulb? Or Einstein and his theory of gravitivity?

MARTY
You mean <u>relativity</u>.

DOC
No, <u>gravitivity</u>! It was his failed theory that led to relativity. These visionaries, my heroes, all had dreams, and they never stopped believing in them.

SO THIS ONE'S FOR THE DREAMERS
WHOEVER TRIED TO MAKE IT
THOUGH VERY FEW
EVER BREAK THROUGH
WE CELEBRATE THEM
WHEN THEY DO
LIONIZE THEM
CALL THEM GREAT
TICKER-TAPE PARADE THEM

BUT THIS ONE'S FOR THE DREAMERS
WHO STRIVE TO BE A WINNER
GO AS FAR AS THEY CAN TAKE IT
EVEN IF THEY DON'T QUITE
MAKE IT
THIS ONE'S FOR THE DREAMERS

LET'S HEAR IT FOR THE DREAMERS
WHO NEVER STOP BELIEVING
ONE GRAIN OF SAND
BECOMES A PEARL
A GREAT IDEA
CAN CHANGE THE WORLD
THEY CAN SEE

ROGER BART (cont'd)

the world as an inventor and as somebody who's going to contribute to society?

BOB GALE

It's the expression of all people who have a dream—to get their movie made, to get their song heard, to get their dance performed, to get their work noticed—and it transcends the trappings of science and invention. The other key aspect, that's not in the movie, is how Marty reacts to it. When Doc sings "It Works!" Marty is caught up in all this manic insanity, but in "For the Dreamers," Marty is getting a much better sense of who his friend really is.

ROGER BART

This was the perfect time and number to let the audience in on how much they care about each other. In the 1985 intro segment and the first-act interactions between the two of them, you see the fully realized great friendship of the first scene, but it goes quickly. In their second scene of the first act [with Marty and 1955 Doc], you see the seeds of what will be a great friendship, even though they're somewhat strangers to each other, at least from Doc's perspective. "Dreamers" is the first time you see them being real friends with each other, active friendship support—"I got you, I believe in you, we got this. We're going to do it." That's a great thing to touch on in the show. It's very human, isn't it?

JOHN RANDO

For something I never expected from the beginning, now it's something I can't imagine the show without. The only issue we had was where to put it in the show. Bob tried it in a few different places, including as the opening of the second act, which didn't work. After the American Church laboratory, I suggested moving it to after Doc watches the video and becomes aware of his own mortality. But it still wasn't right.

DOC (cont'd)
WHAT OTHERS DON'T
TRY THINGS OTHERS WON'T

SO THIS ONE'S FOR THE DREAMERS
WHO LIVE ON INSPIRATION
GO AS FAR AS THEY CAN TAKE IT
EVEN IF THEY DON'T QUITE MAKE
IT
THIS ONE'S FOR THE DREAMERS

AND I KNOW WHAT IT'S LIKE
TO BE MISUNDERSTOOD

AND I KNOW HOW IT FEELS
TO BE TOLD YOU'RE NO GOOD
BUT I COULDN'T GIVE UP
NO, I NEVER WOULD

PEOPLE JUST TOOK
ADVANTAGE OF ME
MY DISTRACTIONS JUST
CONSUMED ME
BUT FOR EVERY ONE THAT
GETS IT RIGHT
THOUSANDS MORE KEEP UP
THE FIGHT
THEY BURN THE FIRES DEEP
IN THE NIGHT
UNTIL THEY LOSE THE LIGHT
AND MOST JUST DISAPPEAR
AND WE NEVER HEAR OF THEM

SO THIS ONE'S FOR THE DREAMERS
WHO HAVE THE GUTS TO RISK IT
TO TAKE A CHANCE
ON WHAT THEY THINK
CAN'T STARE THEM DOWN
'CAUSE THEY DON'T BLINK
RIDICULE THEM
CALL THEM OUT
NO ONE SEES WHAT THEY'RE ABOUT

YES, THIS ONE'S FOR THE
DREAMERS
WHOSE NAMES WE DON'T REMEMBER
THEY WERE CLOSE BUT NO CIGAR
AND WE DON'T KNOW WHO THEY ARE

MARTY
But I know who you are. And
this dream will come true,
Doc. I know it will. Because
I really do believe in you.

Marty hands Doc the model car,
then flips the blackboard back
to the equations.

DOC
Thank you, Marty, I...
appreciate that.

MARTY
Can I get you anything? A
sandwich, maybe?

DOC
(smiles wryly, shrugs)
Just a little more time.
There never seems to be
enough.

MARTY
(sighs with some melancholy)
I hear you. (a beat) G'night,
Doc. Pleasant dreams.

Marty exits, and Doc concludes
the song with new confidence.

DOC
THIS ONE'S FOR THE DREAMERS
THIS ONE'S FOR THE DREAMERS...
LIKE ME

BOB GALE

We had yet to figure out what, if anything, we were going to do about Doc showing Marty his plan to get him back to 1985 with the model of town square and the toy car. Roger had told John Rando that he really hoped we could do it as he loved the scene. When Tim Hatley came up with the concept of the model built on the backside of a blackboard in Doc's lab, it fell into place. The failure of the demonstration made the song naturally follow. I had to rejigger the structure of Act Two to give it its due, but it was the perfect spot in which to showcase both the new song and the vocal and emotional brilliance of Roger Bart.

ROGER BART

It was an appropriate place to frame the number when Doc was showing Marty a failed attempt on how he was going to get him back to 1985. Where was Doc's mental state? His emotional state? If you infuse doubt, what is that doubt about? Is it about being a failure? It plays into a pathology of any person who has any insecurity about themselves. It was a slightly risky venture for three and a half minutes onstage because we abruptly shift from slapstick to pathos. This is a beautiful piece of writing that captures the idea of dreaming big and opening your intellectual world. It works.

Teach Him a Lesson

Since last seeing Biff in a garbage can covered in spaghetti at the end of Act One, audiences had to wait twenty-five minutes into an incredibly jam-packed second act before the bully would reemerge. And Biff, out for vengeance, was delighted to learn where "Calvin Klein" was going to be on Saturday night.

BOB GALE

The true rationale for the scene was to give Marty time to change into his dance wardrobe. In the movie, we did it in a cut, but that couldn't be done onstage. Colin and John suggested having Biff show up at Doc's house and attempt to destroy the DeLorean, but I felt that was out of character, and I didn't want Biff and Doc in the same scene. Ultimately, I wrote a version of the scene from *BTTF-II* in which Biff harasses Lorraine on the street a day before the dance. Seeing Biff learn where he'd ultimately find "Calvin Klein" solved another concern I had. In the movie, Biff's arrival at the car is a total surprise: The audience thinks it's George who is approaching, and we don't see that it's actually Biff until he opens the door. Onstage, there was no way to do the surprise, so telling the audience Biff was coming ahead of time made that a non-issue. This was at the same time Glen added the Biff part to "Something About That Boy," so it made sense to reprise it here, and by the time we got to Sadler's Wells, it was pretty well worked out.

JOHN RANDO

After the public shame and ignominy he suffered at the hands of Marty in "Something About That Boy," we couldn't allow Biff to disappear and not be seen or heard from until he arrives later at the dance for the climactic resolution between him and George. It's a short song, but it also gave us a chance to have even more fun with the goons trying in vain to correct some of Biff's malapropisms.

AIDAN CUTLER

It was originally just referred to as "Something About That Boy Reprise," because it literally started as a reprise, but directly from Biff's perspective, without Lorraine's participation.

GLEN BALLARD

We have a number of reprises in the show. If you have the audience for two and a half hours with a twenty-minute intermission, and if everything they hear is a brand-new song, I think it's too much for them to take in. The reprise is a way of paying things off. If you hear a song for the very first time, and if you strategically repeat and reprise it somewhere along the way,

> **BIFF**
> Well, well, well. Ain't that an interesting redevelopment. Ya hear that, guys? Calvin Klein's going to the sissy dance Saturday. (Calling after Lorraine) Well, <u>we</u> wouldn't be caught dead at a thing like that, would we, guys?
>
> **3-D**   **SLICK**
> Yes!   No!
>
> **BIFF**
> THERE'S SOMETHING ABOUT THAT PUNK
> THAT I DON'T TRUST
> HE'S DANGEROUS
> THERE'S SOMETHING THAT
> DON'T ADD UP
> ARITHMETIC
> AND A HOCKEY STICK
> THERE'S SOMETHING ABOUT THAT GUY
>
> **3-D**
> SINCE HE APPEARED
>
> **SLICK**
> IT'S REALLY WEIRD
>
> **BIFF**
> THERE'S SOMETHING
> THAT'S ALL MESSED UP
> IT DON'T MAKE SENSE
> HOW HE'S DRESSED UP

GLEN BALLARD (cont'd)
it's a huge connective tissue to what started it in the first place. Ultimately, a stage musical should be a big circle. You start in one place and go all the way around, and hopefully you end up with a big character arc, but everything has got to be somewhat familiar to everybody for them to completely digest and enjoy it. With this song, Biff had already acknowledged from the first time we heard it that there was "something" about that boy that he didn't like, but now he's announcing his intentions to go one step further and "teach him a lesson."

SHANE O'RIORDAN (3-D, BIFF UNDERSTUDY)
"Teach Him a Lesson" was the very first number I ever heard from the show, the reason being that I knew Katherine Pearson before I had started the show. When I was auditioning, it was one of the songs I had to perform, so I texted her and asked if there was anything I needed to look out for. She had a recording and she sent it to me. The song went through a number of changes when we were rehearsing for London. In the beginning, when Will [Haswell] and I sing, we were just repeating what Biff says,

213

Play It Again!

As Glen Ballard notes, a number of songs were deemed worthy of a mini-reprise:

- Marty sings "Got No Future" in Lou's Café after meeting young George McFly in 1955, and after he thinks Doc is dead in 1985.

- Lorraine sings "A man should be strong" from "Something About That Boy" to Marty in Doc's lab, and a snippet of "Pretty Baby" before she kisses Marty in the car at the dance.

- "Only a Matter of Time" resurfaces at the very end of the show just before the curtain calls.

- Doc sings a brief refrain of "For the Dreamers" on the ledge of the clock tower as he attempts to reconnect the conducting wires.

SHANE O'RIORDAN (cont'd)
and ultimately, it changed into us trying to correct what he says and turns his part into more of a joke. It's very much fun to play around with that sort of thing and just be a bit goofy. I'd say it's a little more fun playing Biff and doing this number because you get to lead it, and tell off the Goons when they're being too much. At the same time, it's still a lot of fun being a Goon, because we get to do most of the things that Biff does, but I take myself a lot less seriously when I'm a Goon!

AIDAN CUTLER
The writing of this song is so ingenious. It's absolutely brilliant. Glen and Alan have written it in such a way that even in song, Biff is so innately thick that he can't string a simple sentence together, and he manages to muck up all the words in the song. I knew how inspired it was when I was rehearsing in London. Nick Finlow had given me a track of himself playing the number in rehearsals, and I would sing the lyrics in my home. One of my housemates asked me, "Are you singing the right lyrics there? Because the words don't make sense!"

BIFF
I'M GONNA FIND HIM
AND WHEN I DO

I'M GONNA REMIND HIM
OF WHAT A MAN CAN'T DO

I'M GONNA TEACH HIM A LESSON
THAT HE'LL ALWAYS FORGET

TEACH HIM FOR MESSING WITH
A MAN HE WON'T REGRET

YES, I'M A MAN HE WON'T REGRET

TEACH HIM A LESSON
THAT I HAVEN'T LEARNED YET

TEACH HIM FOR MESSING WITH
A MAN HE WILL FORGET

YES, I'M THE MAN

I'M THE MAN

I'M THE MAN

GOONS

AND WHEN YOU DO

OF WHAT A MAN CAN DO

NEVER FORGET

A MAN HE <u>WILL</u> REGRET

<u>WILL</u> REGRET

(spoken)
But you <u>have</u> learned it,
Biff.

A MAN HE <u>WON'T</u>

YOU'RE THE MAN

YOU'RE THE MAN

HE'LL BE DESTROYED!

BIFF & GOONS
THERE'S SOMETHING ABOUT
THAT BOY

BIFF
IT'S HEADS HE WINS
AND TAILS I LOSE

BIFF & GOONS
THERE'S SOMETHING THAT
I'LL DESTROY

BIFF
I'LL PAY HIS DUES
I'LL SHINE HIS SHOES
(spoken)
Saturday night! Ha ha ha ha ha!

They've gone back inside the
door to the school. Biff laughs
malevolently--and then starts
coughing.

Wherever We're Going/ Only a Matter of Time (Reprise)

Alone in Lou's Café, after finishing his letter of warning to Doc, Marty once again checks the photo of himself and his siblings. To his horror, his sister, Linda, completely fades away before his eyes. His dismay turns to alarm when another thought occurs to him: Have his actions also affected Jennifer?

Seeing the Polaroid of the two of them unchanged, Marty breathes a sigh of relief. He appears in the deserted town square and sings of his love for the girl that no amount of time or distance can diminish. Jennifer appears and they serenade each other together, thirty years apart.

BOB GALE

The reprise was Colin Ingram's idea. He deserves the credit for that. There were different versions of how it was going to be staged. We had one version in the early workshops where the first Marty/Jennifer scene takes place in a 7-Eleven, which was the eighties equivalent of Lou's Café. The "across time" duet would have Marty in Lou's Café in the fifties and Jennifer in the 7-Eleven in the eighties. We couldn't afford an extra set, but as we came to learn on more than one occasion, it wasn't necessary. Doing it on the town square worked just fine, and the number does exactly what it's supposed to do.

COLIN INGRAM

I was quite vocal in that I thought we had to see Jennifer again. We couldn't just

ABOVE Jennifer's bench in the West End Production is an easter egg referencing the movie's sequels.

Marty pulls out the Polaroid photo of Jennifer and sighs relief.

> **MARTY**
> Thank goodness <u>you're</u> not collateral damage.

He pockets the photo and stands as the cafe set disappears, leaving Marty, stage right, in a surreal tableau as the 1955 "Welcome to Hill Valley" sign and park bench appear next to him, with a black starlit background.

> **MARTY**
> I DON'T KNOW HOW I ENDED UP HERE
> IT'S SO HARD TO BELIEVE
> THERE'S ONE CHANCE AND THIS MUCH IS SO CLEAR
> IF I MISS IT
> I MAY NEVER LEAVE
> I'LL BE STUCK IN THIS DREAM
> CAN'T WAKE UP
> CAN'T GET FREE
>
> DESTINY
> I'M NOT SURE WHAT THAT MEANS
> AND HISTORY
> WELL IT'S NOT EVERYTHING THAT IT SEEMS
> WILL I BE ON MY WAY
> OR WILL I HAVE TO STAY?
> BUT IT'S ALWAYS A MATTER OF TIME

He plops onto the bench as Jennifer appears stage left along with a 1985 bus bench and streetlight, creating a 1955/1985 split set. She sits on the complementary bench and sings.

JENNIFER
WE'VE BEEN WAITING A LIFETIME,
IT SEEMS,
FOR A CHANCE TO BREAK THROUGH
NOW I KNOW ALL OUR HOPES AND
OUR DREAMS
ARE REAL AND ABOUT TO COME TRUE
IT'S SO EASY TO SEE
THIS IS ALL MEANT TO BE

JENNIFER
WHEREVER WE'RE GOING
IS ALRIGHT WITH ME
THERE'S NO WAY OF KNOWING
JUST WHERE THAT WILL BE
WE'LL GET WHERE WE'RE
GOING EVENTUALLY
WHEREVER WE'RE GOING
IS ALRIGHT

IT'S ONLY A MATTER OF TIME

ONLY A MATTER OF TIME

ONLY A MATTER OF
TIME.

MARTY
THERE'S NO WAY OF KNOWING
JUST WHERE THAT WILL BE
WE'LL GET WHERE WE'RE
GOING EVENTUALLY
WHEREVER WE'RE GOING
IS ALRIGHT
IF YOU'RE THERE WITH ME

ONLY A MATTER

I MAY NOT GET OUT ALIVE

TIME.

COLIN INGRAM (cont'd)
see her in the first act and then she disappears until the finale. Jennifer needs to be there to validate the love story between her and Marty, and for her to be one of the strongest incentives for him to fight to get back to 1985.

COURTNEY-MAE BRIGGS
I love the reprise in the second act, because I think the audience is really ready for that moment. It's beautifully staged in how we're on opposite sides of the stage, and we're hearing each other but in separate worlds, thirty years apart.

OLLY DOBSON
Marty's been on high energy through the whole show and just trying not to lose his head. And then, all of a sudden, he remembers everything he's doing this for. He loves Jennifer, but he hasn't had the time to sit down and think about her. It's very lovely that we see her across

the eeriness and wonderfulness of that moment. And Marty is singing in a way that we haven't seen before. He's really vulnerable and scared, "Will I be on my way, or will I have to stay?" This is a big moment with so much weighing on it. He knows she's OK but he doesn't know if he'll ever see her again.

Deep Diving

Just as the team had replaced the film's "Mr. Sandman" with the original song "Cake," it was decided to replace the cinematic instrumental "Night Train" with another newly created Ballard/Silvestri offering to usher in the Enchantment Under the Sea dance, featuring the musical stylings of Marvin Berry (Cedric Neal) and the Starlighters.

Once again, it was a choice influenced by what the music had done in the film versus what would work best for the musical. In the film, the dance was introduced with close-ups of the band, dolly shots that traveled through the crowd of dancing high-schoolers, the camera finding George McFly taking a few tentative dance steps while waiting for the appointed time in which he'd run out to "rescue" Lorraine from Marty's "advances," as well as Mr. Strickland keeping an eye on the proceedings, all accompanied by the instrumental of the 1952 song "Night Train." Onstage, those separate elements were all immediately on view to the audience as the lights came up in the school gymnasium and the music began.

JOHN RANDO
There were a number of reasons to start off the dance with "Deep Diving." For the scene itself, a song will establish everything more quickly than an instrumental. I was spitballing with Glen, and I was reminded of a song from 1959 called "The Madison," which was a line dance number that had the kind of groove that we needed. Glen got it immediately and came back with this perfect song. It's sexy, there's romance in it, a sensuality painting the picture of the high school guys looking for the right girl. Looking for love. All of that stuff was a great way to introduce the sequence.

ALAN SILVESTRI
"Night Train" in *Back to the Future* was an instrumental, and it served the purpose of having the band playing while setting up the scene. You didn't need it to be sung, in a sense, as it might have taken some of the shine off "Earth Angel." Onstage, it's a totally different environment, where you can't do a slow camera move. When the lights come on, the lights are on—everybody sees everything. And we have Cedric, who is fantastic. This song was an opportunity to have something that sets us up dramatically that is still fun, and is keeping the whole stage, the band, the foreground, alive, and it's great!

BOB GALE
We did have "Night Train" at one time, and John said, "Let's do something original here." And we had Cedric, and in fact, we had promised if he agreed to play both Goldie Wilson and Marvin Berry that we would give him another original song

<u>SCENE 7: INT. SCHOOL DANCE – NIGHT, 1955</u>

The Enchantment Under the Sea dance. Marvin Berry and the Starlighters play on a dais as students dance, while a fidgety George, in a white tuxedo, paces, checks his watch, and interacts with Mr. Strickland.

          MARVIN
Yesterday, I asked my buddy Glen to write a song especially for tonight. Here it is. Hope you like.

IN THE SOUTH SEA ISLANDS
THEY DIVE FOR PEARLS
IN THE USA, THEY DIVE FOR GIRLS
IF YOU TAKE YOUR TIME
AND PLAY IT COOL
THERE'LL BE SOMEBODY WAITING
AT THE END OF THE POOL

AND EVERYBODY SAYS THAT YOU SHOULD
LOOK BEFORE YOU LEAP
AND WHEN I LOOK AT YOU
I'M READY TO GO

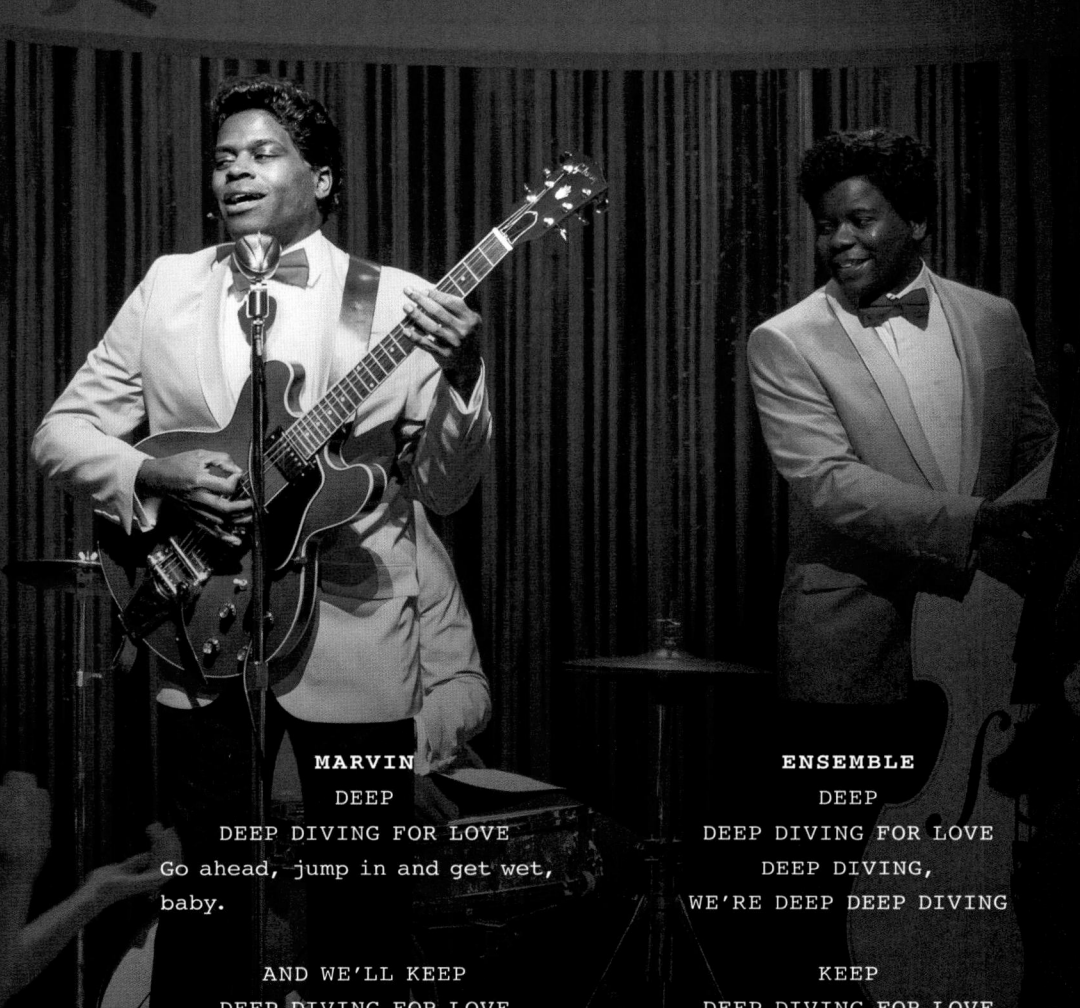

MARVIN

DEEP

DEEP DIVING FOR LOVE

Go ahead, jump in and get wet,
baby.

AND WE'LL KEEP

DEEP DIVING FOR LOVE

Plenty of fish in <u>this</u> sea.

THERE IS JUST SO MUCH

THAT WE'VE BEEN WAITING TO EXPLORE

WE'LL FIND OUR BURIED TREASURE ON

THE OCEAN FLOOR SO

KEEP

DEEP DIVING FOR LOVE

ENSEMBLE

DEEP

DEEP DIVING FOR LOVE

DEEP DIVING,

WE'RE DEEP DEEP DIVING

KEEP

DEEP DIVING FOR LOVE

WE'LL STOP DRIVING,

WE'LL BE LATE ARRIVING

DOO WAPAAH

DOO WAAH

DOO WAAH

OCEAN FLOOR

KEEP

DEEP DIVING FOR LOVE

MARVIN

...at the Enchantment Under the Sea dance...

So thank you, folks, thank you. Right now, yours truly, Marvin
Berry and my band, the Starlighters, are gonna switch over to
records while we take a little break. But we'll be right back,
so don't nobody go nowhere.

AND WE'LL KEEP

DEEP DIVING FOR LOVE

George checks his watch and realizes it's time for him to go.

BOB GALE (cont'd)
for Marvin. Why wouldn't we?
It's also a testament to Glen,
in that people hear it and
think it's a real period song.

GLEN BALLARD
We had a lot of conversa-
tions about what the kids
were going to dance to
before "Johnny B. Goode"
and "Earth Angel." It just
felt right to create this fifties
kind of cruising song and
infuse it with the double en-
tendre—deep diving for love.
And it shows us a different
Cedric than we saw when he
was Goldie.

CEDRIC NEAL
It is so much fun to play
Marvin. My debut in the West
End was in *Motown*, and that
was doo-wop—the groups of
the fifties and sixties. I'm a
very jazzy gospel singer. My
singing is full of melisma, riffs,
licks, whatever you want to
call them. When we started
working on "Deep Diving,"
Nick Finlow came to me and
said, "I know what you can
do, but you need to be true to
the authenticity of 1950s doo-
wop, going back, and trying
to emulate the Four Tops, the
Platters, the Spinners, and
even, from the tail end of the
fifties, the Beach Boys." To be
producing a doo-wop number
for the dance took me back to
1955, and every time I do that
song, I'm actually in the gym
at the Enchantment Under
the Sea dance. I just feel it,
and I love that it was written
specifically for me!

Earth Angel/Johnny B. Goode

The Enchantment Under the Sea dance had always been a daunting piece of the movie to bring to the musical stage. Included amid the music were pivotal action, plot points, last-minute roadblocks, watershed moments, and ultimate resolution—all before leading to the even grander, more thrilling, climactic finale.

- George has just laid out Biff in one punch.
- He takes Lorraine by the hand and leads her into the school.
- Marvin and the Starlighters help Marty out of the trash can, injuring Marvin's hand and rendering him unable to play.

Marty pulls out the fateful photo. We see it projected: Marty is still all alone!

            MARTY
No!!! The photo hasn't changed!
        (checks his watch,
        suddenly realizing)
The kiss! They have to kiss on the dance floor by nine thirty-five!
        (to the Starlighters)
Hey, guys! You gotta get back in there and play!

            REGINALD
Sorry, man, Marvin can't play with his hand like that, and we can't play without Marvin.

            MARTY
But you've gotta play! If there's no music, they won't dance, they won't kiss, they won't fall in love, and I'm history!

            MARVIN
Hey, man, the dance is over--unless you know somebody who can play the guitar.

Marty, Marvin, and the Starlighters all turn directly to face the audience and give them a brief, knowing look. As the scene changes back to the dance, they spin on their heels in unison and take their place on the bandstand.

That knowing look was just another little "wink" to the audience from John Rando, telling them, "We know that you know that we know that we're in a musical and that you know exactly what's coming now."

SCENE IX: INT. THE ENCHANT-
MENT DANCE – NIGHT, 1955

Marty and the Starlighters step onto the dais, Marty playing Marvin's guitar. Students dance as the song intro begins.

George and Lorraine are together, talking, stage right.

            LORRAINE
George. Where have you been all my life?

            GEORGE
Oh. You know, hanging around...

220

Do you want to dance?

                   GEORGE
Yes. Yes.

                      WILL YOU BE MINE?
They begin dancing,   MY DARLING DEAR
awkwardly.   LOVE YOU ALL THE TIME
                        I'M JUST A FOOL
        LORRAINE   A FOOL IN LOVE
Aren't you going to   WITH YOU
kiss me, George?

           GEORGE
Oh, gee, I don't know...

        SMART-ASS GUY
Scram, McFly, I'm cutting in!

A SMART-ASS GUY pushes George aside. M
immediately begins missing chords and s
to collapse onstage.

The guy gropes Lorraine as he "dances"
her. George shuffles off in defeat.

          LORRAINE
George! Help me!

Pulsing UNDERSCORE replaces the song a
situation turns dire.

The underscore was, of course, the work of Alan Silve
he had created for this very moment in the film. Onst
vin and the band freeze, as do all the dancing couples
the first notes of dis-chord begin. With all of the sepa
of action going on simultaneously, Rando needed to f
where he wanted to focus the audience's attention.

JOHN RANDO
"Earth Angel" is a remarkable moment in the show. Th
being sung by Cedric, who's terrific and can sing it so b
He's onstage behind George and Lorraine, but we're in
We don't have a camera up close to put on the two sta
everything is going on around them, and again, becau
is a musical, we don't usually have background music,
was another instance where Alan Silvestri's underscor
movie was really helpful. We worked very hard on that
repeat it, change things, restage—where does George
boy down? Where does he hug Lorraine? Where does h
Where's Marty? How does he wake up?

The issue of how to deal with Marty's impending dis
ance was a troublesome one, with much discussion
to achieve it. Several ideas were explored. "We thou
about using a projection that would be of the world
him, making it look like he was vanishing," says Gale
have smoke coming up from the ground and project

disappearing." Another idea saw the construction of a mechanism that allowed Marty to collapse to the ground, with the guitar remaining behind, floating in midair. Said Gale, "I hated that idea, and I'm glad the mechanism never worked." The solution came to Rando, with the inspiration provided by Silvestri and Robert Zemeckis.

JOHN RANDO

I realized the real story was actually George and Lorraine kissing, and that's where the focus needed to be! That freed me from having to worry about Marty disappearing. In Manchester, he just crumbled and fell to the ground, and we put a little smoke on him. We wanted the audience totally focused on the kiss.

George gets his mojo back and firmly yanks the guy away from Lorraine.

> #### GEORGE
> Excuse me.

George shoves him, Lorraine trips him, and as the music score swells, finally our two lovers kiss.

As George takes Lorraine in his arms, the world comes back to life. In addition to Silvestri's lush arrangement of the final verse of the song, Nick Finlow added a full chorale, bringing the number to an even more passionate crescendo that has George and Lorraine singing the last two lines, because, as every aficionado of musical theater can attest, when a couple is truly in love, they sing to each other:

MARVIN	ENSEMBLE
THE VISION OF	
YOUR HAPPINESS	
WHOA, WHOA, WHOA	
EARTH ANGEL,	
EARTH ANGEL	EARTH ANGEL,
PLEASE BE MINE	EARTH ANGEL
MY DARLING DEAR	OOOOOH
LOVE YOU ALL THE	MY DARLING
TIME	I LOVE YOU

> #### GEORGE & LORRAINE
> I'M JUST A FOOL
> A FOOL IN LOVE
> WITH YOU.

Immediately, Marty stands back up, totally fine, and finishes the song.

When his parents finally kiss, a spotlight hits Marty, who immediately springs up, fully recovered. Note: When the show moved to London, Marty's collapse was enhanced by a slow flicker of the light on him, as conceived by Tim Lutkin. As Olly's collapse became more pronounced, so did the flicker effect, until the kiss and the return of the solid spotlight beam signaled his full recovery.

OLLY DOBSON

It's a rapid scene, and it was all about blocking around George and Lorraine. I always had to make sure my sight was fixated solely on them physically, because if anyone in the audience was looking at me, they needed to see that despite my distress, I was focused on them, and everyone needed to see that kiss. Obviously, the music helps us as well.

The Audience Is Gonna Love It!

Sure, Doc is waiting outside the school with the time machine to send Marty back to 1985, but when Marvin Berry suggests he does another number . . . something that "cooks," Marty figures he can spare another couple of minutes to realize his rock-and-roll dream.

Although the classic "Johnny B. Goode" was slightly condensed for time, the efforts that went into staging and performing the number were not. "One of the things that distinguishes the musical experience from the movie is that we have actors singing the songs live," comments John Rando, "and we want to deliver the 'Earth Angels' and 'Johnny B. Goodes' and to make sure the audience believes what they're experiencing."

Choreographer Chris Bailey agreed, and for all the Enchantment Under the Sea dance numbers he brought in some additional expertise. "Swing dancing is a specific skill," he explains, "one that we don't teach in musical theater school. I did a show directed and choreographed by Susan Stroman in which the whole second act was based on West Coast swing dance. For that show, we had four days of intensive swing 'class,' where we learned all the 'rules' that are inherent in social dancing. I've seen shows that have a swing dance element where it's a bunch of musical theater dancers faking it in the style of swing. I wanted ours to be as authentic as possible, and asked Jenny Thomas, a woman who lives and breathes this style, to come in and teach a class. Darren, Laura [Mullowney, dance captain], and I had already choreographed the routines, but we wanted the actors to have this crash course so it wouldn't feel so foreign in style to them during that part of the process."

Bailey notes that swing dance was used in all of the Enchantment dance numbers, including "Deep Diving" and "Earth Angel," in addition to "Johnny B. Goode," with one of the most important components being "partnering" and the "lift." "They're skills that not everyone is tuned for," says Bailey. "The lifting is so important in terms of learning how to lift and support your partner without hurting them. People sometimes forget their partner is flesh and blood in the moment they're trying to throw them over their head. We have crazy lifts in 'Johnny B. Goode,' and a style unfamiliar to the run-of-the-mill musical theater–trained actor/dancers. I needed to get them more comfortable with it before we added the throwing part. It was a *lot* of fun, and so beneficial to the process. I plan to do this with every subsequent cast!"

Go, Olly, Go!

Olly Dobson loves every musical number in the show, but when he got the role of Marty, one of his most exciting prospects was that he would be singing "Johnny B. Goode."

"I was in a band when I was a kid," he reveals, "and 'Johnny B. Goode' was one of our songs. I've known the lyrics since I was fifteen. It's in my body. Plus, it's Chuck Berry. Like John Lennon once said, 'If it wasn't called rock-and-roll, it would be called 'Chuck Berry.'"

What was also exciting for Olly was that he had the latitude to perform it in slightly different ways. "One of the things I realized about Chuck Berry was that any live recording of his singing that song is not the same as the studio version, so it gives me some license to have fun, and they let me. Sometimes there are shows where I'll just do the studio version. But on a Saturday night, when people have partaken of a drink or two, it might be nice to do a different iteration of it. Either way, I'm always singing it with great love and respect for the man and the music!"

For a brief period of time, Zemeckis and Gale considered adding some other classic rock-and-roll song titles to the dance.

A very, very brief time. "For about ten minutes, way early on, Bob and I discussed the idea that Marty could play a different rock number every night," reveals Gale. "In addition to 'Johnny B. Goode,' we would rotate through 'Blue Suede Shoes,' 'Great Balls of Fire,' 'Hound Dog,' and others. Then we took a reality pill and realized that not only would this add music costs, but it would require the actor and cast to learn more songs. And besides, 'Johnny B. Goode' had become so iconic that it was impossible to imagine *BTTF* without it! After all, it was included in 'Earth's Greatest Hits' on the *Voyager* spacecraft, so if aliens come to see the show, they'll be in on the joke!"

One other thing of interest to fans and musical purists were the instructions that Dobson's Marty gives the band to follow him on the song. In the film, Michael J. Fox calls out "Blues riff in B," when in actuality, the song was written to be played in B-flat major. Dobson corrects the gaffe onstage, but for those who believed the film had disrespected Mr. Berry's classic, Alan Silvestri confirms that in the movie, the song was indeed played in B-flat, as originally intended.

The Power of Love

After he returns to 1985 to find Doc alive and his family life dramatically improved, Marty and the Pinheads finally get to complete the number they started in an alternate universe of the space-time continuum.

As the special guest at the George McFly Day festivities, Marty also gets to play for Jennifer's uncle Huey from the record company.

GEORGE

Friends, today my new novel goes on sale in bookstores across the country, Back to the Future 4: The Further Adventures of Kelvin Klien.

(after some applause) Hollywood already bought the movie rights, but they'll probably screw it up. My success is the result of some very simple advice a young man gave me thirty years ago: You can accomplish anything if you just put your mind to it. And here's proof: may I introduce my son Marty McFly and his band, the Pinheads.

As the stage takes the look of a concert venue with a band logo behind them, Marty joins his assembled band, who are playing the song intro. Marty grabs the center-stage microphone.

MARTY

THE POWER OF LOVE IS A
CURIOUS THING
MAKE-A ONE MAN WEEP AND
ANOTHER MAN SING

CHANGE A HAWK TO A
LITTLE WHITE DOVE
MORE THAN A FEELING,
THAT'S THE POWER OF LOVE.

Uncle Huey enters with a guitar and joins the band.

TOUGHER THAN DIAMONDS,
RICH LIKE CREAM,
STRONGER AND HARDER
THAN A BAD GIRL'S DREAM
MAKE A BAD ONE GOOD,
MAKE A WRONG ONE RIGHT
POWER OF LOVE
WILL KEEP YOU HOME AT NIGHT

Jennifer enters and takes the other microphone.

MARTY & JENNIFER

DON'T NEED MONEY,
DON'T TAKE FAME
DON'T NEED NO CREDIT CARD
TO RIDE THIS TRAIN
IT'S STRONG AND IT'S SUDDEN
AND IT'S CRUEL SOMETIMES

MARTY

BUT IT MIGHT JUST SAVE
YOUR LIFE
THAT'S THE POWER OF LOVE.
THAT'S THE POWER OF LOVE.

Goldie enters with a microphone.

GOLDIE

FIRST TIME YOU FEEL IT,
MIGHT MAKE YOU SAD
NEXT TIME YOU FEEL IT,
MIGHT MAKE YOU MAD

MARTY & GOLDIE

BUT YOU'LL BE GLAD, BABY,
WHEN YOU'RE FOUND
THAT'S THE POWER

GOLDIE

THAT MAKES THE WORLD
GO ROUND

MARTY & COMPANY

DON'T NEED MONEY,
DON'T TAKE FAME
DON'T NEED NO CREDIT CARD
TO RIDE THIS TRAIN
IT'S STRONG AND IT'S SUDDEN
AND IT'S CRUEL SOMETIMES
BUT IT MIGHT JUST SAVE
YOUR LIFE

MARTY	SINGERS
THEY SAY THAT	
ALL IN LOVE	ALL IN LOVE
IS FAIR	IS FAIR
YEAH, BUT YOU	
DON'T CARE	
BUT YOU'LL KNOW	OOOOOOH
WHAT TO DO	WHAT TO DO
WHEN IT GETS	
HOLD OF YOU	

```
    MARTY          SINGERS
  AND WITH A
  LITTLE HELP
  FROM ABOVE      WOOOOAAAAH
  YOU FEEL THE
  POWER OF LOVE
  CAN YOU FEEL IT
```

Lorraine, George, Linda, and
Dave enter and join in.

```
    MCFLYS & COMPANY
   IT DON'T TAKE MONEY,
    DON'T TAKE FAME
  DON'T NEED NO CREDIT CARD
     TO RIDE THIS TRAIN
  TOUGHER THAN DIAMONDS AND
    STRONGER THAN STEEL
    YOU WON'T FEEL NOTHIN'
      TILL YOU FEEL
  FEEL THE POWER (WOOOOOAAHHH)
  JUST FEEL THE POWER OF LOVE
     THAT'S THE POWER--
```

BOB GALE

Very early in the writing, there was a brief conversation about Marty going back to the Twin Pines Mall and having Doc open his eyes. I questioned if it was worth all the logistics of the scene change. One of the lessons I learned from Shakespeare was that in the last scene of a comedy, the entire cast should be together in one place. The town square was that logical place, and George McFly Day was the perfect reason. It meant we could have every single character there, including Goldie Wilson, the Clock Tower Lady, and even Mr. Strickland.

JOHN RANDO

It's a really great song, and I wanted to spread the wealth. We've got some great singers, and Marty getting to have a little duet with his girlfriend is pretty nice. It's just what it should be—a celebration of everybody.

CEDRIC NEAL

I wasn't quite sure why the mayor would be coming out and singing "The Power of Love," and John said, "Cedric, we just want to hear you sing!"

COURTNEY-MAE BRIGGS

We had these handheld mikes, which I'd never used onstage, and you feel like a frickin' rock star with that neon sign behind you and everyone up on their feet! It's so cool!

OLLY DOBSON

I just channel Huey as much as I can. He has so many wonderful different versions of "The Power of Love," but this is definitely the version a lot of people have heard more than any other.

NICK FINLOW

The only thing to say about "Power of Love" is that it had to be "Power of Love." You can't mess with that number. There is, however, an Easter egg in there. There's one and a half bars, six beats of "Hip to Be Square" in that number in the show.

JOHN RANDO

I first thought we were going to have a big dance number for "Power of Love," and it was Chris Bailey who said, "No, we should just do a rock concert."

CHRIS BAILEY

The concept was, the number was planned to be in the town square, but there was something about it that made me question what we were supposed to be doing. Was it that the people in the town square happened to be singing with Marty? It seemed kind of weird. There was also a technical element that needed to be accounted for, and I remember having this revelation where I said, "Wouldn't it be cool if we could

somehow transition into his concert?" We're in a black box space. We have three saxophone players, and three backup singers. They're choreographed. Marty's doing his own thing. Then we stage it where various people come in, and where they go. Tim Hatley brought in the big, massive neon heart, and together it all created this great kind of almost intimate atmosphere that feels like you're suddenly at a Huey Lewis concert.

BOB GALE

I could have never thought of doing it that way, because the transition makes no logical sense at all, but it works brilliantly on an emotional level. All the story issues have been resolved, so now we just want to hear that fabulous song and celebrate.

HUEY LEWIS

I got a big kick out of the whole thing, including Uncle Huey. It's beautifully staged.

```
    MCFLYS & COMPANY
    THAT'S THE POWER--
```

```
Three blinding strobes
accompanied by explosions
and the screech of tires:
the DeLorean reappears!
DOC emerges, in bizarre
futuristic wardrobe, with
appropriate UNDERSCORE.
```

JOHN RANDO

This was definitely a number I had to stop before the song ended and the audience could applaud. I couldn't have everyone thinking the show was over before we gave them a fitting end.

```
        DOC
    Marty!
```

MARTY

Doc!

DOC

You've gotta come back
with me!

MARTY

Where?

DOC

Back to the future! It's
incredible! You have to
see it to believe it!
C'mon, get in the car!

MARTY

Right now? I'm right in
the middle of a song!

DOC

I'll have you back in one
minute. After all, it's a
time machine!

MARTY

You're the doc, Doc.

BOB GALE

We had established that the DeLorean
always announces the destination
time, so during rehearsals, I realized
I had to come up with an appropriate
date. I thought it might be confusing

to use the 2015 date from the second
movie, since it's no longer the future,
and then it hit me—like a bolt of
lightning. I immediately ran over
to John with a crazed look. "John,
I don't know if this is technically
possible, but what if the destination
time is always the date and time of
the very performance the audience is
attending?" He loved it, so I explained
it to Andy Green, our sound guy, who
said it would be no problem at all,
because the DeLorean voice is created
on the fly for every show, and the
performance date is automatically
programmed in. I love the fact that
it always takes a moment for the audience to pick up on it!

DELOREAN

Time circuits on. Desti-
nation time: [today's
performance date].

Marty's family and the
townspeople gather around
the car, totally amazed.

Marty calls to everyone from
the passenger seat.

MARTY

Excuse us, everyone. A
little science experiment
here, please give us some
room...
(as everyone exits,
Marty turns to Doc)
Doc, we're in the town
square. We don't have
enough road to get up to
eighty-eight.

DOC

Roads? Where we're going,
we don't need roads!

The gull wing doors close and
the DELOREAN RISES OFF THE
STAGE and FLIES OUT OVER
THE AUDIENCE, then TURNS
UPSIDE DOWN AND FLIES BACK
TOWARD THE STAGE.

ROBERT ZEMECKIS

Flying cars have been around for
years now. In fact, they were on
the verge of being released to the
public until the dissolution of the Civil
Aeronautics Board in 1985, when we
were making the original *Back to the
Future*. Over the years, we've kept an
eye on the surreptitious work that's
continued on them, and we got our
hands on one of them.

Back in Time

A funny thing happened when the team removed "Back in Time" from the end of the first act and replaced it with "Something About That Boy."

They didn't put it back in the show. Some assumed it was an oversight; others thought it was a way to trim the show's overall running time, but Colin Ingram made it abundantly clear that the song *would* be performed as the encore/curtain call number, just as Bob Gale had originally placed it in the early drafts.

Chris Bailey recalls the producer explaining his position. "He came to us and said, 'Hey, guys, you do realize it's on the poster? When people come to see the show and they see the promotional materials, they think they're going to hear 'Power of Love,' 'Johnny B. Goode,' 'Earth Angel,' and *'Back in Time'*! This is not open for discussion!"

Bailey suddenly found himself in need of some quick choreography. "Everybody was looking to me, and I thought, *OK, I'm going up to the bar with Darren [Carnall] and we'll make something up*, which is never the best way to make a number. So, we've got this music. Let's have some dancing. There was no concept. There was no working out. But even so, it was fun. The song is great, and infectious, and it was in the show the very next night and it got everyone on their feet. Then, after Manchester, I went back and completely reworked it!"

When it had been featured at the end of Act One, the context of the number was that Marty ran back to Doc's lab, where, in song, he begged the scientist to get him "Back in Time," amid a full ensemble, split evenly between iterations of Marty and Doc from other alternate realities.

Bailey honored the memory and spirit of that scene in his revamped version. "We don't have people dressed as Marty and Doc," he explains, "but we do end up with a dance-off between Doc's and Marty's 'people.' For Doc, we bring the DeLorean Girls back, and Marty's gang is all dressed in the orange vests and jeans."

"It became a celebration," notes Darren Carnall of the revised routine. "What makes it more fun in London is that we've incorporated all the principals in a really wonderful way. We even have Strickland going back across the stage on a hoverboard! The ensemble really cuts loose doing it so that the audience can have a good laugh as well." Says Bob Gale, "'Back in Time' ensures that the audience leaves the theater with big smiles on their faces."

CURTAIN CALL

After Doc and Marty take their bows, Biff runs out with a microphone, hands it to Marty, and the band segues into:

MARTY
TELL ME DOCTOR
WHERE ARE WE GOING THIS TIME?
IS THIS THE FIFTIES
OR 1999.
ALL I WANTED TO DO
WAS PLAY MY GUITAR AND SING

SO TAKE ME AWAY,
I DON'T MIND
BUT YOU GOTTA PROMISE ME

The Pinheads backdrop rises, revealing the six DeLorean Girls in front of the Courthouse, who join the number.

MARTY	**DELOREAN GIRLS**
I'LL BE BACK IN TIME	
	TIME
GOTTA GET BACK	GOTTA GET BACK
IN TIME	IN TIME

DOC
DON'T BET YOUR FUTURE
ON A ROLL OF THE DICE

Marty whistles stage right and seven male ensemble members in orange down vests step out with Jennifer and have a "dance off" with the DeLorean Girls.

DOC & MARTY
BETTER REMEMBER
LIGHTNING NEVER STRIKES TWICE

DOC
PLEASE DON'T DRIVE 88

MARTY
DON'T WANNA BE LATE AGAIN

DOC & MARTY
SO TAKE ME AWAY
I DON'T MIND
BUT YOU GOTTA JUST PROMISE ME
I'LL BE
BACK IN TIME

DOC, MARTY & ENSEMBLE	**ENSEMBLE**
GOTTA GET BACK IN TIME	BACK IN
GOTTA GET BACK IN TIME	
	BACK IN TIME
	YOU'VE GOTTA
	GET BACK IN TIME

(The entire cast is now onstage.)

DOC, MARTY & ENSEMBLE
ALL I WANTED TO DO
WAS PLAY MY GUITAR AND SING
SO TAKE ME AWAY,
I DON'T MIND
BUT YOU BETTER PROMISE ME
I'LL BE BACK IN
BACK IN TIME
BACK BACK
OH, BACK IN TIME
BACK BACK
OH, BACK IN TIME
BACK BACK
YOU'VE GOTTA GET BACK IN TIME

Final bows, followed by exit music as the ensemble does some various moves, break dancing, etc.

CODA

IN 2015, WHEN *BACK TO THE FUTURE* REACHED THE THIRTIETH ANNIVERSARY of its release, a new holiday was born. October 21 came to be known as "*Back to the Future* Day," commemorating the date on which Marty and Doc traveled to the "future" in *Back to the Future Part II*, declared by both US president Barack Obama and UK prime minister David Cameron.

For its first *Back to the Future* Day, the musical celebrated with a special guest in the audience, actor/singer/songwriter and creator of the megahit songs "The Power of Love" and "Back in Time," Huey Lewis. He had been on the invited guest list for both the Manchester and London premieres but was unable to attend either, so when Bob Gale approached him about joining them for the October celebration, he leapt at the opportunity.

"Personally, I believe that musical theater is the most demanding, and therefore arguably the most rewarding, form of artistic expression. It's also just the most fun!" said Lewis. The songwriter speaks from experience, having appeared on Broadway in two separate engagements, in the role of shyster lawyer Billy Flynn in a revival of the musical *Chicago*.

BELOW Left: Huey Lewis poses with Justin Thomas, who plays the role of Jennifer's "Uncle Huey." Right: Lewis takes a bow onstage at the Adelphi to the roar of a sold-out audience.

His passion for musical theater was rewarded that night in October as he sat in the audience and fell in love with *Back to the Future* all over again. From the book to the cast to the choreography to the special effects, he has nothing but superlatives for the entire production. With one exception: Ironically, his 2017 diagnosis of Ménière's disease, an inner-ear disorder, left the gifted musician without the ability to hear music. He was able to enjoy the dialogue with the benefit of implants, and a device provided by the theater that broadcasts the sound directly from the show's sound board into a monitor. "But I can't hear the music, I can't hear pitch. I can't tell how good the music is, but I suspect it's fabulous. I do know Glen Ballard's work, and of course, I know Alan Silvestri, and those two guys are amazing."

Despite the handicap, Lewis was able to appreciate, in addition to everything else, how his songs were presented. Olly Dobson was not able to perform that evening, but Huey watched a video of his performance of "Power of Love," followed that evening by Will Haswell's version. Both received high praise, as well as musical arranger Nick Finlow. "They handled 'Power of Love' very faithfully," Lewis observes. "I guess it's a compliment that they didn't try to change it, take it somewhere different. They just do it like I did." As he watched Will Haswell perform under the heart-shaped backdrop of Marty McFly and the Pinheads, "I leaned over

ABOVE When it was decided that Marty and the Pinheads would sing "The Power of Love" in a concert-like setting, Tim Hatley wanted to pay homage to the singer-songwriter with a very familiar logo as the backdrop.

to Bob, and said, 'I think you need to give me a set design credit at the very least!' The logo, the horn section, are you kidding me? It's Huey Lewis and the News!"

In his script, Gale had paid tribute to the musical superstar with Jennifer's "Uncle Huey," a record company executive in search of new talent who was coming to Hill Valley to hear Marty play. "Uncle Huey" makes his onstage appearance at the George McFly Day festivities upon Marty's return from 1955. Ensemble member Justin Thomas remained in the character that he had originated in Manchester, and after the cast took their final bows, Colin Ingram introduced the honored guest, escorted onto the stage by Bob Gale. The entire cast was elated to meet and perform for the musical icon. "Everyone was thrilled to meet Huey Lewis," declares Rosie Hyland. "At this point, we were accustomed to hearing 'Power of Love' and 'Back in Time' as show tunes, so it was a buzz to witness him seeing it all for the first time. I'd been listening to his music my whole life, so it was surreal to perform his music for him. He was so generous with his appraisal of the show.

And the Award Goes to . . .

As the West End continued its gradual reopening from the pandemic, part of the road to normalcy was the return of the time-honored tradition of awards celebrating all things theater across the UK. In November 2021, nominations began for the What'sOnStage Awards. In their twenty-second year, these awards are totally nominated

by, and the winners chosen by, the theatergoing public. After nine days of accepting nominations, *Back to the Future The Musical* racked up an impressive eight: acting nods for Roger Bart, Olly Dobson, and Hugh Coles; technical achievements by Tim Hatley (Best Set Design), Tim Lutkin (Best Lighting Design), Gareth Owen (Best Sound Design), and Finn Ross (Best Video Design); and the overall honor, being one of six titles to compete for the Best New Musical award.

Before the results of voting were finalized, another ceremony held by the UK Casting Directors' Guild honored David Grindrod with the award for Best Casting in Musical Theater.

On February 27, 2022, at the Prince of Wales Theatre in the West End, the winners of the twenty-second annual WhatsOnStage Awards from the *Back to the Future* production consisted of:

- Hugh Coles, for Best Supporting Actor (making his stage debut in the West End, as George McFly)

- Tim Lutkin, for Best Lighting Design
- Gareth Owen, for Best Sound Design

The Best New Musical award went to . . . *Back to the Future The Musical*.

Several weeks later, on March 30, 2022, the winners were announced for the 2021 BroadwayWorld UK Awards, also voted on by the members of the public. *Back to the Future* added the following to the list of award winners—in every category for which they were nominated:

- Olly Dobson, for Best Leading Performer in a New Musical
- Cedric Neal, for Best Supporting Performer in a New Musical

ABOVE (Left to right) Alan Silvestri, Bob Gale, and Glen Ballard are interviewed prior to the Olivier Awards ceremony.

- John Rando, for Best Direction of a New Production of a Musical
- Tim Hatley, for Best Set Design of a New Production of a Play or Musical
- Jim Henson, for Best Musical Direction of a New Production of a Play or Musical
- Mark Oxtoby, for Best Performance by an Understudy/Alternate in Any Play or Musical

The Best New Musical award went to . . . *Back to the Future The Musical*.

It's an Honor Just to Be Nominated...

With the public having twice already made their choices clear, it was time for the theater industry to voice its opinion in the form of Britain's most prestigious stage honor—the Olivier Award, established in 1976. *Back to the Future* received a total of seven nominations, with some repetitions from past awards shows (Olly Dobson, Hugh Coles, Tim Hatley, Tim Lutkin, Gareth Owen) this time joined by legendary composers and songwriters Alan Silvestri and Glen Ballard and orchestrators Bryan Crook and Ethan Popp.

Olly Dobson, Cedric Neal, and the entire ensemble performed to the enthusiastic crowd who filled the majestic Royal Albert Hall.

As the evening progressed, the *Back to the Future* nominees were overlooked, some of them in favor of themselves for other shows! Tim Hatley and Tim Lutkin both claimed Oliviers for their set design and lighting on *Life of Pi*.

"Before the ceremony started, I thought we had a good chance of winning Best New Musical," reflects Colin Ingram, "but I also thought we'd win for set design, lighting, sound, and supporting actor and had a fair chance at the score as well. As the night went on, it felt as if we were being shut out because we're such a commercial production, and generally speaking those don't fare too well at awards ceremonies. I was starting to regret asking Bob Gale, Alan

WINNER! BEST NEW MUSICAL
TIME AND TIME AGAIN...

WHATSONSTAGE AWARDS 2022 · OLIVIER AWARDS 2022 · BROADWAY WORLD AWARDS 2022

BACK TO THE FUTURE THE MUSICAL

BackToTheFutureMusical.com

ADELPHI THEATRE

Silvestri, and Glen Ballard to travel to London, and was not looking forward to having to apologize."

And then the final award to be handed out was for Best New Musical . . .

TOP LEFT Colin Ingram accepts the Best New Musical Olivier Award on behalf of the production.

ABOVE The new recipients of the prestigious Olivier Award (left to right): Alan Silvestri, Glen Ballard, Colin Ingram, Donovan Mannato.

After a mere 225 performances, *Back to the Future The Musical* had captured the hearts of the UK theater industry—it was heralded as the winner.

"I was completely shocked!" continues Ingram. "I've dreamed of winning an Olivier from the first time I attended the awards in 1994, when it was a casual lunch affair. The feeling of going onto that stage was out-of-body . . . I suddenly knew how it felt to travel through the space-time continuum. It meant so much to me, all the hard work we did to make the show happen being recognized by the theater community, and having them acknowledge how hard it is to produce a new musical of this size in these times. With this Olivier, we had won three Best Musical awards, representing the public and the artistic community, and to share the success with Bob, Alan, and Glen in person meant everything. What legends to win an award with!"

Bob Gale was sharing the same experience with Ingram from a few seats away. "When we kept losing the technical awards, I texted my wife, who was watching from California, that we weren't going to win the big enchilada. Having been through a big loss at the Academy Awards in 1986, I prepped myself for the (seemingly) inevitable disappointment, and I could see that the whole *BTTF* team was in the same 'We can see the handwriting' place. I've never been happier to be so wrong! We all felt like Marty did when he thought Doc Brown was dead—and suddenly, there he was, alive and well, and with a bright future ahead—just like our show!"

To the Future!

In 2007, four men sat at a table and collectively agreed to undertake a project that would ultimately take thirteen years to come to fruition. Over that period of time, the quartet would collect a diverse group of artists, artisans, technicians, designers, and erstwhile magicians and dreamers to aid them in their crusade.

The results speak . . . and sing . . . and dance for themselves. And they entertain, astound, amaze, and inspire West End audiences eight times a week.

Back to the Future The Musical surpassed the expectations of its creators. It has delivered a successful new iteration of the favorite film of millions of fans, and, like its cinematic relative, it is creating new fans in every generation, a humbling and gratifying conclusion for franchise co-creators Gale and Zemeckis.

If it had really been a conclusion, that is.

No one would have automatically assumed the show would continue to expand into other markets and touring companies, had there not been a clear mandate from the public and the creative communities as well. Alan Silvestri recalls that as the show neared its premature COVID-related closure, he and Glen Ballard had already begun their West End to-do list.

Since the production had opened in London, fans from around the world began to question if they would ever see the show somewhat closer to their own home, or at the very least, in their own country. Minutes after receiving the Olivier Award for Best New Musical, Colin Ingram confirmed to an interviewer that they were looking for a "parking spot" on Broadway for the DeLorean. "That will be the biggest test of all, because it's the most competitive and costly, and you're either a hero or a zero because of that. I believe American audiences will fall in love as much as British audiences have, especially given this is a piece of American culture."

That's just the beginning of Ingram's plans for the *Future*.

LEFT The "core four" who started it all: Bob Gale, Alan Silvestri, Robert Zemeckis, and Glen Ballard on press night at the Adelphi Theatre, September 13, 2021.

"If you're reading this book in the future, and my calculations are correct, we should have managed to produce this musical around the world," he predicts. "After Broadway, we want to open in Germany, Japan, South Korea, Spain, Mexico, Brazil, Scandinavia, and Australia and will be launching a touring version for the UK and North America. Bringing this musical to all these countries will be a thrilling ride for myself, Bob Gale, and all the creative team. To be continued . . ."

Despite the fact that Glen Ballard was not involved with the original *Back to the Future* film, his work on the musical made him an official citizen of Hill Valley. He's ready for more: "This musical represents one of the longest and most joyful journeys of my career, and it's still going! The mythical environs and characters of Hill Valley are as familiar to me now as if I had grown up there. My partners created the flawless source material—Robert Zemeckis, Bob Gale, and Alan Silvestri—and to be invited to help move it to the stage is one of my greatest privileges. The DeLorean is waiting, flux capacitor fluxing, twenty actors onstage, fourteen musicians in the pit . . . ready to take you to Hill Valley and beyond!"

John Rando, who shares equally in the success of the show, also subscribes to the theory that theater never ends.

ABOVE Home again: The cast and crew celebrate the winning of Olivier Awards on their home stage at the Adelphi Theatre.

"Before we move on to the next location from London, we'll be able to evaluate, examine where we are, and determine if there's anything else we want to do for all future productions of the show."

Alan Silvestri's enthusiasm and love for *Back to the Future* remains as strong today as it was in the very beginning, with his score for the motion picture, the two sequels, the theme park attraction, the animated series, and *Back to the Future in Concert*. "This story goes on," he avows. "It continues to transform, change, grow, and adapt and be exciting. Bob and Bob have always been amazing about their openness to let their 'child' live its life and see what life brings it next. They're amazing like that, and I'm proud to be a part of that life's journey." Silvestri stands by with his Broadway to-do list at the ready.

For Bob Gale, it has come down to one very simple principle, adhering to the philosophy of Doctor Emmett Brown (which Gale himself wrote!). "At the end of *Part III*, Doc says, 'Your future is whatever you make it, so make it a good one.' I think we all made *this* musical future a *great* one . . ."

Franchise co-creator Robert Zemeckis wants to go even further than that. "I honestly think it's one of the greatest musicals ever made," he declares. "I would like to see the show tour the entire world, and then I'd like it to be performed in high schools and in grade-school theatrical productions from now on, up there along with *Annie* and *The Wizard of Oz* and *The Producers*. I'd like it to live forever."

AFTERWORD

by ROBERT ZEMECKIS

N 2005, AFTER MY WIFE, LESLIE, SUGGESTED WE explore a theatrical musical based on *Back to the Future*, there was one thing Bob Gale and I knew for sure: If such a musical never happened, the world be just fine. By 2005, the movies had risen in stature, and we didn't want to compromise that stature. More importantly, as theater neophytes, a musical was not just a total unknown to us; it was a serious risk. We risked alienating our fans and squandering the goodwill the world had for our franchise. We could not only fail, we could fail spectacularly.

No one would ever criticize us for *not* making *Back to the Future The Musical*. Clearly, aborting the idea was the one safe choice, with absolutely no downside.

And yet . . . seeing a great musical is an experience like no other. There's an energy in live theater that you can't get with cinema. And there was the lure of trying something outside our comfort zone. Could we actually pull it off? Would we kick ourselves years later for not even trying it? How could we not at least explore it? We went back and forth on the subject. And that's where our secret weapon came in. "The Red Button."

Because *Back to the Future* was an original screenplay, *we* owned the theatrical rights. Not Universal, not Amblin. No, this was Zemeckis & Gale, all the way. And that put us in the driver's seat. So we came to a simple decision. If at any point we thought the musical wouldn't be worthy of being called *Back to the Future*, we would push the red button, kill the entire project, and never look back. That was our protection against "spectacular failure."

More than once on the roller coaster of the development process, we considered pushing it. The time I recall most clearly was when we had trouble finding a director.

I actually flirted with the idea of directing the show myself. Then, good sense prevailed when I realized that if I got into serious hot water, I'd have to fire myself and that would redefine "spectacular failure." At that point, the red button seemed very enticing.

But, as you all know, we never pushed it. I credit the creative team for helping to keep our fingers safely away. Bob and I would get depressed and fatalistic, and then Alan Silvestri and Glen Ballard would bring us a wonderful new song that reminded us of what the show could be. Our 2017 Showcase, when I first got to hear many of our songs performed properly, was a revelation. After that, we had the enthusiasm of producer Colin Ingram and the passion of director John Rando, whose collective experience put any setbacks in proper perspective. They brought in an incredibly talented cast and crew and, with Bob Gale always there to keep the train on the tracks, that red button was soon left far behind. Thanks, everyone, there could be no better creative team!

Writing this in 2022, I now think the world actually might be a little better because *Back to the Future The Musical* exists. It certainly is for me, and I think it's true for the vast majority of those who've seen it. I literally had tears in my eyes on opening night in Manchester; that's how happy I was (and still am) with the show. And now, when I encounter that rare person who has never seen the movie who asks me, "Which version should I see, the movie or the musical?" I answer, "The musical!" And then I add, "But the movie's pretty good too!"

ROBERT ZEMECKIS
Santa Barbara, California
September 2022

ACKNOWLEDGMENTS

I have, in the time it's taken to write this book, had the fortune to observe the process of the creation and production of *Back to the Future The Musical* from the "best seat in the house."

The man who ushered me to that seat was Bob Gale. This book doesn't exist as it appears before you without Bob Gale. Since 1988, he has encouraged, trusted, endorsed, and generously given his time and guidance to my every effort in the world of *Back to the Future.* It is a world that has enhanced my life, and continues to do so. Bob has my eternal thanks for allowing me to be a part of it. I am honored to be able to call him my mentor and friend.

It has also been a pleasure to reconnect with Robert Zemeckis, and to thank Leslie Zemeckis for her idea that sparked a momentous new chapter in *Back to the Future* history!

I have always loved spending time with Alan Silvestri, and his participation in this book has only reinforced those feelings. Over this time, I was also fortunate enough to get to know his wife, Sandra, whom I heartily thank for access to her exclusive photography, which I couldn't have gotten from anyone or anywhere else.

When Alan was first paired with Glen Ballard on *The Polar Express,* he found a new partner, and a close friend. I'm delighted to call Glen a new friend, and thank him for all his help.

I thank both Colin Ingram and John Rando for a revelatory education in musical theater, and for allowing me unfettered access both to them and to the show itself. From In Theatre Productions: Phoebe Fairbrother, Matthew Green, Simon Delaney, Felicity Caffyn, Lottie Bauer.

To watch a group of performers give the residents of Hill Valley new life has been breathtaking. Every single one of them has claimed their characters and imbued them with their own special gifts. Their collective contributions are a significant part of why the show has been so enthusiastically embraced by film fans and musical theater fans as well. My most sincere appreciation and admiration to: Roger Bart, Olly Dobson, Hugh Coles, Rosanna Hyland, Cedric Neal, Aiden Cutler, Courtney-Mae Briggs, Mark Oxtoby, Will Haswell, Emma Lloyd, Rhianne Alleyne, Amy Barker, Matthew Barrow, Joshua Clemetson, Jamal Crawford, Morgan Gregory, Ryan Heenan, Cameron McAllister, Alessia McDermott, Laura Mullowney, Nic Myers, Shane O'Riordan, Katharine Pearson, Melissa Rose, Justin Thomas, Tavio Wright.

Everyone involved behind the scenes, onstage, backstage, and even under the stage, has been incredibly approachable, gracious, welcoming, and informative. Their generous and copious contributions have honored me. Thank you: Tim Hatley, Chris Bailey, Nick Finlow, Hugh Vanstone, Tim Lutkin, Finn Ross, Gareth Owen, Chris Fisher, Ethan Popp, Bryan Crook, Stephanie Whittier, Simon Marlow, Gaz Wall, Maurice Chan, Jonathan Barnard, David Grindrod, Jim Henson, Richard Fitch, Christa Harris, Josh Chalk, Darren Carnall, Chris Marcus, Jonathan Hall, Reese Kirsh, Ross Edwards, Felipe Carvalho, Mark Marson, Wendy Phillips, and Mr. David Massey.

A book about anything *Back to the Future* wouldn't be complete without a contribution from Michael J. Fox and Christopher Lloyd. They have my sincere gratitude for their participation, as does music legend Huey Lewis. My hearty thanks as well to Lisa Lloyd, Lauren Moger, and Nina Bombardier.

No less important are the contributions and support of the following, to whom I express my appreciation: Piers Allardyce, Kath Ball-Wood, BroadwayWorld.com, Sean Ebsworth Barnes, Camille Benett, Dave Benett, Bonnie Britain, Leo Bruce, Darren Chadderton, Stephen Clark, Owen Chaponda, Lora Colver, Josh Gad, Samantha Gale, Tina Gale, Adam Gradwell, Oliver and Terry Holler, Aisha Jawanda, Paul Kolnick, Nathaniel Landskroner, Justin Lubin, David McGiffert, Ken Norwick, Oliver Ormson, Bethany Rose Lythgoe, Antonia Paget, Laura Radford, Jemma Revell, Jamie Richardson, Tony Ruscoe, Peter Sciretta, Jake Small, Angela Smith, Phil Tragen, Joe Walser, Steven Wickendon, Mitchell Zhangazha, Chloe Rabinowitz.

Thanks to Comic Relief (www.comicrelief.com), DeWynters Limited, Keith Lemon, Sarah White, Amanda Malpass, Alex Buchanan, Ginny Bootman, Sarah Wharton. At Universal Pictures: Roni Lubliner, Peer Ebbighausen, Rachel Parham, and to Jessica Wright and the staff of the Adelphi Theatre.

At Abrams Books, my editor, Eric Klopfer, deserves a great deal of thanks for his enthusiasm, his expertise, his guidance, and his patience! Thanks as well to Liam Flanagan, Diane Shaw, Lisa Silverman, and Denise LaCongo.

If I've inadvertently missed someone, I apologize. Everyone who worked on this show is a rock star!

Dedicated again, and always, to Ardemis Freeland

MICHAEL KLASTORIN
Los Angeles, 2022

ADELPHI PRODUCTION CREDITS, 2021

PRODUCERS

LEAD PRODUCER Colin Ingram
Donovan Mannato, Ricardo Marques,
Hunter Arnold, Nick Archer, CJEM,
Bruce Carneigie Brown
FRANKEL/VIERTEL/BARUCH/ROUTH GROUP
GAVIN KALIN PRODUCTIONS
PLAYING FIELD
CRUSH MUSIC
TERESA TSAI
IVY HERMAN/HALEE ADELMAN
ROBERT L HUTT
UNIVERSAL THEATER GROUP

ASSOCIATE PRODUCERS

Kimberly Magarro
Stage Productions
Glass Half Full/Neil Gooding Productions

MUSICAL DIRECTOR Jim Henson
ASSISTANT MUSICAL DIRECTOR Steve Holness
KEYBOARD Rob Eckland
GUITAR 1 Duncan Floyd
GUITAR 2 Ollie Hannifan
BASS GUITAR/DOUBLE BASS Iestyn Jones
DRUMS Mike Porter
PERCUSSION Jess Wood
OBOE/COR ANGLAIS Lauren Weavers
ALTO SAX/TENOR SAX/FLUTE/CLARINET Simon Marsh
FRENCH HORN Richard Ashton
TRUMPET/FLUGEL Pablo Mendelssohn
TRUMPET/FLUGEL Graham Justin
TROMBONE/BASS TROMBONE Simon Minshall
MUSIC TECHNOLOGY Phij Adams
ORCHESTRAL MANAGEMENT Sylvia Addison

COMPANY MANAGER David Massey
STAGE MANAGER Gary Wall
PRODUCTION STAGE MANAGER Graham Hookham
ASSOCIATE DIRECTOR Richard Fitch
DEPUTY STAGE MANAGER Josh Chalk
ASSISTANT STAGE MANAGERS Scarlett Hooper,
Robert Allan, Jack Roberts
RESIDENT DIRECTOR Christa Harris
HEAD OF SOUND Reese Kirsh
SOUND DEPUTY Jav Pando
SOUND ASSISTANT Ben Smith
HEAD OF LX Jamie Povey
LX/VIDEO DEPUTY Piers Illing
HEAD OF VIDEO Oliver Hancock
HEAD OF AUTOMATION Jack Wigley
AUTOMATION DEPUTY Stuart Sneade
SWING TECH Erin Thomson
HEAD OF EFFECTS Ben Stevens
HEAD OF WIGS Katy Lewis
WIGS DEPUTY Lilian Komor
WIGS ASSISTANT Ellesia Burton
WIGS ASSISTANT Amelia Ball
HEAD OF WARDROBE Wendy Phillips

WARDROBE DEPUTY Ian Jones
WARDROBE ASSISTANT Hannah Boggiano
DRESSERS Janine Cartmell Hull, Marianne
Adams, Jena Berg, Christopher Palmer,
Ross Carpenter, Gemma Atkinson
COSTUME ASSOCIATE Jack Galloway
COSTUME SUPERVISOR Holly Henshaw
PROPS SUPERVISORS Chris Marcus, Jonathan Hall
WIGS, HAIR & MAKE-UP Campbell Young
Associates
WIGS, HAIR & MAKE-UP ASSOCIATE Mark Marson
ASSOCIATE SET DESIGNER Ross Edwards
ASSOCIATE ILLUSIONS DESIGNER Filipe Carvalho
ASSOCIATE VIDEO DESIGNER Henrique Ghersi
**ASSOCIATE LIGHTING DESIGNER &
PROGRAMMER** Chris Hirst
ASSOCIATE SOUND DESIGNER Andy Green

PRODUCTION CREDITS

SOUND EFFECTS ASSOCIATE Steve Jonas
ASSOCIATE LIGHTING DESIGNER Charlotte Burton
VOICE OF RADIO NEWS BROADCASTER
Nicolas Colicos
ASSOCIATE FIGHT DIRECTOR Jonathan Bernard
HEALTH AND SAFETY Chris Luscombe
MERCHANDISING The Araca Group
PRODUCTION CARPENTERS Michael Murray,
Phil Large, Jonothan Smith, Oliver Ellerton
WORKSHOP CARPENTERS Mark Sutton, Mo Bower
SENIOR PRODUCTION ELECTRICIAN Fraser Hall
PRODUCTION ELECTRICIANS Scott Carter,
Suzi Futers, Richard Mence, Phill Giddings,
Chris Hirst
PRODUCTION SOUND ENGINEER Dan McIntosh
SOUND ENGINEERS James Melling, Jon Reynolds,
Richard Pomeroy, Jonnie Westell, Ben Giller
ANIMATOR Grace Arnott-Hayes
PRODUCTION VIDEO ENGINEER Sam Jeffs
VIDEO ENGINEERS Neil McDowell Smith,
Matt Somerville, Sam Gough
TECHNICAL VIDEO ASSOCIATE Jon Lyle for
Ammonite
PRODUCTION RIGGER Mark Davies
RIGGERS Danny Brookes, Dave Curtis,
Liam Gough, Nick Hill
RIGGING CONSULTANT Emily Egleton
PRODUCTION AUTOMATION ENGINEER Andy Biles
AUTOMATION ENGINEERS Simon Wait, Andy Biles,
Tim Klaassen, Chris Harvard
**SET ELECTRICS AND SPECIAL EFFECTS MANAGEMENT
BY** Ammonite Ltd
SCENERY BY Souvenir Scenic Studios and
All Scene All Props
ENGINEERING AND AUTOMATION BY Silicon Theatre
Scenery
FLYING DELOREAN BY Twins FX
SET ELECTRICS BY Made by Mouse, Lamp
and Pencil, Electric Foundry, Junction and
Howard Eaton Lighting Ltd
PYROTECHNICS BY Encore SFX
SCENIC CLOTH PAINTED BY Emma Troubridge
SCENIC PAINTING BY Souvenic Scenic Studios
VIDEO EQUIPMENT BY Blue I Theatre
Technology Ltd

LIGHTING EQUIPMENT BY Hawthorn
SOUND EQUIPMENT BY Orbital Sound
RIGGING BY Unusual Rigging Ltd

DOMINION/SADLER'S WELLS WORKSHOP PERFORMERS
Kelly Agbowu, Cameron Blakeley, Natalia
Brown, Nicolas Colicos, Georgia Carling,
Matt Corner, Nicole Deon, Olivia Hibbert,
Ashley Irish, Aisha Jawando, Lemuel Knights,
Emily McGougan, Oliver Ormson, Ayesha
Quigley, Clancy Ryan, Parisa Shahmir,
Tino Sibanda

WORKSHOP MUSICAL DIRECTOR Danny Wirick

THANKS TO

Lounici Abdel, Michael Afemare, Richard
Appiah Sarpong, Nicki Barry, Simon
Batho, Ashley Birchall, Charlie Burn, Will
Burton, Scott Campbell, Laura Caplin, Ed
Carlile, Aaron Cawood, Collectif, Lily Collins,
Tommaso Creatini, Frances Dee, Lauren
Elphick, Joe Evans, Kate Forrester, Robert
Fried, Joe Frost, Phil Gleaden, Ruben Gomez
Bustamante, Eve Hamlett, Henry Harrod,
Jack Heasman, Fionnuala Hills, Ian King,
Natasha King, Phil Knights, Petra Luckman,
Jade MacIntosh, Rebecca Maxwell, Poti
Martin, Steven Mijailovic, Sonja Mohren,
Michael Nelson, Georgina Niven, Kirsty
Nixon, Nathalie Perthuisot, Justin Quinn,
Stuart Ramsay, Sammie Richards, Aaron
Rogers, Suzanne Rogers, Pedro Seguro, Jo
Serbyn, Sam Schwartz, Kim Sheppard, Laura
Singleton, Emma Smith, Jake Smith, Lou
Stobbson, Sharon Trickett, Evan Thompson,
Stuart Thorns, Spencer Tiney, Angela Vicari,
Zoe Weldon, Katie Whatman, Chris Whybrow,
Steven Wickenden, Martin Wilkinson, Harriet
Williams, Isobel Wood, Bleu Woodward,
Adam Young – Notch Artist

Editor: Eric Klopfer
Designer: Liam Flanagan
Design Manager: Diane Shaw
Managing Editor: Lisa Silverman
Production Manager: Denise LaCongo

Library of Congress Control Number:
2021946828

ISBN: 978-1-4197-5652-8
eISBN: 979-8-88707-195-4

Image Credits
Piers Allardyce: pp. 114 (left), 230; **Chris Bailey:** p. 202; **Kath Ball-Wood:** pp. 58 (bottom), 60; **Glen Ballard:** p. 23 (courtesy of); **Sean Ebsworth Barnes:** pp. 4–5, 8, 14, 17 (middle), 18, 25, 30, 32–34, 35 (top; bottom right), 52 (both), 55 (b&w), 74 (top left; bottom), 81–83, 86 (bottom), 87, 89 (top left; right), 93 (bottom), 94 (bottom), 95 (right), 100, 108–109, 111, 112 (bottom), 122, 126 (middle left), 132, 142, 146, 148, 150, 152–53, 155, 157–58, 160, 163–64, 166, 168–70, 172, 175–78, 180–81, 186, 188, 190, 193–94, 196, 199–201, 203, 205–206, 209–10, 213–14, 217–18, 220, 222–24, 227; **Roger Bart:** p. 6; **Dave Benett:** pp. 134–37 (all), 234, 236; **Bob King Creative:** p. 131; **Felicity Caffyn:** p. 235; **Matt Crockett:** p. 11; **Bob Gale:** pp. 2–3, 10 (courtesy of), 72, 73 (middle), 80, 96 (bottom), 103 (top left; right), 112 (top left), 123 (bottom left), 128 (top left; middle), 129 (top row, middle), 130 (middle left; right; bottom right), 176 (inset), 182, 198 (top; bottom), 204 (bottom right), 216; **DuJonna Gift-Simms:** p. 42; **Will Haswell:** p. 113; **Tim Hatley:** pp. 35 (bottom), 64–66, 67 (bottom two), 68 (right), 70–71, 73 (bottom), 84–85, 96 (top left; top right), 97 (right), 124 (top right), 130 (top), 175 (inset), 231; **Leo Bruce Hempell:** p. 22; **Graham Hookham:** p. 97 (top left); **Michael Klastorin:** p. 73 (top right), 74 (top right), 75, 98 (bottom), 104 (bottom), 110 (bottom), 124 (top left), 126 (top; bottom), 127 (all), 128 (top right; bottom, both), 129 (bottom), 130 (bottom left), 133, 161, 185, 188 (inset), 189 (inset), 192, 204 (bottom left), 229; **Paul Kolnick:** p. 92; **Tim Lutkin:** p. 67 (top right); **Chris Marcus:** pp. 97 (bottom), 101 (all); **Nederlander Theaters:** p. 47 (bottom left); **Gareth Owen:** pp. 68 (left), 69 (both), 102 (top right), 118; **Laura Radford:** p. 117; **John Rando:** pp. 77 (top, middle, right), 187 (inset); **Finn Ross:** p. 98 (top right;

middle), 110 (top three), 125 (graphics); **Sandra Silvestri:** p. 17 (bottom), 78, 79 (bottom), 89 (bottom), 90 (top), 104 (top right; middle), 121, 232–23; **Phil Tragen:** pp. 12–13, 16, 63 (both), 90 (bottom), 91, 103 (bottom), 106 (all), 114 (right), 115–16 (press night); **Hugh Vanstone:** p. 67 (top left), 99 (middle right), 102 (bottom right); **Stephanie Whitter:** pp. 28, 29 (bottom), 46 (bottom), 47 (top; left), 48; **Steven Wickenden:** pg. 77 (bottom); **Danny Wirick:** pp. 55 (bottom), 56–57; 58 (top); **contributors:** Matthew Barrow, Will Haswell, Ryan Heenan, Emma Lloyd, Alessia McDermott, Shane O'Riordan, Katherine Pearson, Tavio Wright: p. 140; **contributors:** Sandra Silvestri, Amy Barker, Justin Thomas-Verweij: p. 141.

Photos from *Back to the Future* by **Ralph Nelson:** pp. 17 (top), 88, 93 (top), 94 (top), 95 (left), 139. **Courtesy of Universal Studios Licensing LLC**
Original songs from *Back to the Future The Musical:* Lyrics reprinted by Permission of Alan Silvestri and Glen Ballard
"The Power of Love" and **"Back in Time":** Lyrics reprinted by Permission of Huey Lewis
"Earth Angel": Words and Music by Jesse Belvin.Copyright © 1954 (Renewed) by Embassy Music Corporation (BMI) International Copyright Secured All Rights Reserved.
Reprinted by Permission of Hal Leonard LLC

Printed and bound in the United States
10 9 8 7 6 5 4 3 2 1

Abrams books are available at special discounts when purchased in quantity for premiums and promotions as well as fundraising or educational use. Special editions can also be created to specification. For details, contact specialsales@abramsbooks.com or the address below.

Abrams® is a registered trademark of
Harry N. Abrams, Inc.

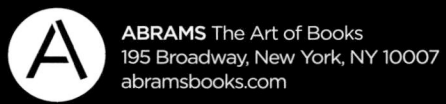

ABRAMS The Art of Books
195 Broadway, New York, NY 10007
abramsbooks.com